Praise for *A Guide to Documenting Learning*

In *A Guide to Documenting Learning*, the authors seek to qualify, rather than quantify, what contemporary learning is all about: looking for, capturing, reflecting, sharing, and amplifying the learning that is taking place. In this text, they break down these actions and how they apply to before-, during-, and after-learning moments and describe a new way to approach contemporary work and self-determined learning.

—**Michael Fisher, Author and Consultant**
The Digigogy Collaborative
Amherst, NY

I love the idea that students can be aware of their learning. It can be documented, reflected on, curated, and shared in order to garner feedback, and the student owns the learning every step of the way.

—**Kathleen Rodda, Literacy Coach Affiliation**
Eucalyptus Elementary
Hawthorne, CA

This book touches upon information that would be useful to any school system because it scaffolds ways that educators can help students make their thinking known, which will only improve their future reasoning skills.

—**LaQuita Outlaw, Principal**
Bay Shore Middle School
Bay Shore, NY

Educators trying to create compelling learning experiences confront the daunting challenge of content-coverage requirements and expectations of teaching to the test. Students and their thinking are often invisible as the only representations of learning made public are marks and rankings. Tolisano and Hale take the inspirational Reggio Emilia approach and scale it into new contexts to create deep learning experiences for today's learners, with an eye on the future of learning as well.

—**Cameron Paterson, Head of Learning and Teaching**
Shore School
North Sydney, Australia

This book will become an important guide for schools and educators to have on their shelves. The content is original and highly organized, and it presents many new ideas on documenting learning. This book takes what is happening in the world of teaching right now and elevates it to a coherent pedagogical process. The graphics are a fantastic resource.

—**Andrea Hernandez, Educational Consultant**
amplifiEDucation and edtechworkshop.blogspot.com
Jacksonville, FL

A Guide to
Documenting Learning

Silvia Rosenthal Tolisano

*To my father, Jochen Rosenthal,
who showed me the importance of
where I come from and where I am going.*

Janet A. Hale

*To my lifelong friends,
Lisa Frederick, Linda Isaac, and Rondi Little,
who love and support me unconditionally.*

A Guide to Documenting Learning

Making Thinking Visible, Meaningful,
Shareable, and Amplified

Silvia Rosenthal Tolisano

Janet A. Hale

Foreword by Alan November

CORWIN

A SAGE Publishing Company

FOR INFORMATION:

Corwin
A SAGE Company
2455 Teller Road
Thousand Oaks, California 91320
(800) 233-9936
www.corwin.com

SAGE Publications Ltd.
1 Oliver's Yard
55 City Road
London EC1Y 1SP
United Kingdom

SAGE Publications India Pvt. Ltd.
B 1/I 1 Mohan Cooperative Industrial Area
Mathura Road, New Delhi 110 044
India

SAGE Publications Asia-Pacific Pte. Ltd.
3 Church Street
#10-04 Samsung Hub
Singapore 049483

Acquisitions Editor: Ariel Bartlett
Senior Associate Editor: Desirée A. Bartlett
Editorial Assistant: Jessica Vidal
Production Editor: Amy Schroller
Copy Editor: Lana Todorovic-Arndt
Typesetter: C&M Digitals (P) Ltd.
Proofreader: Dennis W. Webb
Indexer: Maria Sosnowski
Cover Designer: Gail Buschman
Marketing Manager: Margaret O'Connor

Printed in the United States of America

Library of Congress Cataloging-in-Publication Data

Names: Tolisano, Silvia Rosenthal, author. | Hale, Janet A., author.

Title: A guide to documenting learning : making thinking visible, meaningful, shareable, and amplified / Silvia Rosenthal Tolisano, Janet A. Hale.

Description: First edition. | Thousand Oaks, California : Corwin, a Sage Company, [2018] | Includes bibliographical references and index.

Identifiers: LCCN 2017041327 | ISBN 9781506385570 (pbk. : alk. paper)

Subjects: LCSH: Educational evaluation. | Curriculum planning. | Student participation in curriculum planning.

Classification: LCC LB2822.75 .T65 2018 | DDC 379.1/58—dc23
LC record available at https://lccn.loc.gov/2017041327

This book is printed on acid-free paper.

SFI label applies to text stock

19 20 21 22 10 9 8 7 6 5 4 3 2

Contents

Foreword

I am very proud to write the foreword for this book. Every once in a while, a really important, practical book comes along that can make a difference every day for a wide range of learner abilities. *A Guide to Documenting Learning* is just such a book. This step-by-step guide provides a framework for helping students and professionals to "learn how to learn." Specifically, these pages can help students and teachers capture their learning, reflect on their learning, share their learning, and ultimately, amplify their learning.

My own experience as a teacher, administrator, and now a consultant who has had the opportunity to visit schools around the world has convinced me that many learners are not aware that documentation is a valuable strategy or do not know how to document their learning well. As I am sure you are aware, there has been an explosion of tools and platforms available on every device that, when used creatively, can organize, share, and amplify learning. Silvia and Janet's book provides educators with a framework for introducing these tools and platforms to learners and, most importantly, documenting phases and learningflow routine steps to use them well every day. Making sense of tools to purposefully capture learning and understanding how to manage the learning evidence can be overwhelming for even the most tech-savvy educators. Silvia and Janet have done years of experimentation with students and professionals and various tools to provide a clear road map for success.

On a personal note, Janet and Silvia have shared these ideas at my summer conference in Boston for the past few years to educators from around the world. Teachers walk out of their workshops on fire.

I have had the pleasure of collaboratively working with Silvia on the concept of the Digital Learning Farm where students have responsibility to research and create content that adds value to peers. Examples of the jobs associated with the digital learning farm that are specifically presented in *A Guide to Documenting Learning* are The Official Scribe, The Tutorial Designer, Global Communicators, and Collaborators. I have been working for years using an action research model for many of the main process concepts presented in these pages.

Another concept that Silvia and I have been collaborating on is a powerful framework called the *First Five Days of School* where a specific skill set is frontloaded during the first five days of school that has a learning payoff throughout the year. Almost all educators agree that how you begin the school year can make a huge difference to the success of the entire school year. While there are applications for all five days, Day One and Day Five are of particular note. Day One is where the daily discipline of *carefully documenting learning* is introduced. Day Five is where students begin to understand the *power of sharing their work authentically with a global audience.* Authentic presentation of ideas can be highly motivating and provide invaluable feedback. I am always amazed at how some students will work harder and with more care for an authentic audience than if the work is only for themselves. Of course, the learning strategies of the first five days extend naturally to the first five weeks, the first five months, and throughout the school year. The documentation learning phases and learningflow routine that Silvia and Janet explain in detail and articulate through helpful examples and implementation suggestions are perfect for supporting and expanding all of the *First Five Days of School* skills and strategies.

Although Silvia and Janet advocate the *use* of technology, their book is *not* about technology. They leverage the use of tools and platforms for the sole purpose to amplify learning and to share learning beyond an audience of one (the student or professional) or few classmates or colleagues. It is their belief that documenting OF learning becomes more than display of "What did we do?" and moves into the realms of documenting FOR learning and documenting AS learning.

We need to help teachers make their students' thinking visible. One of the most powerful results of implementing the ideas in *A Guide to Documenting Learning* is the constant opportunity to do just that—making learners' thinking visible. As we all know, every student does not ask for help at the moment it is needed. Many students do not even know what questions to ask sometimes, or they think they do not need any help when they are heading down a wrong path. Once the concepts of this book are applied in any learning environment, teachers, administrators, and professional development leaders will have a deeper understanding of how their learners are making meaning. There will be very clear evidence of where learners need help and where learners can help one another! Silvia and Janet's book is jam-packed full of ideas to use tools, platforms, and thinking routines that allow learners to make their thinking visible, reflect deeper, and prepare to share their learning-thinking artifacts with an authentic global audience.

All of us are concerned about the ethics and moral ground of helping learners gain awareness of how to navigate the potentially treacherous course of social media. The majority of our students will not have been guided by an adult on how to use *Facebook*, *Twitter*, *Instagram*, *Pinterest*, and more that are yet to come. For those of you who are concerned that our students must have the high moral ground of adult guidance, this book points out clearly and in detail how to provide students with sophisticated social media skills for learning opportunities.

Ultimately, what *A Guide to Documenting Learning* is about a framework that can be applied to lifelong learning. The ongoing results of the documentation work can also inform teachers of the impact of their own work that can be in turn shared in Professional Learning Communities and Professional Learning Networks. This book should be essential reading for all veteran and prospective teachers, as well as administrators and educational leaders. Enjoy!

—Alan November, Founder, November Learning
Author, *Empowering Students With Technology*
Marblehead, MA

Preface

When you need to innovate, you need collaboration.

—Marissa Mayer

A COLLABORATION INVITATION

Silvia and I met in person for the first time in 2010 at a Curriculum21 summer conference. I knew of her innovative documenting work due to following her on Twitter, reading her *Langwitches* blog posts, and interacting with her virtually in preparation for the conference. I had been inspired (and still am) by Silvia's forward-thinking around evidence of learning, and especially challenged by her stance on the act of documenting to go beyond merely displaying what had been learned at the end of a unit, lesson, or activity.

About two years later, I made an offer to Silvia, "If you ever want to write a how-to book based on your documenting learning concepts, I'd love to coauthor it with you!" I knew that her ideas needed to be articulated and shared via a professional book and I felt I could be of service, given my professional-writing experience with Corwin and ASCD. Silvia shared that she was not ready at the moment, given her life was busy with moving to Brazil, teaching, coaching, consulting, and blogging.

Fast forward to the fall of 2015. I received a phone call that began a virtual collaborative writing and image-creating journey that we would not trade for the world. You are about to embark on the result of our journey. Before you begin reading, we want to share a quick glimpse into our collaborative process.

Silvia created the majority of the visuals based on our frequent Skype and Facetime calls, Google Doc comments, and text messages. Our decision-making process involved agreement on the placement of images and the written text for each visual.

The majority of the QR codes in this book will take you to specific *Langwitches* blog posts for extended reading and viewing. Given Silvia has been working on the action-researched documenting learning framework we share in this book for over 10 years, there were plenty of posts for us to read through together to determine the one that best enhanced a particular key point.

When I asked Silvia what she felt I contributed to our book's collaboration, she shared insights that included:

> There is no denying that I am a blogger at heart. I love the immediacy of being able to link, embed, publish, edit, and add to posts at any time. I love my forgiving blog audience with my tri-lingual spelling and grammar errors that naturally occur. With Janet's book-writing experience and meticulous attention to detail, I was reminded often throughout our drafting, revising, and editing process that her patience,

explanations, and editing of my German run-on sentences and Argentine culturally influenced metaphors helped to make us the perfect writing team for this project.

Just as the opening quote suggests, one learns and grows through collaboration with others. Growth for both of us as textual writers and visual communicators was invaluable. Our hope is that as you read through the chapters and begin to apply what you discover and realize about our documenting learning ideas, phases, and routine, you will find a colleague (or two) with whom to collaborate. Together, you can grow wiser as you begin or make advancements in your classroom and professional documenting learning journeys.

A Guide to Documenting Learning Rationale

We believe, and have found in practice, that the documenting learning framework—making thinking about learning processes *visible, meaningful, shareable,* and *amplified*—provides students and educators (*as active learners*) with an interconnected, metacognitive approach for creating evidence of their learning.

Our framework aids learners in owning their learning process, as well as assisting others in their learning growth. When deep learning experiences are visible and involve students directly in the documentation process, it enables them to identify moments worth remembering. When teachers are co-creators with their students, both gain valuable insights that inform future learning and empower students as engaged learners.

Educators will find the information shared in this book thought-provoking and invaluable for improving pedagogical and heutagogical practices, including those involved in

- personalized learning and ensuring student voice,
- contemporary learning and assessment alternatives,
- competency-based classrooms,
- technology integration that transforms teaching and learning,
- social-media engagement to foster learning and teaching,
- Reggio Emilia's framework for pedagogical documentation, or
- becoming a National Board Certified teacher.

As the title indicates: This book is a *guide*: a *how-to* that provides insights into contemporary learning and teaching documentation practices in classroom and professional learning environments. There are other documenting learning books available that have a similar call for observing, recording, interpreting, and sharing to positively impact student engagement and learning. While we were inspired by Reggio Emilia's early learning philosophy, and affirmed by the book *Visible Learners,* which shares practices for fostering K–12 learning through documentation, *A Guide to Documenting Learning* is unique because it

- Extends the use of documentation for all learners—pre-K through lifelong learners
- Uses the power of technology to amplify teaching and learning beyond the walls of classrooms and schools
- Expands students and teachers sharing beyond displaying and discussing their learning with peers at the same school
- Focuses on amplifying to reach from parents and a local community to a global community in dynamic ways

- Takes advantage of transformative teaching and learning opportunities through authentic uses of social media
- Encourages educators to document, reflect, and share their professional learning beyond same-site colleagues to inform immediate or future teaching and learning

Disclaimers

While the documenting learning framework is not meant to be considered an add-on,

- we are not advocating you document everything every day, every lesson, or in every unit; and
- we acknowledge that documenting is a process. There is a learning curve involved, and putting it into practice will help you and your students improve its use and application.

Documenting learning is not the answer to all teaching and learning problems:

- We do not have every answer related to documenting learning figured out. We are continuing to search, research, pilot, revise, retry, share, and ask for feedback to become better at our documenting work.

Assumptions

- We will rely on your imagination and inspiration to tweak the examples and vignettes sprinkled throughout the chapters for you own purposes and personalized situations.
- We will count on your willingness to push yourself outside of your comfort zone to observe, reflect, and share your work openly and transparently.
- We will trust in your readiness to be (or continue to be) a globally connected educator who disseminates his or her own learning to collaborate, communicate, and connect with learners outside your zip code.

Acknowledgments

- Thank you to **Alan November** for his vision that pushes our thinking. Thank you for being provocative and continually questioning the ways learning and teaching have always been done.
- Thank you to **Heidi Hayes Jacobs** for being a mentor, coach, guide, and inspiration. She started it all with her collaborative book, *Curriculum21*. We are honored to keep the collaboration going.
- Thank you to **Mike Fisher** for taking any idea we come up with, getting passionate about it, and adding your genius spin and out-of-the-box thinking to push our thinking even further.
- Thank you to these **educators and learners from around the world** who have contributed their work, thinking, and curiosity to dive deeper into documenting OF, FOR, and AS learning: Claire Arcenas, Gabriela Bechmann, Catalina Behrens, Verónica Behrens, Andrea Berteloot, Joel Bevans, Jamie Bielski, Jocelyn Blumgart, Rivka Cohen, María del Carmen Correales, Ana Paula Cortez, Graciela Cusman, Mark Engstrom, Lily & Charlie Fisher, Florencia Gavelio, Marisa Gonzalez, Shana Gutterman, Karin Hallett, Marissa Heavener, Gaby Holm, Cata Horny, Maggie Hos-McGrane, Laurel Janewicz, David Jorgensen, Bena Kallick, Karin Klingspor, Deb Kuhr, Evelyn Mahler, Cristina Massen, Jon Mitzmacher, Mónica Müller, Heidi Musterós, Alejandra Oberbeil, Andy Raitt, Judy Reppert, Esteban Gonzales Rittler, Marjie Rogozinski, Edna Sackson, Mechi Schenzle, Uschi Schwartz, Melina Seifert, Mariana Sturmer, Laura Tagliabue, Stephanie Teitelbaum, Luciana Vallejos, Emily Vallillo, Arlene Yegelwel, and Shelly Zavon.

SILVIA

- Thank you to my grandchildren, **Elena** and **Benjamin**, for allowing me to look for, see, and capture the wonders of learning through your eyes.
- Thank you to **Andrea Hernandez**, **Katrin Barlsen Jurado**, and **Silvana Scarso** for always lending a listening ear when I spill over with thoughts, ideas, and plans.
- Thank you to my teacher cohorts from the **Goethe Schule** in Buenos Aires for their dedication to building windmills instead of walls in times of change.
- Thank you to my fellow bloggers, specifically **Donna Miller Fry**, **Jackie Gerstein**, **Diane Kashin**, and **Angela Stockman**, for their work in advancing heutagogical and pedagogical documentation and sharing it.
- Thank you to my Langwitches **blog readers** who show me that documenting and sharing learning amplifies around the world.
- Thank you to **Janet Hale** for suffering through my German run-on sentences, and for caring about the stories behind them.

JANET

- Thank you to **Silvia Tolisano** for continually stretching my thinking and understanding. Drafting, revising, and refining our words, images, concepts, and examples so that educators and students around the world can grow from their own documenting opportunities has created special memories that I will treasure forever.
- Thank you to **Valerie Lyle** for your willingness to drop everything multiple times to review and make recommendations that definitely improved our chapters.
- Thank you to **Mike Fisher** for your friendship, laughter, energy, passion, and love for your family that continually inspires me and always makes me smile.
- Thank you to my husband, **Johnny Hale**, for always encouraging me to grow in my learning, including the time-consuming world of professional writing.

PUBLISHER'S ACKNOWLEDGMENTS

Corwin gratefully acknowledges the contributions of the following reviewers:

Michael Fisher, Author and Consultant
The Digigogy Collaborative
Amherst, NY

Andrea Hernandez, Educational Consultant and Co-Director of edJEWcon
amplifiEDucation.com and edtechworkshop.blogspot.com
Jacksonville, FL

LaQuita Outlaw, Principal
Bay Shore Middle School
Bay Shore, NY

Cameron Paterson, Head of Learning and Teaching
Shore School
North Sydney, Australia

Kathleen Rodda, Literacy Coach Affiliation
Eucalyptus Elementary
Hawthorne, CA

About the Authors

Silvia Rosenthal Tolisano is a Third Culture Kid (TCK). She was born in Germany, raised in Argentina, lived shortly in Brazil, and is now planted in the United States. Her multicultural upbringing fueled her passion for languages, travel, global awareness, and global competencies.

Silvia holds a bachelor's degree in Spanish with a minor in International Studies, and a master's degree in education with an emphasis in instructional technology. She has worked as a world language teacher, technology integration facilitator, 21st century learning specialist, social media coordinator, and professional development and educational consultant.

She is a Curriculum21 faculty member, co-founder of edJEWcon, author of *Digital Storytelling Tools for Educators* (Lulu, 2010), and coauthor of *Mastering Digital Literacy* and *Mastering Global Literacy* (Solution Tree, 2013).

Her passions include globally connected learning, technology integration, contemporary upgrades, amplification of curriculum and instruction, blogging as a pedagogy, developing and maintaining a personal learning network, and documenting learning.

Visit Silvia's consulting website: *globallyconnectedlearning.com*; amplifiEDUcation website: *amplifieducation.com*; documenting learning website: *documenting4learning.com*; and blog: *Langwitches.org/blog*; and follow her on Twitter *@langwitches*.

Janet A. Hale grew up in a military family, which allowed her to see the world. When she was 12 years old she volunteered to teach swimming lessons to children with special needs and English to Korean children who were blind, while her father was stationed in Seoul. She was hooked and has been involved in education ever since.

Janet earned a bachelor's degree with dual majors in elementary education and special education, as well as a master's degree in educational leadership with an emphasis in curriculum development. She also graduated from the Institute of Children's Literature.

She has worked as a special education high school teacher and a general education elementary teacher. Janet also worked as a seminar/workshop creator, presenter, and trainer for Teacher Created Materials, and authored or contributed to 40 books for Teacher Created Resources. She is the author of *A Guide to Curriculum Mapping* (Corwin, 2008), coauthor of its companion, *An Educational Leader's Guide to Curriculum Mapping* (Corwin, 2010), and coauthor of *Upgrade Your Curriculum* (ASCD, 2013). She has been an independent educational consultant for more than 20 years.

Janet presents at national and international conferences, and works with schools, districts, and dioceses as a consultant, trainer, and coach. She also assists for-profit companies and non-profit organizations to align their curriculum and materials to standards.

Her passions include systemic curriculum design and curriculum mapping; standards literacy and alignment; modernizing curriculum, instruction, and assessment; and documenting learning.

Visit Janet's consulting website: *CurriculumDecisions.com*; documenting learning website: *documenting4learning.com*; and blog: *CurriculumDecisions.com/blogs*; and follow her on Twitter *@janet_hale*.

Introduction

Reading is to the mind what exercise is to the body.

—Joseph Addison

CHAPTER DESCRIPTIONS

Our book contains 13 chapters (see Image Intro.1) that can be read in sequential order or by reading and applying the chapters that most interest you. That said, it is recommended you begin with the first three chapters simply because they lay a documentation foundation that

- explains the nuances among three types of documenting—OF, FOR, and AS learning;
- expresses the need for learners to embrace and put into practice the *now* literacies; and
- addresses the differences between pedagogy and heutagogy in the context of learning evidence.

Chapters 4 and 5 provide in-depth information regarding learner engagement and the gradation of sharing and amplifying when planning for and implementing documenting learning opportunities.

The core of our framework is found in Chapters 6 and 7, which consist of the three documentation phases—*pre-documentation*, *during-documentation*, and *post-documentation*; and the five steps involved in the *documenting learningflow routine*. You will discover that the phases and routine are not completely separate components, as there are times when the two overlap.

Chapters 8 and 9 contain activities and narratives that help you put the phases and routine into practice with a variety of media platforms and tools, while Chapter 10 explains how to unpack collected media.

Chapter 11 features a documenting learning vignette based on the three phases and routine steps coupled with specific learning focuses and goals.

A school's or district's collective visible evidence of learning helps to convey its mission, vision, and values. Chapter 12 focuses on the concept of branding as an identity tool through the use of sharing and amplifying documentation artifacts.

Chapter 13 addresses three questions related to implementing or expanding the use of the documenting learning framework: *What to cut? What to keep? What to upgrade?* The first question is viewed through the lens of mindsets and attitudes; the second through the lens of academic necessities; and the third through the lens of upgrading assessments and grading practices.

The Appendix includes sketchnote and infographic planners to aid you in summarizing the phases and routine for your documenting learning opportunities. It also contains a KWHLAQ template to assist you in your planning process.

Given a word or phrase may be unfamiliar to you while reading, a Glossary of Terms is also included.

Throughout the book, there are images and infographics to aid your understanding, as well as QR codes that lead to additional reading on a particular topic or concept. Given some QR codes take you to public materials, we do not have control over whether these sites are removed or edited. We hope we have selected ones that are timeless, but one never knows!

Lastly, you are invited to contribute using the #documenting4learning hashtag on Twitter, Facebook, or Instagram; or by mentioning @documenting4learning on Facebook and Instagram, and @doc4learning on Twitter.

Image Intro. 1

1

Documenting Learning Types and Purposes

Telling will never be as effective as experiencing.

—George Couros

Outside of the brick-and-mortar or virtual school day, we are living and thriving in a time when *where* we learn, *how* we learn, *when* we learn, and *with whom* we learn changes based on what we are currently curious or passionate about learning. More and more, these contemporary learning characteristics and experiences are being replicated within school time.

We are living and thriving in a time when *where* we learn, *how* we learn, *when* we learn, and *with whom* we learn changes based on what we are currently curious or passionate about learning.

We can no longer rely on any one tried-and-true methodology or practice because what it means to teach and learn is evolving exponentially. As mindful documenting learning educators, we must purposefully have the

- self-motivation of *life-long learners*, who are never satisfied with the status quo and see continued learning as part of their regular work and life;
- restless hearts of *adventurers* and *pioneers,* who are willing to try new things and step outside of their comfort zones and thrive on exploring uncharted territories;
- inquisitive minds of *scientists,* who push beyond what they can see with their eyes and imagine what could be by articulating their ideas, generating new theories, and providing evidence to dispute or confirm their thinking and reasoning;

- curiosity of *researchers,* who continuously search—and search again, try, test, and document their journeys to contribute to a larger purpose of advancing understanding and practices;
- courage of *innovators,* who continuously wonder "*what if . . . ,*" and are not afraid to fail as part of the creation process;
- imagination of *storytellers,* who paint in vivid color a wide variety of narratives and share them with the world;
- passion of *mentors,* who instill and nurture a voracious love for learning and inquiry; and
- unselfishness of *parents,* who unconditionally love their learners and role of sharing and nurturing without expecting anything in return.

Documenting means more than being organized or supporting learning by providing evidence. It involves accessing and reflecting on one's own learning processes and articulating what is taking place throughout a learning journey.

Documenting informs students and teachers about what needs to be in focus, whether coaching, mentoring, or providing direct instruction. Implementing the documenting types and purposes positively affect how teachers see their students (and themselves) as engaged learners. It naturally fosters and creates historic growth-timelines for students, and professionally for teachers and administrators.

While anyone can document a moment in time by recording a video, taking a picture, or writing down verbatim what is being said, documenting learning needs to be *strategic* and *purposeful.* A learner needs to be aware of what type of learning evidence he or she accepts and desires to capture. Teachers and students need to learn how the sharing of their documenting affects the quality of their documentation. Skills need to be developed to aid learners in understanding how media tools and platforms aid in capturing and sharing learning, as well as how media choices affect one's ability to demonstrate thinking and learning visibly and/or auditorily.

Documenting learning creates purposeful and meaningful evidence. These artifacts play a critical role in conveying thinking and learning through four aspects: *visibility, meaningfulness, shareability,* and *amplification.* These aspects are components, in varying degrees, of the three documenting learning types: Documenting OF Learning, Documenting FOR Learning, and Documenting AS Learning (see Image 1.1).

Documenting learning creates purposeful and meaningful evidence.

DOCUMENTING LEARNING TYPES

There are *documenting nuances* among the three types that teachers need to be cognizant of when planning documenting opportunities for their students and for themselves.

Documenting OF Learning

Documenting OF learning uses documenting as *snapshot* product or performance artifacts that *display* learning moments. This is often the first type of documentation educators utilize. It conveys that a documenter or learner is beginning to think about the importance of documentation.

Image 1.1

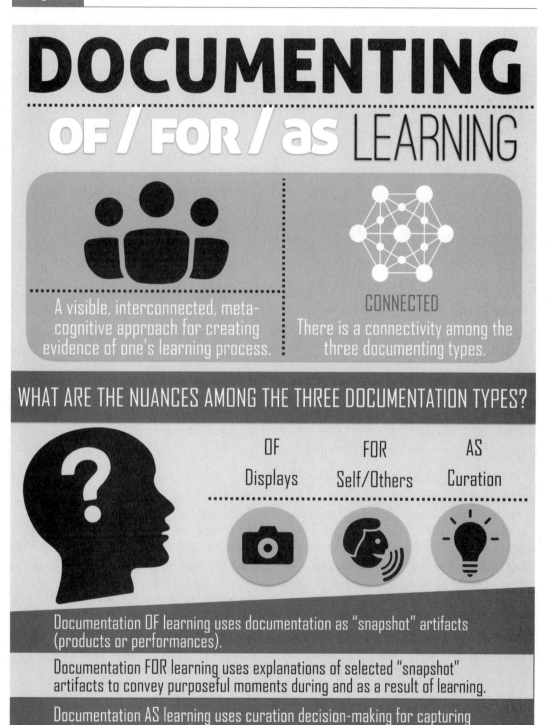

Truth be told, documenting OF learning is often overused. Learners often record everything and anything, without necessarily interpreting what has been captured. Table 1.1 provides a few examples of common documenting OF learning artifacts.

Table 1.1   Documenting OF Learning Examples

Photography	Videography	Textual Recording	Audio Recording
Student brainstorming with others during his passion-project work time.	Student explaining the steps she took to create a culminating project with display board behind her.	Student's writing sample placed in a portfolio by the teacher.	Student singing a song.
Group of students presenting in front of a screen.	Group of students appearing giddy about their participation in an activity.	Three students wrote a Reader's Theater script and posted it on their class website.	Two students interviewing an Iraqi war veteran.
Group of teachers talking at a table.	Group of teachers talking at a table and hearing their verbal exchanges.	Teacher's blog post about his latest science unit, including photos of his students in action.	Teacher explaining highlights of attending a recent workshop for her professional-learning portfolio.

Documenting OF learning focuses on *the product* and attempts to answer these questions:

- What did the learner do?
- What is the result of the learning?

The answers are artifacts that are observable, visible, and/or audible to an onlooker. They are explicit representations of what was experienced. They are simply captured moments in time, whether shared in person, digitally, or on social media.

To aid in understanding the nuances among the three types of documenting learning, an iceberg metaphor may be helpful. Documenting OF learning is *the visible portion* of the iceberg that is above the water (see Image 1.2). It is explicit. It is known. No depth of cognitive or metacognitive thought processes are necessary regarding what is displayed.

Documentation, when done too often only at this surface level, often feels like extra work for students and teachers, who see no real benefit or purpose beyond compliance. It is therefore imperative that learners have ample opportunities to experience and explore the two remaining types of documenting, which supports cognitive and metacognitive processes to take place while the learning is happening, and even before it happens.

Documenting FOR Learning

Documenting FOR learning uses *interpretations of purposefully selected* snapshot artifacts to convey evidence of meaningful visible and audible moments that take place *during, or because of,* the learning process. It is designed to *raise awareness* of a learner's changes, trends, or patterns over time. For example:

- During his makerspace project time, Mikeal has been purposefully taking and reflecting on a series of captured moments (photographs). Based on his reflections, he

Image 1.2

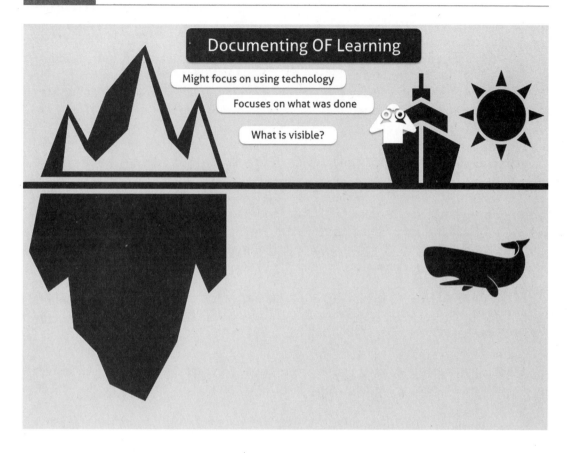

notices a trend in his behavior. He regularly gravitates toward particular partnerships for input on new iterations of his makerspace object. Mikeal annotexts several selected photographs as evidence of his reasoning for why these two peers are his consistent "go tos."

- Mrs. Gilmore collects and studies samples of her students' writing over four weeks as evidence of their application of a writing skill she has taught and supported during Writer's Workshop. She observes steady improvement in all of her students except for one, Nathaniel. While Mrs. Gilmore applauds the visible improvement by sharing some writing samples with the class, she holds a private conference with Nathaniel to discuss his artifacts. She asks him if he would like a peer to join them to discuss what the classmate is doing to apply the skill effectively. Nathaniel asks Marjorie to join the conference. Mrs. Gilmore explains to Marjorie why she has been asked to join them. As Nathaniel and Marjorie dialogue, she observes them comparing and analyzing their personal writing artifacts as they discuss potential ways Nathaniel may choose to improve his writing.

Documenting FOR learning goes beyond simply capturing evidence of learning by *digging deeper into the interpretation and application of what the artifacts convey*. This type of documenting can be divided into two categories, which can take place simultaneously:

1. Documentation for one's own learning purpose. For example, someone learning a new metal braiding technique and working toward mastery of the technique films herself while conducting the braiding process to track progress over time.

2. Documentation wherein a learner makes his or her thinking and learning visible in order to help others learn when it is shared. For example, the metal-braiding learner films herself attempting the new braiding technique and angles a camera just so to capture the step that is proving to be the most difficult for her. While recording, she verbally shares the specifics regarding her frustration and asks viewers for suggestions to improve her braiding capabilities. She posts her video via Twitter with the hashtag #kumihimobraiding. In doing so, she is not only benefiting herself as a learner, but she is also benefitting the learning of those with whom she is sharing.

Documenting FOR learning focuses on *interpretation* and attempts to answer these questions:

- How is what I am learning now related to something I have previously learned?
- How will this learning influence and inform my future learning?
- Why do I accept this artifact as evidence of my learning process and progress?
- How could someone else learn from my experience—both my failures and my successes?
- What would I need to do to best document (capture) my learning today and at the end of the year related to _____ for me to see and hear evidence of my growth over time?

Note: While the pronouns *I* and *my* were used in the questions above, if a learner is involved in a collaborative learning experience, the pronouns would simply be changed to *we* and *our.*

Since documenting FOR learning asks learners to interpret, reflect on, and connect artifacts along a learning journey, this type of documentation often makes visible that which learners are *not even aware of* and provides time to interact with and examine artifacts to make connections and discover patterns or trends.

Continuing the iceberg metaphor, documenting FOR learning is the waterline *connecting the visible to the invisible*. It is in this space that hidden or implicit learning is cognitively explored, explained, and expressed (see Image 1.3). This occurs using multimedia platforms and tools that help learners strategically document to:

- freeze moments in time,
- rewind moments that passed by too quickly,
- unwind moments that cannot be seen easily by the naked eye, or
- capture moments taking place in two or more places simultaneously.

Students and teachers express that this type of learning opportunity is authentic and worthwhile, especially when they can share their learning process with others. Contributing to a community of learners deepens one's understanding, meaning, and purpose.

Documenting AS Learning

Documenting AS learning takes the documenting FOR learning process to an even deeper depth wherein the documenting process *becomes a critical facet* of the learning journey. This type of documenting uses *searching, filtering, and purposeful decision-making about what to capture* to express specific moments as evidence of one's learning process. Whether

Image 1.3

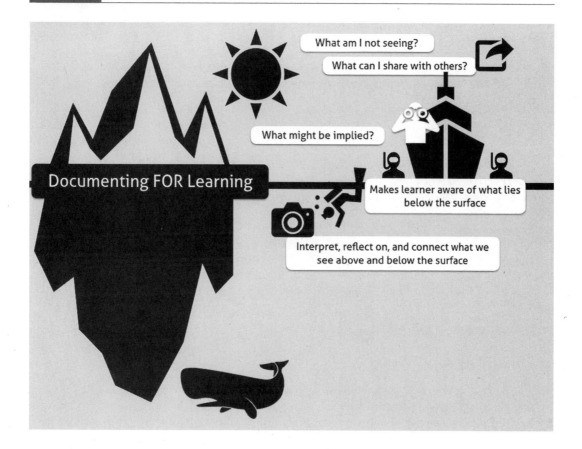

It's Time to Take Action!

You will encounter a recommended action step in each chapter. These steps are intended to connect you with other readers as you collectively generate examples and resources beyond what we can share with you in the timeframe that this book was written.

Through social media and the use of #hashtags and @handles, we encourage you to contribute your examples and experiences in documenting learning with a global community, while also gaining access to an ever-growing crowdsourced pool of ideas and resources.

There are multiple platforms you can choose from to provide your action steps' evidence of learning:

Twitter

Create an explanation tweet in 280 characters or less that shares the documenting learning opportunity. Include an image or video as the learning evidence, as well as the hashtag #documenting4learning, and/or mention @doc4learning.

(Continued)

(Continued)

Instagram

Upload an image or a video that express your learning evidence from your documenting opportunity. Include the hashtag #documenting4learning, and/or mention @documenting4learning.

Facebook

Create a post explaining your documenting opportunity. Include one or more artifact images or videos with your text; include the hashtag #documenting4learning and mention @documenting4learning.

Your Personal/Professional Blog

Create a blog post explaining your documenting opportunity and include images and/or videos as learning evidence. Tweet a link or share a link on Facebook to your published blog post using the hashtag #documenting4learning.

Now, it is time for your first action step . . .

Chapter 1 Action Step

Share an artifact from a documenting OF learning opportunity that your students experienced, or you experienced professionally. Change it to a documenting FOR learning artifact by posting a descriptive tweet with attachment, Instagram description, Facebook post, or blog post, include annotations* and/or annotexted** artifacts that aid in answering one of these questions: *How will this learning influence and inform my future learning? How could someone else learn from my experience—both my failures and my successes?*

Notes or comments alongside text, image, video to aid in processing or explaining the media content.

**Act of annotating an image or video digitally by overlaying text, highlights, directional arrows, frames, or freehand drawing.*

personalized professional learning or student choice-making, central to this type of documenting is the inclusion of

1. Active and reflective metacognitive opportunities as action researchers

2. Engagement in a connected learning community to share insights and discoveries

3. Authentic feedback and new considerations locally and globally

For example, Mr. Henkle is a member of a professional learning community (PLC) in his school and is stretching himself to grow and develop his project-based learning teaching practices. He strategically selects and annotates multimedia artifacts focused on *student voice and choice* from his class's four small groups. He consistently shares and amplifies his professional-learning evidence and realizations on his blog and via Twitter. He interacts with his blog commenters, as well as with participants in Twitter chats he attends. He applies several of the suggestions made by his PLC and professional learning network (PLN) throughout the unit of study.

There is a deeper level of critical-thinking and metacognition involved when someone needs to make choices about what best portrays evidence of learning. Some of these choices will need to be made prior to capturing the desired evidence.

Documenting AS learning focuses on *the learning process* and attempts to answer these questions:

- What is worthy of being looked for and captured during this learning opportunity?
- What media platforms and tools will provide the maximum effect for capturing, reflecting on, curating, sharing, and amplifying my personal learning or the evidence of others' learning?
- How can my/our thinking be best conveyed visibly and audibly when considering the audiences who will be experiencing my/our shared and amplified learning?

When documenting moves from being a *product or cognitive tool to a metacognitive process*, it enters the depths wherein the iceberg is totally hidden beneath the surface (see Image 1.4). Documenting AS learning is not immediately visible or tangible. It is only viewable *with strategic preparation and implementation*. It is about the actions and metacognitive thinking taking place *while the learning is happening*. It is about exploring the what and how below the visible surface that aids learners *immediately and over time*. It also invites and engages others to join in the learning process through *sharing and obtaining feedback*.

Image 1.4

SUMMING UP

Based on a Google search, *documentation* is defined as material that provides official information or evidence, serves as a record, or the process of classifying and annotating texts, photographs, and so on.

While documenting OF learning is a valid place to begin purposeful documentation, moving to documenting FOR learning makes thinking about one's learning visible and/or audible, which leads to an awareness of what is involved in the learning process. Documenting AS learning adds a subtle, yet powerful, layer of metacognition that engages learners in determining how to best capture the learning process in preparation for purposefully sharing and amplifying new or expanded thoughts or ideas with a worldwide community of learners. (see Image 1.5). Casa-Todd (2017) quotes a student who shared from a personal experience, "I never realized that impact that your voice can have on others, but once I began observing the number of people that listened to me, I felt empowered as a student" (p. 17).

DOCUMENTING LEARNING PURPOSES

Before digging into the purposes, please note that documenting OF learning, documenting FOR learning, and documenting AS learning are *not* direct synonyms for assessment OF learning, assessment FOR learning, and assessment AS learning, although there are similarities regarding overall purpose.

The first two assessment types are associated with the work of Stiggins, Arter, Chappuis, and Chappuis (2006), who describe these terms as:

> Assessments OF learning are those assessments that happen after learning is supposed to have occurred to determine if it did. They are used to make statements of student learning status at a point in time to those outside the classroom. . . . State assessments, local standardized tests . . . [and] within a classroom when we gather evidence to determine a student's report card grade. (p. 31)

> Assessments FOR learning happen while learning is still underway. These are the assessments that we conduct throughout teaching and learning to diagnose student needs, [and] plan next steps in instruction, provide students with feedback they can use to improve the quality of their work, and help students see and feel in control of their journey to success. on these occasions, the grading function is laid aside. This is not about accountability. . . . This is about getting better.

Assessment AS learning is described by Earl (2006) as,

> The process of developing and supporting meta-cognition for students . . . as active critical thinkers, make sense of information, relate it to prior knowledge, and use it to construct new learning. . . . It occurs when students personally monitor what they are learning and use the feedback from this monitoring to make adjustments, adaptations, and even major changes in what they understand. (p. 47)

They are involved in determining *the next* in their learning (e.g., strategy, learning focus), as well as providing descriptive feedback to peers and to themselves as they grow in their capabilities to be reflective learners.

Image 1.5

PEDAGOGICAL & HEUTAGOGICAL
DOCUMENTATION

OF LEARNING	**FOR** LEARNING	**as** LEARNING
 Product	Interpretation	Process
 What did we do?	Where do we go from here?	How are we learning?
 Observable	Reflective	Meta-Cognitive
 Summative Assessment	Formative Assessment	Summative & Formative Assessment

The three *documenting* types have unique components and characteristics when compared to the three *assessment* types. While assessment is an integral part of documenting, the documenting learning framework serves purposes beyond assessment. The overarching purpose for documenting learning, especially documenting FOR and AS learning opportunities, is to allow learners to fully participate in their own learning processes, whether a young student or adult learner.

The overarching purpose for documenting learning is to allow learners to fully participate in their own learning processes.

As mentioned previously, documenting is often times based on an *OF learning* perspective. Fry (2016) refers to this as "flashy busywork." Fry reflects on how learners can be more meaningfully engaged by producing, "Examples of visible student and educator learning," rather than simply displaying the results of a learning experience. Ritchhart, Church, and Morrison (2011) mention that, "Documentation must serve to advance learning, not merely capture it" (p. 38). Please note: Documenting OF learning is not wrong. There are times when sharing a display to celebrate accomplishments is appropriate and worthwhile. What is problematic for students is when teachers allow time for only this type of documenting.

At first, documenting FOR and AS learning can feel timeconsuming. Hale and Fisher (2013) mention that modernizing, or upgrading, student learning should happen, "one unit at a time." In other words, after reading this book, do not feel that *everything* related to student learning must be accomplished via documenting. If you begin by applying the documenting techniques, tools, and tips conveyed in this book *once a semester or quarter*, you will have begun an amazing and worthwhile journey! Yes, it will be time consuming early on—not just for you, but for your students as well. It is a new way of thinking about one's thinking. Two benefits to using FOR and AS learning opportunities is witnessing students' authentic engagement and sense of empowerment.

Collaboration plays an important role in documenting FOR and AS learning, which Hale and Fisher (2013) also convey is an important aspect when modernizing learning:

> We based *Upgrade Your Curriculum* on the premise that moving from *me* to *we* is an ongoing and essential process. Slow-and-steady upgrades or transformations, in which teachers (and students) work collaboratively to make strategic and specific modifications to current curricular elements, lead to modern, meaningful, and engaging experiences. We have found that once a collaborative culture is in place, participating in curriculum transformation continues to have positive effects on both teachers and students. (p. 3)

Documenting strategically and purposefully supports all aspects of one's learning process. The specific purposes for documenting learning are fourfold: to make one's cognitive—and most importantly, metacognitive—thinking *visible*, *meaningful*, *shareable*, and *amplified*.

Do not feel that *everything* related to student learning must be accomplished via documenting learning. If you begin by applying the documenting techniques, tools, and tips conveyed *once a semester or quarter*, you will have begun an amazing and worthwhile journey!

Making Learning and Thinking *Visible*

Clark (2017) states that, "Visible thinking doesn't always mean visual." While there are many images and videos on blogs and other social media platforms, it is important to not fall into a visual trap and focus solely on conveying ideas or thoughts through infographic or photographic images. The heart of documenting is capturing the learning and thinking *while it is happening*, not simply the act of capturing what is happening or happened. Capturing one's or a group's thinking can happen via textual responses, narratives, or illustrated note taking, as well as audio reflections, interviews, or presenting video-recorded oral arguments to name a few.

The reality is that many young and adult learners are not aware of their own thinking when learning and do not proactively use thinking strategies and techniques to capture how learning is occurring. That is why it is imperative for learners to have ample opportunities in exploring how to make their thinking and learning visible, which awakens both cognitive and metacognitive processing.

To make thinking and learning visible involves breaking down the learning into self-awareness process steps. Project Zero (2017) states that, "When thinking is visible in classrooms, students are in a position to be more metacognitive, to think about their thinking. When thinking is visible, it becomes clear that learning is not about memorizing content but exploring ideas."

Martinez and Stager (2013) add that,

> Teachers should be concerned with making thinking visible, or making private thinking public. *Making* is a way of documenting the thinking of a learner in a shareable artifact. Stages of a project 'under construction' offer important evidence of productive thinking or scaffolding opportunities. (p.157)

Educators define and recognize learning acquisition differently. Some teachers will say that a student who gets all ten spelling words correctly on a test has learned how to spell the words, while other teachers will say it is simply an act of rote memory and will most likely be unable to spell the words correctly in a week without assistance. Some teachers may claim that reading a chapter in a book represents learning specific subject material, while others will say that is an assumption.

To bridge the gap of what a group of educators recognize as learning, the *learning-thinking* needs to be made visible. It is important for teachers to explore what constitutes learning-thinking in general, as well as for a particular focus or goal. They need to come to an agreement on the answers to such questions as:

- How do we recognize and acknowledge that our students have truly learned something?
- How can we recognize and acknowledge that we as adult-learners have truly learned something? Is it the same for students and adults?
- How can we recognize a pattern or trend of learning-thinking in our students over time?
- How can we teach/model the awareness and processes involved in learning-thinking?

Ritchhart et al. (2011) researched what it meant to capture learning-thinking discernibly. Ritchhart and some of his colleagues identified eight *thinking moves* that are, "Integral to developing understanding, and without which it would be difficult to say we had developed understanding of the learning":

1. Observing closely and describing what's there

2. Building explanations and interpretations

3. Reasoning with evidence

4. Making connections

5. Considering different viewpoints and perspectives

6. Capturing the heart and forming conclusions

7. Wondering and asking questions

8. Uncovering complexity and going below the surface of things (pp. 11, 13)

Each of the eight thinking moves is supported in strategic documentation and moves documenting from a display to a documenting learning process. To expand on each of these thinking moves, consider:

- **Observing closely and describing what's there**

  Observing is more than simply looking. It is homing in on what is taking place with a deliberate purpose. Being charged with articulating and describing what is being observed concerning oneself and/or others throughout a learning opportunity elevates cognition and metacognition processes when documenting.

- **Building explanations and interpretations**

  Embedding explaining and interpreting the meaning behind an action, behavior, belief, or phenomenon provides clearer evidence of one's thinking and ownership of the learning. As learners document through creating explanations and interpretations of their artifacts, they experience how the *act of documenting* aids in the learning itself. One's interpretation of a captured artifact can articulate background knowledge, viewpoints, and potentially, bias.

- **Reasoning with evidence**

  While it appears relatively easy to capture documentation artifacts and present them as evidence of learning, there is often no visible-thinking reasoning to support the evidence's claims. It takes thoughtful actions, such as annotexting a series of images over time.

  For example: A kindergarten teacher, Mr. Flagg, shares insights into his classroom's learning and discoveries through weekly class blog posts. Currently, his students are learning more about the interdependent relationships in ecosystems. Given his students live in Ventura, California, a study of the monarch butterfly is relevant and meaningful to them. He creates an initial post explaining the purpose and science-specific focuses for the unit of study. Mr. Flagg includes images (labeled drawings) of a few students' original mental models of how the monarch butterflies interact with the ecosystem in Camino Real Park after they ate a picnic lunch there in mid-October.

  While gaining knowledge about the life cycle of monarch butterflies and the *why* behind their migration patterns to California locations, Mr. Flagg continues to include iterative evidence of his students' models (ongoing photographs of their evolving labeled drawings) in his blog posts. His final post includes their representation and explanation of the relationship between the butterflies and their choice of wintering among the park's Eucalyptus trees and nearby milkweed.

Important note: While Mr. Flagg also includes photographs of his class caring for and observing monarch butterflies in the classroom (e.g., looking intensely at a caterpillar munching on a milkweed leaf in their butterfly camp), these photographs do not provide actual evidence of learning. Only when comparing the initial, iterative, and final drawing models does the evidence of learning actually convey the learners' sophistication of understanding and reasoning at a kindergarten level over time.

- **Making connections**

    Krechevsky, Mardell, Rivard, and Wilson (2013) express that, "Documentation is largely about building connections—temporal, relational, and conceptual" (p. 75). When capturing artifacts, learners have two choices:

    - Amass hours of recordings, hundreds of photographs, and piles of text snippets that can fill up analog or digital folders. These may or may not ever be used thoughtfully to aid in making connections.
    - Strategically capture and organize artifacts to purposefully create connections between and among the artifacts that aid in deepening understanding. The act of learning is alive and visible to oneself and to others.

- **Considering different viewpoints and perspectives**

    Taking advantage of artifacts captured by others allows learners to view their learning from multiple viewpoints. Documenting from varying perspectives allows learners to view and review moments in time, as well as study vantage points that could be outside their comfort zone (think of movie stars who do not like to view their own work) or beyond their isolated perspective, which deepens the acquisition process and allows the learners to articulate their thinking beyond themselves.

- **Capturing the heart and forming conclusions**

    While documenting learning could involve capturing everything seen, heard, or read, it is counterproductive. A learner must contemplate how to best capture evidence of the learning process, failures and successes alike, which is the heart of one's learning-thinking. A learner needs to be able to answer these questions when planning what needs to be captured: *how will I use the documentation artifact to form conclusions about my current/future learning? How will the documentation artifacts inform what I need to learn (or teach) next?*

- **Wondering and asking questions**

    Documenting is seen as a constant quest of wondering (looking) and finding potential answers. Through intentional documentation, learners and teachers conduct research through the inquiry process by posing questions, interpreting captured information, reporting on the findings, and asking more questions. Sheskey (2010) proposes learning is not about, "The answer anymore—it's the question." He continues, "At this point in the history of formal education, a change is occurring. Whereas before we gathered knowledge to become intelligent, now intelligence is measured by how well we apply knowledge to ask the right questions about how to solve the world's problems" (pp. 208–209).

- **Uncovering complexity and going below the surface of things**

    While it is easy to set up a camera and record an event or a moment in time, it does not capture thinking. Taking a photograph captures the surface—what is visible and desirable to the eye of the recorder. It cannot convey complex underlying assumptions, perspectives, interpretations, or explanations. How someone may interpret what is being seen or heard may be influenced by such factors as cultural beliefs, prior experience, what just happened moments before and after the image was taken or video recorded, or what was happening just off screen. When students and teachers observe their learning, and need to make their thinking and meaning visible, it aids in uncovering the complexities in their learning processes.

Making Learning and Thinking *Meaningful*

Making learning and thinking meaningful is not an easy task. For the documenting process to be meaningful, learners need to ask themselves questions such as:

- How do I know this documenting process has a worthwhile purpose?
- How will this process be useful to myself, as well as to others?
- How will this process support my ability for creating learning-thinking evidence?
- How will this process communicate information that cannot be expressed explicitly?

Learners must see an intentional link between the act of documenting and a meaningful focus or goal. Documenting purposes can be thought of as *usefulness*. For example: *Does the documenting action support growth? Does the documenting action move learning forward? Does the documenting action tell a story about the learning?* Table 1.2 provides questions pertaining to potential purposes.

Table 1.2   Sampling of Documenting Learning Purposes

Does the documenting action . . .		
. . . support growth? • *Does it provide intentional emphasis on demonstrating growth over time?* • *Does it show strategic and/or individual stages of learning over time?*	**. . . move learning forward?** • *Does it capture more than just "what is," so that it truly serves the purpose of moving the learning forward?* • *Does it provide an indication of the direction the learning can, could, or should take?*	**. . . tell a story about the learning?** • *Is the thinking and learning part of a larger story that the learner is telling?* • *Can it break down the learning process into individual components wherein each component makes the nuances of learning visible?*
. . . give learners a voice? • *Does it authentically allow learners to share their unfiltered thoughts, ideas, and conclusions?* • *Does it empower learners to be self-motivated and self-directed, and convey that the learners are being taken seriously?*	**. . . cause ownership of one's learning?** • *Does it play an integral part in taking ownership of my own, or our, learning?* • *How does it make a difference to the learner concerning wanting to learn versus waiting to be taught?*	**. . . create opportunities for feedback?** • *Does sharing it invite feedback by encouraging conversations that validate the work—whether ideas, questions, or conclusions?* • *Does it provide opportunities to obtain encouragement, constructive criticism, or interest-awareness levels?*
. . . encourage reflection and metacognition? • *Does reflection play a vital role in the documenting process versus simply an add-on, if only time permits?*	**. . . make meaningful connections to future learning?** • *Does it help in bridging gaps of isolated and disconnected learning moments currently or over time?*	**. . . support collection through curation?** • *Does it aid in preserving, maintaining, and archiving evidence and reasoning of personal/collaborative learning?*

Does the documenting action . . .		
• *Does it convey a cognition and/or metacognition learning-thinking process?*	• *Can it serve as an anchor moment that can be linked to future learning?*	• *Does it aid in creating artifacts worthy of potential curation?*
. . . encourage community communication?	**. . . embrace communication with a global audience?**	**. . . create professional learning opportunities?**
• *Does it encourage community involvement and authentic audiences?* • *Does it communicate transparently how educators are responding to the needs of their modern learners and willingness to continually transform teaching and learning?*	• *Is it created with a global audience in mind and respects varying perspectives and multicultural awareness?* • *Is it presented in multicultural, multilingual-friendly formats?* For example: using military time 16:00, instead of 4 p.m.; provide both standard and metric measurements: write out the date instead of including numerically (e.g., in most countries 3/7/2018 [March 7, 2018] will be read as July 3, 2018).*	• *Does it embrace educators as action researchers?* • *Does it embrace a teacher's desire to improve curricular content or areas of passion and interest?*

Making Learning and Thinking *Shareable*

In addition to content knowledge being learned in schools, there are critical skills and *now* literacies (which are addressed in Chapter 2) that learners of all ages need to build fluency in. Students and teachers are being asked to learn *how to learn*. The *now* literacies combined with the purposeful use of media platforms and tools require learners to apply strategies and techniques to aid them in *acquiring* and *sharing* their evidence of learning with others:

- **Sharing thoughts, ideas, creations, and connections to help make sense of what is being learned.**

    Global conversations are taking place on the immediacy to transform teaching and learning, including the necessity for authentic sharing. These conversations often lead to collaborations, fueled by educators who are passionate about impacting and empowering their students in meaningful ways. Learners gain leverage when they are given access and invitation to view other's learning, as well as ask for insight and feedback for their own learning. It is imperative that teachers also share their professional learning and growth to learn from their documentation artifacts and engagement with others.

- **Sharing allows thoughts, ideas, creations, and connections to be disseminated quickly beyond traditional avenues.**

    Appreciation for instant responses via an email or text versus snail-mail especially resonates with an older generation. Younger generations do not know what waiting for information really means. People around the world depend on instant, up-to-date information due to the ease of sharing, editing, and publishing technologies. Likewise, the ways that news, books, entertainment, and other kinds of information are now delivered and shared is staggering, especially when one realizes the sharing is accomplished at no or a low cost for the recipients or end users.

- **Sharing successes and failures/mistakes digitally extends and expands learning.**

  Twenty-first century teachers and students are pioneering new trails of what learning is and what it looks like using social media and digital curation. To *curate* in this context means the act of determining a resource's or artifact's value for a current or future learning need or task. Traditional learning pathways are not as they once were due to the reality that the world is advancing digitally in leaps and bounds. Just as pioneers of the past shared their success and failure stories as they journeyed to new lands to inform those who would blaze new trails after them, documenting while learning and sharing those journeys locally and globally aids and supports the journeys of others.

- **Sharing purposefully using social media can reach hundreds (and even thousands) of people instantly, and supports a learning-thinking model for others.**

  Social media avenues continue to grow at an exponential rate because people want to share their thinking, reasoning, experiences, latest work, and resources. While this is beneficial, there is a difference between sharing for sharing's sake versus sharing strategically to gain desired insights and feedback from expertise around the globe. The latter is what needs to be incorporated and modeled by teachers and students who are participating in documenting opportunities.

November (2010) emphasizes that, "Collaboration and sharing knowledge are the highly prized skills. . . . Teachers will be valued for their ability to share their knowledge and solve problems about teaching and learning that an individual teacher could not solve alone" (p. 50). Educators need to shift from a traditionally isolated learning process to include sharing strategies and techniques that support more meaningful learning opportunities, which lead to better retention and connection capacities.

Sharing can take on many forms, especially in today's world. What was once difficult to share with people who did not live or work on the same floor, in the same building, or geographically in the same area can now be contacted and connected via an email, DropBox downloadable files, or an impromptu FaceTime conversation. Shirky (2011) makes the point that even the notion of sharing is evolving due to myriad social media and networking tools that allow anyone to produce, publish, and comment:

> Expanding our focus to include producing and sharing doesn't even require making big shifts in individual behavior to create enormous changes in outcome. The world's cognitive surplus is so large that small changes can have huge ramifications in aggregate. We are increasingly becoming one another's infrastructure. This may be a cold-blooded way of looking at sharing – that we increasingly learn about the world through stranger's random choices about what to share – but even that has some human benefits. Our ability to balance consumption with production and sharing, our ability to connect with one another, is transforming the sense of media from a sector of the economy to a cheap and globally available tool for organized sharing. (p. 327)

Ritchhart et al. (2011) express that "Students need to see how others plan, monitor, and challenge their own thinking in ways that move them forward. Students need to see that all learners make mistakes and that learning often occurs from reflecting on those mistakes" (p. 29). Therefore, it is important to note that artifacts do not equate perfection. They are often works in progress designed to aid in gaining knowledge and understanding.

The act of documenting and creating artifacts naturally lends itself to making documentation shareable. What was once invisible becomes visible and allows moments in time to be captured, replayed, organized, archived, and retrieved. It also aids in making meaning and deepening meaning.

When documenting learning with a sharing perspective in mind, consider incorporating the following:

- Keep the sharing short and summarize or highlight the salient points. For example: Do not share hours of recorded video clips; instead, share short snippets that capture the thinking and learning in focus.
- Consider creating infographics to explain data and thinking about that data.
- Have an audience in mind who will be receiving or viewing the shared artifacts and anticipate potential questions, points of interests, and necessary clarifications.
- Determine the media platforms and tools that best aid in sharing the learning-thinking artifacts.
- Be conscious of privacy concerns when sharing personal or other learners' artifacts.
- Be globally aware and culturally sensitive when sharing artifacts with the world.

Making Learning and Thinking *Amplified*

When sharing thinking and learning beyond an *audience of one*, a sharer becomes acutely aware of the impact his or her artifacts can have on a larger audience. Therefore, the act of amplifying needs to be purposeful as well.

Amplifying personal or group learning-thinking is similar to a speaker's voice is amplified and reaches a larger audience, especially when the learners are strategic about using social media to reach the desired audience. Learners who want to gain knowledge and deeper understanding from those with whom they share find amplifying to be enriching and enlightening. It encourages active participation in globally connected communities of learners, professional educational conversations, and communication among thought leaders.

Transformational thinking and learning are positively affected through amplification because learners meaningfully interact with others *while their learning is still taking place.* Collaborating via amplification with experts from around the world provides evidence of its worthiness when witnessing the interactions students have with those who, in the not too distant past, where unreachable.

For example, a fifth-grade class was about to study the American Revolution. Their teacher wanted them to experience a learning opportunity beyond the pages of their textbooks and her own expertise. With Silvia's assistance, the class posted a collaboration want ad on her *Langwitches* Blog and tweeted her professional learning network asking for interested experts, teachers, and classrooms who would like to work with the students and provide varying perspectives concerning this time period in American history.

It did not take long before receiving inquiries and comments from experts, colleagues, and peers who were eager to connect and share with the class. Due to the want ad amplification, the class was able to skype and learn from:

- Travis Bowman, a sixth-generation descendant of Peter Francisco, a famous American patriot and soldier in the American Revolutionary War, who authored a historical novel about Francisco's life titled *Hercules of the Revolution.*

QR Code 1.1

Scan this QR code to read the *Wanted: Collaboration Partner for American Revolution* blog post.

http://langwitches.me/americanrevolution

- Richard Byrnes, a previous high school history teacher and well-known creator of the *FreeTechnology4Teachers* website.

While local interactions with peers and colleagues within school and district learning communities cannot be underestimated, it is imperative that educators realize the power of participating in a living, breathing learning culture that amplifies to reach a global audience using social media platforms and tools. Documenting that includes amplification embraces and encourages modern forms of learning that accesses expertise, receives meaningful feedback, and connects beyond the limitations of zip codes and language barriers. When learners become acutely aware of how their learning grows due to amplification, it transforms their pre-planning for how to best amplify learning and thinking.

When learners become acutely aware of how their learning grows due to amplification, it transforms their pre-planning for how to best amplify learning and thinking.

QR Code 1.2

Scan this QR code to read *Framing a Skype Learning Experience.*

http://langwitches.me/learning-experience

Amplifying learning often brings unexpected and memorable surprises. For example, fourth graders created book trailers for fiction books they had read. They published the trailers via their student blogs by embedding their book-recommendation videos. The author of one of the recommend books received a Google alert that someone had posted something about her literary work. She was able to locate the specific student's blog and video trailer about her book. She contacted the student's teacher to see if she could use the book trailer on her own website. The teacher, knowing an incredible opportunity to continue the amplification was possible, asked the author if she would be willing to skype with her class to talk about being a professional writer and share her thought process when she wrote the recommended book. The author accepted without hesitation. Based on the actions of sharing the online book review and someone else unrelated to the class amplifying the student's recommendation, an extended amplification learning opportunity now benefited the entire class and author.

Sharing learning-thinking strategically online creates greater degrees of amplification—both expressively and receptively. Here are a few amplification considerations:

- **Digitize an artifact.** Digitizing allows learners to be able to share their artifacts online. Digitizing is the act of converting images or sound into a digital format. When the digital content is uploaded, sharing and amplification have begun. An audience—beyond one or a few who are physically present—who view and/or hear what the documentation artifacts are conveying allows thinking and learning connections to be enhanced.
- **Consider different media.** Choosing to produce evidence of learning using a variety of media and social media applications allows online audiences to read, look at, watch, and listen to learners' artifacts in multiple forms. Amplification happens when learners purposefully and strategically go beyond traditional media, which primarily has been text-based, to embrace different media forms, including the mixing of mediums to create new forms.
- **Extend learning opportunities.** Amplification can extend the learning time beyond a traditional school day or professional development hours. It is designed so the

learners' reach is 24/7 accessible. Traditionally, the only expert in the room was the teacher. Magical learning moments happen when teachers see themselves as learners and allow students to express their current knowledge—both accurate and inaccurate, plus pose inquiry questions that invite peers, experts, and eyewitnesses globally to interact with them and their documentation artifacts.

- **Extend the reach.** Until recently learners have not had a reach beyond their personal scope of families, friends, teachers, professors, and classmates. Today, extending one's reach is multifaceted. For example, an extended reach happens when a blog post is uploaded, cross-posted, and linked strategically to others using social media, such as Twitter. By using strategic social networking, connections, collaborations, and dissemination paths can be immediately beneficial to learners. *Disclaimer: Oftentimes the act of uploading content online is not enough to successfully extend the reach. The student or teacher must participate in building and interacting with professional learning networks (or know someone who does) to alert, contact, and disseminate the documentation.*

- **Connect with a global audience.** Learners' reach can be considered amplified when artifacts are created or uploaded in a password-protected environment (e.g., accessible only to classmates, colleagues, or limited community members). A broader amplification happens when artifacts and inquiries are sent out to the world. A global audience affords students to hear and learn from differing perspectives, viewpoints, and obtain resources that are unavailable when confined to a controlled local audience. Understandably, when learners are permitted to share and amplify globally, it comes with responsibilities for both students and teachers.

- **Have your voice heard.** Making a difference in the world is possible through amplification and reaching a global audience. Even children as young as four and five years, with the help of their parents or teachers, are finding their voice and being heard. More and more children are being asked to be keynote speakers at educational and business conferences. This is because the traditional limitations of age, physical capabilities, and financial limitations are melting away due to the access that social media and network connections allow. Amplification is a learning strategy that allows student and teacher voices to be heard. It is a powerful realization that anyone, young or old, has something valuable to share with the world. For example, search for either of these hashtags and explore the amplification taking place: #kidscanteachtoo, #studentvoice.

SUMMING UP

Teachers must see themselves as active learners—both in the classroom alongside their student-learners and professionally with their colleagues. When all learners are provided ample documenting opportunities to transfer their learning and understanding from *within a content area, one content area to another, one class or course to another, and one year to the next,* their understanding of how they learn and what they are learning is purposeful and meaningful. Making meaning emerges and evolves naturally when documenting opportunities requires ownership of one's learning actions. This is because the act of documenting the learning is occurring while the learning is taking place, not as a result of it.

Being cognizant of one's strategic actions to capture, share, and amplify learning-thinking artifacts at specific moments in time, coupled with revisiting artifacts over time, are essential to the documenting learning framework.

GOING BEYOND

To amplify your reading beyond this book's pages, we have created *discussion questions and prompts* for this chapter, which are located at *www.documenting4learning.com*. To extend your thinking, reactions, and responses, you can connect with other readers by leaving comments on individual chapter's discussion posts on our documenting4learning blog.

We also invite you to contribute and share your artifacts in other social media spaces to connect with and learn from other readers around the world using the #documenting4learning hashtag on Twitter, Facebook, or Instagram; or by mentioning @documenting4learning on Facebook and Instagram, and @doc4learning on Twitter.

Documenting Learning and the *Now* Literacies

Let us make our future now, and let us make our dreams tomorrow's reality.

—Malala Yousafza

To provide learners with a deeper understanding of how documenting learning benefits their awareness, skills, and routines, they must be cognizant of and continually improve their *now* literacies:

- Basic literacy: reading, writing, listening, speaking
- Media literacy
- Digital citizenship
- Global literacy
- Information literacy
- Network literacy

Now does not imply *preparing for the future* because the future is here. It is *now* (see Image 2.1).

RELATIONSHIP BETWEEN DOCUMENTING LEARNING AND *NOW* LITERACIES

The point of a formal or informal education is to become *literate*—the ability to read, write, and communicate thoughts and ideas—regardless of chosen profession or passion. To be literate is to be a productive contributor to society.

Basic Literacy

How does documenting learning support and foster the development of basic literacy? Preparing for and creating documentation artifacts enable thoughts and ideas to move from one's mental thinking to shareable thinking using text and images. Artifacts aid in visibly conveying connections of otherwise isolated thoughts, reflections, events, and projects, to create meaning making. Likewise, they provide learners with pattern-and-trend timelines that enable learners to describe, explain, illustrate, and interpret their learning journeys.

Artifacts can involve various text types and purposes for both student and professional learning. Table 2.1 provides information concerning ten text types from a documenting perspective, including an example of each from Silvia's blog posts.

It is important to remember that the documenting process and creation of artifacts capture what oftentimes goes unnoticed. This is beneficial to learners as they are working toward becoming stronger readers, writers, listeners, speakers, and thinkers.

Whether the learning process is taking place through passionate pursuits or required content, it is important for learners to realize they are

Image 2.1

- becoming action researchers involving both active and reflective opportunities;
- engaging with connected learning communities to share their insights and discoveries; and
- gaining authentic feedback and new considerations related to current or future learning.

Table 2.1 Documentation Artifacts Using Various Text Types and Purposes

Narrative artifacts allow documenting learning to be read, heard, or viewed in the context of storytelling, which aids in creating a learning storyline.

QR Code 2.1

Scan this QR code to read *The Story Behind Langwitches.*

http://langwitches.me/langwitches-story

Description artifacts provide specific characteristics, details, and features that capture the sights and sounds, and possibly even textures and tastes, of a learning journey.

QR Code 2.2

Scan this QR code to read *Digital Learning Farm in Action: Mystery Skype.*

http://langwitches.me/learning-farm

Informational artifacts present information or aspects of an event related to the content being acquired, processed, or internalized using clear facts and no personal opinions.

QR Code 2.3

Scan this QR code to read *Copyright a Little Fuzzy?*

http://langwitches.me/fuzzy

Expository artifacts provide explanations and relevant evidence, as well as share ideas, wherein the learner does not assume readers/viewers have prior knowledge.

QR Code 2.4

Scan this QR code to read *What Are the Best Ways a Teacher Can Demonstrate Leadership in the Classroom?*

http://langwitches.me/leadership

(Continued)

Table 2.1   (Continued)

Persuasive artifacts try to convince readers/viewers to change their minds or participate in an action; hence, when learners share their personal reactions to an experience or event they may influence others to consider change or take an action.

QR Code 2.5

Scan this QR code to read *3 Reasons Why You Should Share and 3 Things You Can Do to Start Sharing.*

http://langwitches.me/share

Explanation artifacts contribute articulations related to content, actions, or how/why something works (or possibly does not work). Explanations also aid in breaking down and supporting steps in a procedure, which is an important cognitive process to put into practice.

QR Code 2.6

Scan this QR code to read *Action! The Digital Learning Farm.*

http://langwitches.me/action

Recount artifacts convey what has taken place in chronological order. It is oftentimes combined with explanations to articulate specifics related to the events or actions.

QR Code 2.7

Scan this QR code to read *Evolution of Note Taking: New Forms.*

http://langwitches.me/notetakingevolution

Procedure artifacts provide step-by-step instructions for how to do or create something, which supports learning by having to break down the process and articulate each step.

QR Code 2.8

Scan this QR code to read *Step-by-Step: How to Create a Collaborative Class eBook.*

http://langwitches.me/collaborative-ebook

Research artifacts play an integral role in documentation when learners realize they are investigative reporters who are expected to own their own learning and convey their learning processes to aid in improving their learning or facilitate the learning of others.

QR Code 2.9

Scan this QR code to read *Quad Blogging Reflection.*

http://langwitches.me/quadblogging

Social media artifacts support reading and writing in new forms through the use of online features such as hyperlinks, @mentions, and #hashtags to connect to the world. Using social media platforms and tools also allows for nonlinear and asynchronous learning to occur.

QR Code 2.10

Scan this QR code to read *Unpacking a Twitter Conference Feed.*

http://langwitches.me/unpacking-feed

For example, all three realizations are present when a middle school teacher strategically selects and annotates multimedia artifacts from her fourth period's small-group teams focused on student voice when writing and conveying one's ideas succinctly. Using the artifacts as evidence, she shares and amplifies her professional learning observations and realizations using her blog and Twitter. From her shared introspections coupled with the insights shared by others, she realizes that while she continues to encourage her students to improve their voice capabilities, she needs to make a few adjustments and improvements to her instruction and her students' writing expectations.

Media Literacy

How does documenting learning authentically incorporate media literacy? Media literacy expresses an informed, critical understanding of the explicit and subliminal purposes and influences of mass media. It also includes the ability to understand and create visual messages. This *now* literacy enables learners to analyze, evaluate, and create messages using a wide variety of media modes, genres, and formats, including text, image, video, audio, or a mixture thereof. This literacy is also based on the premise that visual images can be read both for comprehension (making meaning) and inferencing (interpreting and negotiating meaning).

Documenting is tightly connected to media literacy because the documentation process involves making the learning visible to the learner and to others. Therefore, documenting allows learners to *see* the learning in action, especially when engaging in the interpretation and analyzation of artifacts. Questions to pose while planning to capture media-based artifacts include:

- What will the learning look like?
- Will I recognize learning when I see it?
- How can one image or series of images represent that can't be touched or easily seen?
- How can a video clip become evidence of a learning process?
- How can I become aware of, and on the lookout for, the absence of learning?

Since documenting is about capturing the invisible and making it visible to oneself and others, the process over time points out learning patterns, trends, and unconscious points that are often missed. Wien, Guyevskey, and Berdoussis (2011) state that

> Graphic design principles and processes are important to pedagogical documentation, along with an understanding of visual literacy—how the human eye reads images and how people interpret those images. Also helpful is an awareness of the ways that combining text and image, or text and audio, or video and still image can convey information effectively. A grasp of how digital technologies can be used in visual design may also be applied to documentation.

Given their points:

- How could I make learning and thinking visible?
- How can I capture a potential absence of learning?
- How can the contributing *invisible* factors be captured and made visible (e.g., motivation, engagement, trust, curiosity)?
- How could a process over time be captured in strategic short clips or images?
- What media are best suited to communicate and convey my message?
- What techniques for capturing media will I incorporate?
- How can I mix media to best communicate evidence of learning?

Media literacy is not only about reading, writing, and creating media. It is equally about interpreting, analyzing, evaluating, and make meaning of the media:

- Do the media I captured demonstrate evidence of, or lack of, learning?
- What media can be shared (considering digital citizenship)?
- Which media will help convey my message?
- How do I connect related or contrast captured media?
- What media do I keep? What media get cut/deleted?
- How will I need to edit the media to make it appealing to my viewing audience?
- How does the captured media influence how I will express what was experienced?
- Did what was captured inform me about what I need to look for or pay attention to next?

It is important to document to aid one's own learning, but when sharing learning strategically with others, it creates a new dimension. Preparing documentation media to share and communicate a message requires technology capabilities and considering how the sharing will aid in one's learning process:

- Why would I share this learning documentation?
- What message do I want to share with my potential audience?
- How do I best present my documentation to receive feedback about my learning and current understanding?
- How do I prepare the media to make them easily sharable?
- What types of media are best suited for specific platforms of dissemination?
- How should I disseminate the created media to best share and amplify them with my intended audience?
- How do I prepare my learning-thinking message so it is seen/heard by my intended audience?
- What are the best ways to prepare my media artifacts and message so that they can be interactive (liked, re-shared, retweeted, or re-mixed)?
- How can my shared artifacts become a source of learning for others?

Digital Citizenship

How does documenting learning ask learners to actively display digital citizenship? Heick (2013a) describes digital citizenship as, "The quality of habits, actions, and consumption patterns that impact the ecology of digital content and communities." MacMeeking (2013) notes that, "The more our students are online, the more information they will encounter. It is important for them not only be able to access this information, but also to be the best digital citizens that they can be."

Documenting is based on the premise that students and teachers will display quality habits and actions throughout, and beyond, their academic learning opportunities as they display respectfulness and lawfulness, while contributing to an ever-growing digital world as thoughtful digital citizens.

Here are ten digital citizenship characteristics that the documenting learning process fosters (see Image 2.2):

Privacy in Respecting Confidentiality

Maintaining privacy becomes a necessity when documenting learning. *What is appropriate to share with others and the world? Where is the invisible line that may not be crossed?* When

Image 2.2

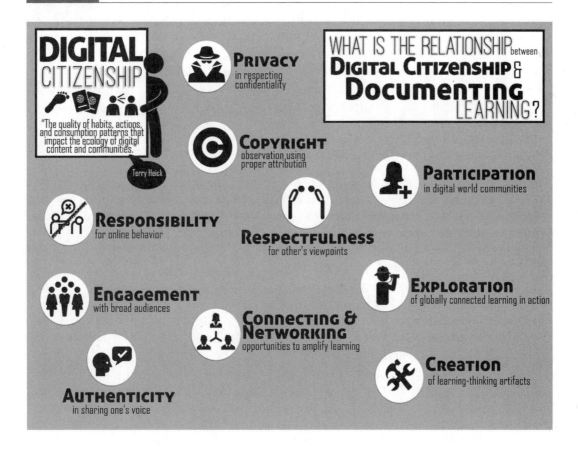

artifacts are being readied to be shared or amplified, one's own privacy as well as others in the artifacts must be considered. Students and teachers need to learn how to capture learning without showing people's faces (e.g., recording backs of heads, or using a pixelating tool prior to sharing) unless given written permission. Likewise, it is important to be conscientious about sharing any information that could be exploited by others (e.g., location, name, phone number, address, interests).

Copyright Observation Using Proper Attribution

When engaged in the learning process it is not uncommon to use resources, ideas, and works created by others. It is therefore important to ensure that copyright attribution becomes a natural part of the process when curating, sharing, and amplifying artifacts. When one's learning-thinking is made visible—whether text, image, or multimedia—it is required by law to reference the original owners of any included content, as well as provide reference to authors and their intellectual properties. If this is an area that has been ignored or overlooked in your classroom or school, it needs to be addressed head-on to ensure learners and teachers are modeling correct behavior and being mindful digital citizens concerning their actions when conveying their documentation to the world.

Responsibility for Online Behavior

When placing artifacts online, it is imperative that it is done so respectfully. Documenting raises awareness of the learning process, including the need to embrace failures and mistakes.

This vulnerability must be protected. Allowing malicious or hurtful comments orally or textually must never be permitted. Documenting the learning of oneself or others is not about shaming, but about embracing and correcting misunderstandings, gaining new perspectives, progressing one's understanding by sharing and amplifying the learning, and celebrating and showcasing the learning. Just as with privacy, there is an invisible line that is not to be crossed when deciding what can be shared to accurately and strategically represent the learning process without embarrassing learners. *Netiquette* is a term often used by school and districts to express the need for responsible behavior and expected protocols as Internet consumers or producers.

Respectfulness for Other's Viewpoints

Learners will most likely deal with more subjective comments versus objective ones when sharing and amplifying their artifacts with the world. For example, when a student posted his thoughts concerning a current-event issue in a blog post, he was quite shaken when a commenter made a strong, rather personal attack concerning his main points. When the student showed the comment to his teacher, she did not immediately remove it or tell him to, "Just ignore it." Instead, she asked him some thought-provoking questions: *Why do you think this person may have had such an intense emotional response? Where does this person live? What life experiences may be influencing his comments?* By clicking on the commenter's avatar, they eventually got to the commenter's Facebook page and began to put two-and-two together. The student drafted a response and asked his classmates for their thoughts and input. Eventually, he posted a response to the commenter. Soon after, the commenter posted a new comment in the thread wherein he apologized for his harshness and shared insight into why he used the tone he did when expressing his thoughts.

Participation in Digital World Communities

The digital world has bridged the gap between consumers and producers. In an analog world, it was difficult and expensive to join the ranks of publishers and purveyors of thoughts and ideas, but in today's online world, information is freelance and accessible to anyone with an Internet-enabled device and a connection. Documenting amplifies the notion of what it meant to be learning collaboratively regarding who is teaching, and when and where learning takes place. Participating in and contributing to a global learning community allow learners to be digital-world citizens. For example, we can learn about how to dubstep from a preteen (scan QR Code 2.11).

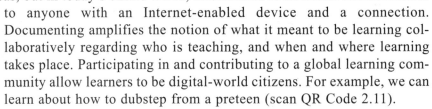

QR Code 2.11

Scan this QR code to view *This amazing girl mastered dubstep dancing by just using YouTube.*

http://langwitches.me/dubstep

Engagement With a Broad Audience

Engaging with an audience beyond oneself live or digitally can vary due to what is being documented, how it is being documented, and how the learners are sharing and amplifying the artifacts. Social media feedback by the target audience can range from active forms of conversation (e.g., comments on a blog, writing or replying to a tweet) or passive forms (e.g., receiving likes, reactions, retweets). Both students and adult learners need to learn how to engage in active forms of digital communication and providing meaningful feedback.

Connecting and Networking Opportunities to Amplify Learning

Participating in digital world communities implies a commitment to not simply joining existing communities in a passive manner, but actively connecting and networking with its members. Documenting learning was originally based on the Reggio Emilia-inspired pedagogical documentation model, which did not consider the ability and need to share, amplify, and obtain feedback in real time in a digital world because these capabilities and technologies were not available and accessible at the time. New applications and opportunities for connecting learners to share their thinking around the world is becoming commonplace. Proactively and strategically sharing and disseminating artifacts that represent thinking in visible ways empowers students and teachers during the school day, and most importantly, beyond.

Exploration of Worldwide Learning in Action

As Heick (2013a) suggested in his definition of digital citizenship, it is about an ecology of digital content and communities. An ecology is focused on the organisms' relationships—one to another and to their physical surroundings. There is a need to explore how other learners are learning beyond the limitations of one's own classroom walls, country, or continent. Likewise, learners should be available to "be discovered" by others who want to learn from them. Documenting allows a local learning organism to interact with worldwide learning organisms who are technically living and breathing in the same ecosystem and desire to gain insights into how one other thinks, believes, acts, and reacts to similar topics or themes.

QR Code 2.12

Scan this QR code to view a variety of Sylvia Duckworth's sketchnotes.

http://langwitches.me/duckworth

Authenticity in Sharing One's Voice

When documenting over time, a learner develops his or her own style, which becomes recognizable by others. For example, two well-known sketchnoters' images are recognized just by quickly scanning their work. Each has her own voice that is conveyed through a personalized use of font, color, images, and layout (scan QR Codes 2.12 and 2.13).

As learners are involved in multiple opportunities to express their visible thinking, they begin to have a recognizable style and voice. When sharing and amplifying artifacts, one's voice needs to be truthful and forthright, including answering the following questions: *What do I see in myself as I observe my learning at this moment in time? How can I best convey my understanding of what I am learning and where I am in my learning process?*

Creation of Learning-Thinking Artifacts

Documentation artifacts are creations that include interpreted information and explanations of the visible thinking and understanding. Anderson et al. (2000) conveys that the highest level of the revised Bloom's Taxonomy of Educational Objectives is *creation*. Today's digital world consists of an ongoing exchange of *both* consumers and producers (contributors). If learners never have documenting opportunities that involve creating digital content to be accessed and interacted with locally or globally, they will forever remain consumers, which means being only a partial digital citizen.

QR Code 2.13

Scan this QR code to view a variety of Silvia Tolisano's sketchnotes.

http://langwitches.me/langwitches-sketchnotes

It's Time to Take Action!

Chapter 2 Action Step

So far in this chapter, you have read about three *now* literacies: *basic literacy*, *media literacy*, and *digital citizenship*. Share a documenting opportunity (even if you would not have called it that before reading this book) that involved your students or yourself applying one or more of these three literacies during a learning experience.

In your tweet, Instagram description, Facebook post, or blog post, include annotations and/or annotexted artifacts that express characteristics of your selected literacy or literacies.

Remember to use the #documenting4learning hashtag on Twitter, Facebook or Instagram, or by mentioning @documenting4learning on Facebook and Instagram, and @doc4learning on Twitter.

Global Literacy

How does documenting learning support global literacy? Asia Society (2015) defines *global competence* (literacy) as the toolkit a productive, involved citizenry used to meet the problems and opportunities of the world. In addition, they state:

> In the curriculum, global competence challenges students to investigate the world, consider a variety of perspectives, communicate ideas, and take meaningful action. A globally focused curriculum engages students in their own learning and motivates them to strive for knowledge and understanding. And a curious, inspired student strives to learn more in school and beyond.

Notice the last sentence: *And a curious, inspired student strives to learn more in school and beyond.*

Documenting learning is about just that: providing phases, routine, platforms, and tools that inspire student and adult learners to strive to learn more academically, personally, and professionally in and outside of school time.

Here are nine global literacy characteristics that the documenting learning process fosters (see Image 2.3):

Awareness of Self in Context of World's New Knowledge

As students and teachers document their learning, abstract concepts related to beliefs, perspectives, understandings, and practices become visible. This can be frightening at times as it causes oneself to become cognitive, and metacognitive, regarding who he or she is within a cultural context of the world and the people who inhabit it. Identification of one's own cultural uniqueness may not meaningfully occur unless learners are engaged in documenting opportunities that encourage reaching out to and learning form a global audience.

When learners can articulate their cultural identity, they are more likely aware of what influences their motivation, desire, practice, and decision making. The ability to stand back from oneself and become aware of other's cultural learning values, beliefs, and perceptions (why they learn, what they are learning, and what they plan on doing with the learning) is important for students and teachers to experience. Identifying and reflecting on what comprises the attitudes, actions, products, and performances of one's culture in light of a

Image 2.3

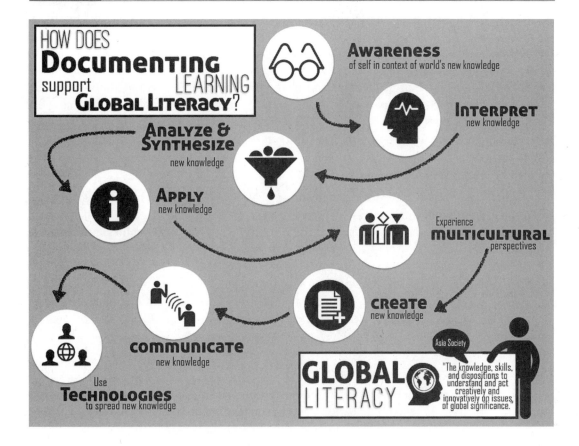

growing awareness of the similarities and uniqueness of other cultures can be enlightening. A strategic component to creating artifacts in terms of global awareness is for learners to be conscious of how their artifacts may explicitly or implicitly convey personal cultural points of view when making thinking visible that may be different than other's cultural viewpoints.

Interpret New Knowledge

Learning from and with others takes place via reading, viewing, hearing, and interpreting artifacts from around the globe. Learning also takes place through a symbiotic relationship among the owners of the artifacts: the thinking conveyed and interpretations made by the learners engaged in the documentation process. Background knowledge and cultural beliefs play a role in interpreting new knowledge. The realization of cultural differences expands one's understanding that there are multiple ways to express facts, ideas, opinions, and arguments than may have been initially thought. Documenting opportunities cognitively and metacognitively deepens the understanding of one's own practices via interpretation. This reflection process goes even deeper when learners engage in knowledge and interpretation discussions with learners and experts from around the world.

Analyze and Synthesize New Knowledge

Analyzing can be defined as the act of *critical examination to determine the elements and specific features for the act of explanation or interpretation.* Documenting learning gives students and teachers opportunities to do so by examining the captured learning in detail for nuances, patterns, trends, and implications for future learning and teaching. Synthesizing can be defined as *the act of combining what is known to create a new or more complex understanding*. The exchange of the thinking created, shared, and amplified around the world enables learners to analyze and synthesize varying perspectives, content, and resources that expand and challenge their own thoughts, ideas, and beliefs. This is true for students, as well as teachers and administrators. Many teachers we have worked alongside have commented on how their repertoire of pedagogies and instructional techniques and methods have been affirmed, challenged, and expanded by transparently sharing their professional learning and growth with educators around the world. The same has been true for administrators who have been willing to share and amplify their own professional documentation artifacts.

Apply New Knowledge

The better the artifacts portray evidence and interpretation of the learning being captured, the easier it becomes for readers, listeners, and/or viewers to gain insights that can be applied to their own learning. When learning through analyzing and synthesizing artifacts, whether one's own or others, learners grow in their own understanding as they apply their new or deeper knowledge to new situations, problems, or issues. Documenting is especially important during the process of creating new information, such as piloting new ideas or action research. It is critical that learners know how to document their own learning and apply their gained knowledge in meaningful ways with intended audiences.

Experience Multicultural Perspectives

As mentioned previously, documenting learning from one's cultural perspective influences the learning and understanding conveyed in artifacts. The term *global* simply means *outside of one's locality*. Learners in one town, city, or state can learn much from students and teachers living in another. Students' and teachers' understanding broadens in terms of histories, values, and viewpoints of global citizens. For example, skyping with a classroom halfway around the world who is also struggling with a similar water-conservation problem adds perspective for both classrooms, and will most likely influence considerations and solutions for the task at hand in both locations.

When connecting and experiencing other's cultures it does not take long to discover people are more similar than different regarding love, lifelong desires, and values. Take an amplified video created as an experiment by a high-school student in an arts-focused high school in Chicago titled: *People react to being called beautiful* (scan QR Code 2.14). When watching the video, a viewer cannot help but notice the surprised looks and emotions conveyed based on the simple act of being told they are beautiful inside and out. After viewing this video, a teacher in an Arkansas high school decided to do the same, but this time asked teachers to capture shared moments of why particular students make them want to come to school. The same physical and verbal expressions are evident in both videos (scan QR Code 2.15). The visible action of touching the hearts of students in Chicago being shared and amplified led to students in Arkansas knowing they are loved as well. *(If you would like to participate in this project, use #beautifulpeople and #documenting4learning when sharing and amplifying your video on your selected social media platforms.)*

QR Code 2.14

Scan this QR code to view the video *People react to being called beautiful.*

http://langwitches.me/beautiful

QR Code 2.15

Scan this QR code to view the video *Students react to being called important.*

http://langwitches.me/important

Create New Knowledge

If you have chosen to take the #beautifulpeople challenge, you will be creating/producing new knowledge and sharing it with the world through amplification. Whether videoing veterans, family members, synagogue attendees, or administrators in your district, when documenting the reactions of those being told of their worth and value, it also informs audience viewers as learners as well. Documenting opportunities provide avenues for creating artifacts that convey new knowledge and bring awareness of global issues. For example, in March of 2017, Cable News Network (CNN) launched a project #MyFreedomDay, "When students around the world did amazing things to raise awareness of modern-day slavery. . . . Students at hundreds of schools, spread across six continents, came together to form a global community, shining a light on [this issue]." From school panels and presentations to silent film-videos and black-and-white photographs, students as contributors created, shared, and amplified their voices, while acting on behalf of those whose voices are often silenced.

Communicate New Knowledge

Communication of new knowledge is not meant to be passive. It is meant to be active—mutually expressive and receptive. Documenting asks learners to formulate and articulate not only *what* will be shared, but *how* it will ask audiences to communicate their knowledge, thoughts, opinions, and perspectives. Thoughtful decision-making regarding media types (text, image, audio, video) and platforms that promote responsive communication (e.g., Twitter—hashtags and direct messages; blog posts, YouTube, SlideShare—comment threads; Snapchat geofilters—sharing one's location) to reach the desired global audience need to be made.

QR Code 2.16

Scan this QR code to view *Obvious to You. Amazing to Others*.

http://langwitches.me/obvious

It is not uncommon for learners of all ages to believe they do not have anything new or special enough to share. Sivers (2011), calls this phenomenon, "Obvious to you. Amazing to others" (scan QR code 2.1.6). The belief that *I do not have anything worth sharing* is not an uncommon hurdle that needs to be overcome early on when learners are first asked to document their learning. This is true especially for older learners, given younger learners have not yet experienced non-acceptance, or created a personal fear of failure.

Use Technologies to Spread New Knowledge

When learners share and amplify their artifacts, the feedback and new knowledge and ideas gained create an *added value* to their documentation being meaningful and purposeful. Using text, images, and multimedia communication technologies to reach a worldwide audience supports action research and innovation. By sharing across the globe, as opposed to only with local classmates or colleagues, amplification degrees widened and often lead to deeper learning experiences.

The imperative for sharing learning and discovery globally are becoming the norm. The Oxford Dictionary (2017a) defines *crowdsourcing* as obtaining information or input into a task or project by enlisting the services of a large number of people. Therefore, it is important to be aware and take advantage of crowdsourcing and the ability to learn from and with the world. The barriers of traditional publishing technologies have been removed by the accessibility to self-publishing devices and networking platforms that can reach millions.

Information Literacy

How does information literacy relate to documenting learning? Unfortunately, living in a digital age leads to the inability to

- determine meaningful materials and resources due to information overload,
- discern truth from false information due to fake news reports,
- comprehend and inference multimedia forms due to beyond-text communication, and
- create, re-mix, and disseminate new forms of information due to the implication that online users *both* consume and produce.

These *inabilities* need to become *abilities.* To do so builds informational literacy, which consists of four abilities:

- Identify and search effectively for information.
- Locate, filter, discern, evaluate, and analyze the quality of information.
- Tag, categorize, re-mix, and create new types of information.
- Effectively use and communicate findings on a topic, theme, problem, or issue.

Here are nine informational literacy characteristics that the documenting learning process fosters (see Image 2.4):

Image 2.4

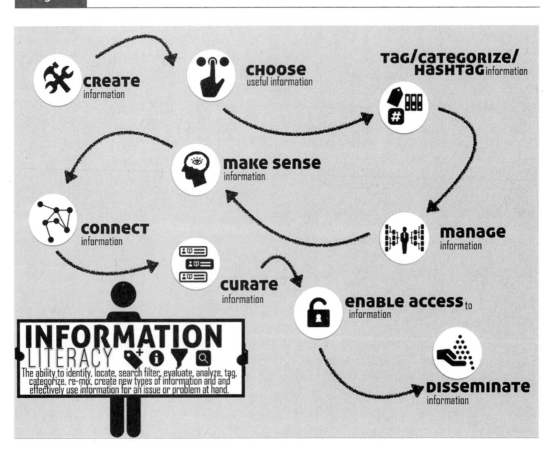

Create Information

Documenting involves looking for learning, capturing visual and auditory evidence, reflecting on the meaning of the captured evidence, and making that meaning visible, shareable, and amplified. As producers, learners are turning data into information and creating new knowledge based on that information. Documenting learning overall focuses on creating information about a learner, his or her learning process, and how the learning plays a role in a bigger picture of learning over time.

Choose Useful Information

Learners need to continually improve their capabilities to evaluate what information needs to be gathered: *What characterizes useful and worthwhile information as evidence of learning at various stages of the learning?* Documenting is about much more than snapping a photograph or recording a few moments in time. It involves being strategically selective about collecting the most useful information that captures evidence of the learning.

The ability to make choices between *useful* and *useless* information is a learned art. Student and adult learners need multiple opportunities before they can make cognitive and metacognitive documenting decisions that are consistently useful. Likewise, learners need to gain insights into figuring out what is the most beneficial information during their learning experience. For example, if students are learning about how the common cold virus is spread in their community, this would not be the best time to reach out globally. What would be beneficial is contacting and interviewing local health agencies and learning about regulatory guidelines for their local public environments.

Tag, Categorize, and Hashtag Information

With the amount of information being created, shared, and amplified worldwide daily, it is paramount that learners know how to tag, categorize, and hashtag information to make their artifacts easily searchable and accessible for themselves and others. Students and teachers need to be consciously aware of how to best curate and catalog each artifact. By doing so they begin to see relationships across and among content and skill areas, as well as create connections to their stored artifacts that can be accessed during future learning opportunities.

Manage Information

Learners need to manage information created by others, as well as the information they create. Downes (2013) predicts that, "Increasingly in the future, students will be responsible for managing their own online learning records and creative products. . . . They will need to manage these resources, index them, and enable access to them." For example, managing information and artifacts via cloud storage provides learners with experiences in using systems and platforms that facilitate the management of online resources. The ability to archive artifacts promotes the capability to track and document their learning over time. Another example of managing one's learning evidence can be through the use of blogfolios. The blogging platform used will have management features, such as chronological posting, archiving, tagging, and categorizing capabilities.

Make Sense of Information

People are bombarded with information 24/7, without even asking. Think of the ads that pop up when searching that just so happen to reflect a search topic or website you visited just a few hours ago. With the capabilities of businesses and nonprofits to share, disseminate, re-mix, and create any type of information they wish, learners as consumers need to be cognizant of the critical thinking necessary when confronted with a constant stream of information.

Given that documenting focuses on capturing and highlighting the learning process, not every image, audio, video, or text collected will be useful as evidence. Learning to discern and making sense of what is worthwhile is an important skill to practice. As learners gain fluency in information literacy, they will begin to make better and wiser choices about what and how to best capture and convey learning.

Connect Information

Information literacy involves how to filter the extraordinary amount of information available online and make connections between and among the worthwhile information. Learners need to be able to see patterns and trends in information gained as a consumer, as well as a producer when creating their artifacts. Documenting embraces learners articulating the connections and relationships evident and visible in their artifacts (e.g., annotexted video or image, hashtagged crowdsourced conversation, blog posts with embedded media collage).

Curate Information

Wikipedia defines digital *curation* as

> The selection, preservation, maintenance, collection, and archiving of digital assets . . . which establishes, maintains, and adds value to repositories of digital data for present and future use. This is often accomplished by archivists, librarians, scientists, historians, and scholars.

An important aspect of being a digital curator is becoming a responsible information filter for others. Curating implies more than just collecting resources or artifacts. It requires organizing and articulating the importance of the information. Documenting develops and calibrates cognitive thought processing that goes beyond being simply collectors of information to being thoughtful curators. When students and teachers are expected to include reflections, recommendations, and relevant connections related to the learning, it adds value to the learning process. It also causes learners to be reflective about their evidence of learning, and how to make those reflections visible to others.

Enable Access to Information

Most likely you were a consumer of information in your formative education years wherein you read books, newspapers, articles, and magazines written, edited, and published by a select few. A mindset of privacy, protection of intellectual property, password-protected content, and copyright restricting licenses have all contributed to information being kept behind digital firewalls. This is changing due to society becoming prolific producers of information and enabling easy access to that information by others.

When sharing and amplifying artifacts learners are producers who are allowing access to their work, thinking, reflections, failures, and successes, which is modernizing what teaching and learning looks like *now* and into the future. As students and teachers are contributing to the information available online, it is important that they understand the connection between digital citizenship and network literacy when preparing their artifacts to be accessed by a local and global community.

Disseminate Information

Disseminate means to spread information widely. Documenting involves disseminating through sharing and amplifying. Simply sharing artifacts by publishing the information online does not mean the learning is spreading like wildfire and reaching desired targeted audiences. The saying: *If you build (share) it, they will come,* does not necessarily hold true in this hyper-information age.

Think of disseminating as scattering seeds widely. *Who really knows where the seeds will land and if they will take root?* Learners must strategically disseminate their artifacts in such a way so that they know they are connecting with their desired audience. Discernment in disseminating information requires a new set of skills that are tightly connected to both the network and media literacies.

Network Literacy

How does documenting learning embrace network literacy? Hellweg (2012) explains that network literacy consists of, "The abilities to [1] obtain a basic understanding of network technology, [2] being able to craft one's own network identity, [3] understand network intelligence, and [4] understand network capabilities." These four network abilities involve:

- **Networking platforms**—media that connect people and ideas synchronously or asynchronously without geographical restrictions or time limitations
- **Network connectivity**—person's voice, tone, and expression of ideas through text, images, and multimedia that create a connection between self and his/her part in a network
- **Network intelligence**—person's ability to identify, examine, and make connections among online interactions involving users, networks, platforms, applications, and protocols
- **Network capabilities**—focused on communities and networks and how the members can aid in gaining and/or creating content

Here are four network literacy characteristics that the documenting learning process fosters:

Obtaining a Basic Understanding of Network Platforms

As more and more network communities are being birthed, evolving, and expanding, the more important it becomes for learners to be able to understand these platforms in terms of how each could possibly best convey the information being shared or amplified. For example: *When would it be better to share artifacts via a blog post versus a Twitter post with a strategic hashtag? If wanting to gain insights into an aspect of game programming, would participating in a hashtag chat or following an expert on Twitter be the best given the project's timeline?*

Posing network technology questions is a natural component of the documenting process, both as a consumer and producer. Contemplating what network technologies and communities would be the most beneficial for both gaining knowledge and obtaining feedback, pushback, collaboration opportunities, and curated resources are part of the decision-making process. When preparing to share and amplify artifacts, learners put into practice their network technology skills when considering audience possibilities based on their learning focuses and goals.

Crafting a Network Connectivity

To have a voice and tone that expresses his or her ideas and thoughts through text, image, and multimedia, a learner must move beyond passively lurking in network communities. A *lurker* is someone who reads the work of others and takes advantage of the resources that are being shared, but never contributes. All of the *now* literacies expect learners to be receptive and expressive.

Establishing and building network connectivity that others choose to follow and learn from based on quality content takes time and strategic effort to develop. Being part of a network community also involves building trust among its members. *What do you want others to know about you as a member of a particular community? What do you stand for and believe in? What niche do you fill informationally? What content represents your area of interest or expertise? What do you want to be known for in a particular network community?*

When purposefully documenting and developing an understanding of the value of sharing and amplifying learners are constantly in need of making cognitive and metacognitive decisions concerning

- what to share,
- whom to share it with,
- what message is going to be conveyed, and
- what type of feedback is desired.

Someone's network identity attracts specific types of followers based on what he or she is authentically producing, sharing, and amplifying for a connected and targeted audience.

Understanding Network Intelligence

One of the biggest shifts in recent years in terms of accessing learning information and networking is that restrictions have been removed regarding what and how information is accessed, and who is providing the information. Consider the networking possibilities during a conference breakout session. If someone asks, "Who is the smartest person in this room?" oftentimes the presenter would be indicated. The accurate answer is *the collective room*. This alludes to the power of network intelligence versus the mindset of standalone intelligence.

It is hard to understand the positive impact of this shift if learners have never experienced the power of networking to gain, filter, create, and disseminate information. Learners of all ages need to have multiple experiences in taking advantage of crowdsourcing, a phenomenon impossible without participating in network communities.

Leveraging Network Capabilities

When involved in document learning over time, learners develop skills and strategies to best leverage network intelligence related to their learning. They become active researchers, applying their intelligence to aid in figuring out how their learning communities and networks can add leverage to their own and others' learning. For example, a teacher helps out a colleague by posting a tweet containing a specific hashtag. She attaches her colleague's student-created argument-based video and asks her network to post comments concerning the students' claims. She reminds her network to post their tweets using the included hashtag.

As in many of the other *now* literacies, in network communities its members are contributors, not just consumers. This is the heart of networking. If no one contributes, the network system ceases to function. When sharing and amplifying artifacts via networks to disseminate documentation strategically; chances of receiving feedback and push-back are leveraged.

This capability transforms documenting OF learning into documenting FOR and AS learning. Networking capabilities embrace learning *with* others by contributing perspectives, voices, and reflections with like-minded global audiences.

SUMMING UP

Documenting learning supports content curriculum and the application of the *now* literacies through the process of making learning and thinking visible, meaningful, shareable, and amplified. As learners embrace the *now* literacies and apply them thoughtfully in their documenting opportunities, students and teachers become strategic consumers *and* producers. They learn *how* to learn by applying contemporary mindsets that involve purposefully accessing, leveraging, and contributing online in meaningful ways through reaching and interacting with global audiences.

GOING BEYOND

To amplify your reading beyond this book's pages, we have created *discussion questions and prompts* for this chapter, which are located at *www.documenting4learning.com*. To extend your thinking, reactions, and responses, you can connect with other readers by leaving comments on individual chapter's discussion posts on our documenting4learning blog.

We also invite you to contribute and share your artifacts in other social media spaces to connect with and learn from other readers around the world using the #documenting4learning hashtag on Twitter, Facebook, or Instagram; or by mentioning @documenting4learning on Facebook and Instagram, and @doc4learning on Twitter.

3

Documenting Pedagogy and Heutagogy

If we want to change how students learn, we have to change how teachers learn.

—Katie Martin

It is important when documenting that teachers and administrators have a clear understanding of the distinctions between teacher-centered pedagogical and learner-centered heutagogical documentation.

DEFINING THE DIFFERENCE BETWEEN PEDAGOGICAL DOCUMENTATION AND HEUTAGOGICAL DOCUMENTATION

What Is Pedagogical Documentation?

Pedagogy encompasses the methods, techniques, and strategies teachers use to facilitate learning. Pedagogical documentation is teacher driven and focuses on aiding this facilitation via the documenting process. Wien (2013) explains that:

> We have always documented as a society–from cash register slips to medical records, family photo albums to report cards. But pedagogical documentation offers more than a record. It offers a process for listening to children, for creating artifacts from that listening, and for studying with others what children reveal about their competent and thoughtful views of the world. To listen to children, we document living moments with images, video, artifacts, written or audio recordings of what children

have said, or other digital traces. These documented traces of lived experience, when shared with others, become a tool for thinking together. To hear others' thoughts makes us realize there are many viewpoints. Pedagogical documentation goes beyond the foundation of the developmental continuum to welcome both children's perspectives and our study of their views.

Kashin (2017) adds, "Meaning making is an opportunity to think deeply about the content of documentation so that it can become pedagogical." In other words, by default documentation is not pedagogical. For example, some may describe documentation as the act of taking a photograph of students that captures a moment during an activity. To be considered *pedagogical documentation*, the action must *facilitate* learning. The photograph would need to be used in a strategic way to inform students on how they are doing, while moving toward exhibiting the learning focus or goal. If a teacher annotexts the photograph and gives it to the appropriate students to aid them in their reflection, the documentation now facilitates learning. Likewise, if a series of *moment in time* photographs are bundled to provide learners with an opportunity to reflect on what the visual snapshot timeline conveys, the photographs collectively facilitate meaning making about one's learning growth.

How Does Pedagogical Documentation Correlate With the SAMR Taxonomy?

As mentioned previously, this book distinguishes itself from the Reggio Emilia documentation philosophy and other documenting frameworks by using technology strategically to share and amplify learning. It is the use of technology for the dual purpose of transforming and redefining teaching and learning. The SAMR model supports the awareness and application of using technology authentically to allow for such creations and innovations.

Puentedura's (2008) SAMR model describes a taxonomy that aids in classifying four levels of technology, pedagogy, and content knowledge infusion and how each level impacts teaching and learning. Application at each level is viewed through the lens of learner tasks and how the technology affects accessibility and transformative learning:

- **Substitution**: Technology acts as a direct tool substitute, with no functional change.
- **Augmentation**: Technology acts as a direct tool substitute, with functional improvement.
- **Modification**: Technology allows for significant task redesign.
- **Redefinition**: Technology allows for the creation of new tasks, previously inconceivable.

This taxonomy has been interpreted in various ways by educators and educational groups. Therefore, it is critical that a team or network comes to consensus on what each level represents when students are engaged in documenting learning tasks. If the SAMR taxonomy is new for those involved, Image 3.1 can be used as a conversation-starter for coming to agreement on what each SAMR level represents. The image is based on the bulleted SAMR definitions, plus the inclusion of amplification as conveyed by Hale and Fisher (2013).

Educators may claim that having students create book video trailers is a modern form of conducting traditional book reports. They may say that because students are going to be

Image 3.1

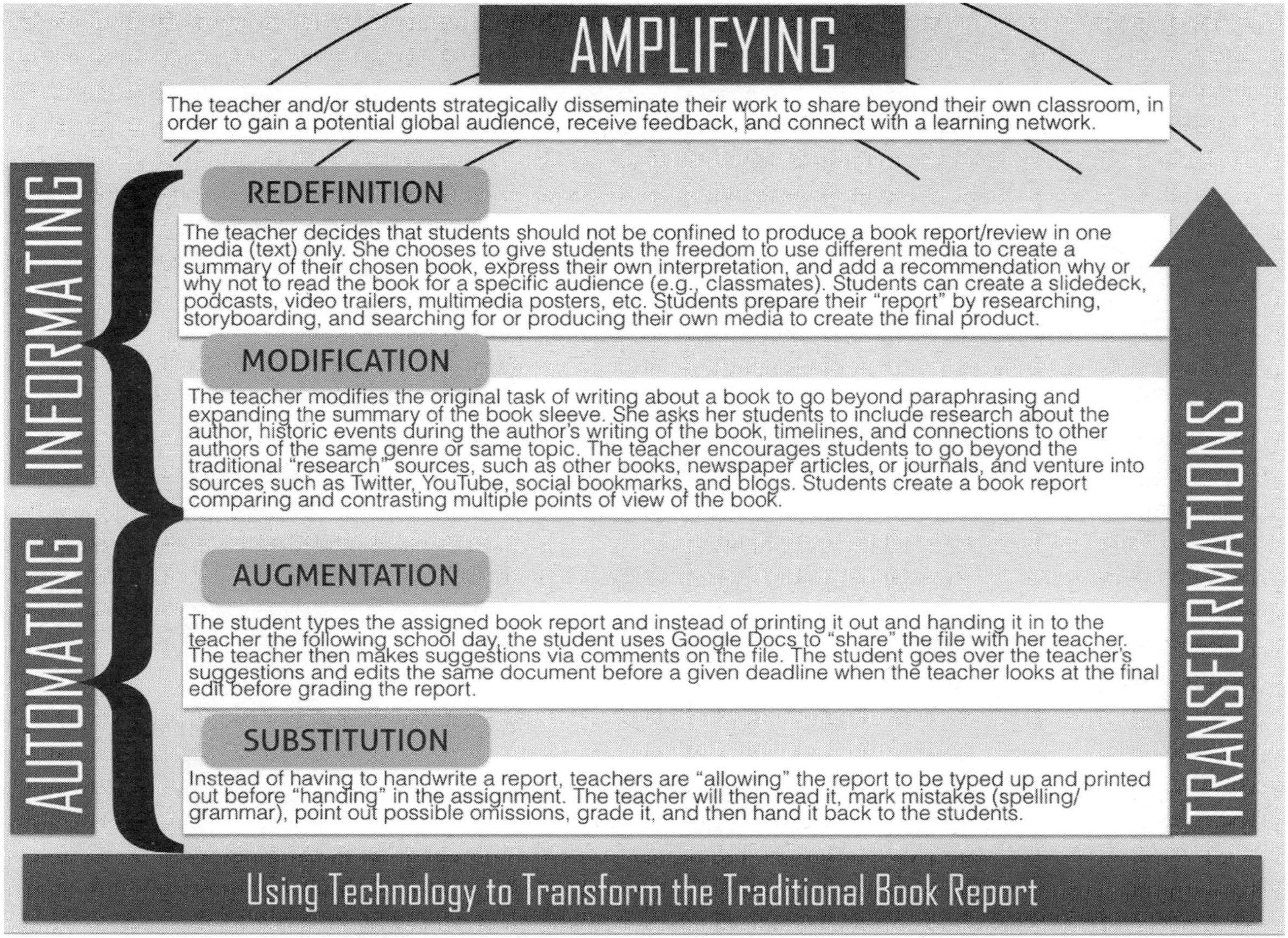

AMPLIFYING

The teacher and/or students strategically disseminate their work to share beyond their own classroom, in order to gain a potential global audience, receive feedback, and connect with a learning network.

TRANSFORMATIONS

REDEFINITION

The teacher decides that students should not be confined to produce a book report/review in one media (text) only. She chooses to give students the freedom to use different media to create a summary of their chosen book, express their own interpretation, and add a recommendation why or why not to read the book for a specific audience (e.g. classmates). Students can create a slidedeck, podcasts, video trailers, multimedia posters, etc. Students prepare their "report" by researching, storyboarding, and searching for or producing their own media to create the final product.

MODIFICATION

The teacher modifies the original task of writing about a book to go beyond paraphrasing and expanding the summary of the book sleeve. She asks her students to include research about the author, historic events during the author's writing of the book, timelines, and connections to other authors of the same genre or same topic. The teacher encourages students to go beyond the traditional "research" sources, such as other books, newspaper articles, or journals, and venture into sources such as Twitter, YouTube, social bookmarks, and blogs. Students create a book report comparing and contrasting multiple points of view of the book.

INFORMATING

AUGMENTATION

The student types the assigned book report and instead of printing it out and handing it in to the teacher the following school day, the student uses Google Docs to "share" the file with her teacher. The teacher then makes suggestions via comments on the file. The student goes over the teacher's suggestions and edits the same document before a given deadline when the teacher looks at the final edit before grading the report.

SUBSTITUTION

Instead of having to handwrite a report, teachers are "allowing" the report to be typed up and printed out before "handing" in the assignment. The teacher will then read it, mark mistakes (spelling/ grammar), point out possible omissions, grade it, and then hand it back to the students.

AUTOMATING

Using Technology to Transform the Traditional Book Report

Based on the SAMR Model by R. Puentedura (2011) built on ideas shared by A. November (2010). Visual adapted by S. Rosenthal Tolisano (2011)

uploading their trailers to an online site (e.g., YouTube) they are functioning at the Redefinition and Amplification levels. Their reasoning may include that the video trailers are online where hundreds of people could potentially view them and provide feedback to their students. While this reasoning at first appears plausible, *where is the evidence that the original book report task has been transformed due to the strategic use of technology?* The act of publishing student work online does not guarantee that a transformative or amplified learning moment has taken place. Teachers and students need be strategic concerning how their desired audiences will be accessed (e.g., a tweet using specific hashtags geared toward a specific professional learning network). Without this purposeful pursuit, targeted feedback will not happen, unless by chance.

Teachers and students must be strategic concerning how their desired audiences will be accessed (e.g., a tweet using specific hashtags geared toward a specific professional learning network). Without this purposeful pursuit, targeted feedback will not happen, unless by chance.

Teachers do not have to start a task at the Substitution level and progressively move toward the Redefinition or Amplification level. Consideration for the entry point should be based on why teachers desire to use the SAMR taxonomy in relationship to how it will impact students' learning and their instruction.

Decisions should also be based on a teacher's experience with various forms of technology. If he has never used a collaborative Google Doc with his students to support the writing process, implementing the use of this technology will redefine the task he is proposing for his students (e.g., collaborative editing, multiple authors). On the other hand, another teacher may already have experience using Google Docs. Simply asking her students to use this tool to collaborate will not redefine the learner task.

To use a Google Doc as an Augmentation entry point, the teacher would ask students to not only collaborate with their classmates in writing a research paper, but would also require them to share their work publicly vis social media and request feedback and further resources via comments. The task of writing a research paper has now been redefined because it does not only rely only on the collaborative Google Doc technology, but it is also dependent on accessing human expertise and resources beyond the original authors via crowdsourcing.

Regardless of entry point, here are considerations for how the documenting process correlates to the SAMR taxonomy:

Substitution. Technology devices are used to capture learning. It could be a camera taking a photograph of an analog object, such as a picture of a LEGO marble maze created by a young learner (see Image 3.2). The use of technology did not change the learner's task (getting a marble to travel from an entry point to an exit point through the maze).

Image 3.2

Likewise, nothing further was done with the captured image beyond it representing the student's marble-maze creation. It serves only as a snapshot of *what happened.*

When students have reached the age or stage of learning where they are required to keep track of their research for purposes of proper quoting or citing, traditional quotes and citation references are noted as either a bibliography page or footnotes. With substitution when posting a blog or a tweet, quote or cite references still happen at this level, but due to technology capabilities there is hyperlinked text that takes reader directly to the quoted or cited resource. Likewise, substitution includes replacing index note cards to archive and access resources with bookmark applications, such as Diigo and Google Bookmarks.

Augmentation. The nuance at this level of the SAMR taxonomy is that the technology is still a direct tool substitute, but now there is recognizable *function improvement* in conveying information. For example, instead of a photograph conveying assumptions, what it captures and conveys is summarized and made visible using a screenshooting tool to annotate the image. This is especially important when creating artifacts related to learners' tasks.

Image 3.3 now includes annotexted information that informs viewers of the student's thinking while performing the maze task. In this example, the annotations do not convey the student's thinking, but provides the documenter's explanation to aid viewers understanding of what is happening so there is no guesswork as to what is taking place at this moment in time. By including annotations when an image is shared or amplified, the documenter does not need to be present to convey the evidence of learning.

Another example of an augmented task involving functional improvement is collaboratively collecting digital links, while researching those that are saved using a social bookmarking platform. This adds a functionality that allows accessibility from any device on any browser at any time for the learners to continue to collect, organize, tag, search, and retrieve their saved links. When considering this level in context of the digitally bookmarked reference links, it involves the learners needing to be *curators.* The act of curating resources cognitively demands more than the act of collecting because learners must make meaning of their choices, connect them to the chosen resources, and add value by including their reasoning for themselves and others.

Modification. While learners benefit immensely by sharing their documentation artifacts with classmates, other classes, and colleagues, using technology strategically supports sharing beyond classroom walls and school boundaries and transforms interactive possibilities. It is not simply about actions such as tweeting an image or video out to the Twittersphere. It is about conscientiously reaching out to and connecting with strategic members in an analog or digital learning community to gain their input, feedback, and crowdsourcing assistance.

Image 3.4

The use of a central hub plays an important role when learners as documenters are able to take advantage of technology devices to capture, reflect on, archive, and share their artifacts at anytime, anywhere, and in any form.

Strategic use of technology, including the metacognition of what to choose and how it benefits the learner, aids in making thinking visible in ways not possible in the past. A decade ago, there was no technology available for even the youngest learners to create annotexted images, screencasts, podcasts, infographics, and digital sketchnotes. All of these technologies promote modifications and make thinking visible and shareable.

Image 3.4 captures moments that convey the young learner interacting with her created marble maze. Her teacher has used a collage tool to create an artifact that reflects a timeline of the student designing and modifying her maze, including a key *I Wonder* question that she kept asking herself as she modified her design, which led to adjusting, rebuilding, applying, and failing until finally she succeeded.

At the modification level, documentation is not simply displaying what was done. It transforms artifacts into making the learning process and thinking visible to the learner, as well as sharing it with a wider audience. When transforming learning and teaching in the context of documentation that functions at the Modification level or Redefinition level, the learners' artifacts become increasingly metacognitive.

QR Code 3.1

Scan this QR code to view young learners in action with their marble mazes.

http://langwitches.me/ marblemaze

Redefinition. While the marble-in-a-maze documentation example concludes at the Modification level, for it to be functioning at a Redefinition level, with the addition of amplification, the teacher-documenter could co-create a step-by-step tutorial video where the young learner shares recommendations for how to best build a marble maze and suggests ways to successfully navigate a marble through the maze.

The teacher could share it on YouTube and add hashtags such as #kindergartentutorials or #kinderchat to strategically connect the student's insights with others interested in learning from and with young learners or with preschool or kindergarten teachers.

Redefinition's call for using a wide range of technology to create new tasks that were previously inconceivable, documenting's call for sharing and amplifying plays an integral role. For example, in the not too distant past, students and teachers could not have dreamed of documenting their learning using digital portfolios and crowdsourcing to ask for comments and feedback via various social media platforms.

Experiencing *transmedia documentation*, which Heick (2013b) defines as, "A narrative that extends beyond multiple media forms that also plays to the strength of those forms," embraces documenting and the need for learners to make their learning and thinking visible in multimedia forms. Using a variety of media (text, image, audio, video) throughout a documenting opportunity not only captures the explicit learning taking place, but often highlights hidden aspects, perspectives, and interpretations of the learning.

Take a moment to study Image 3.5. The first two levels of the SAMR taxonomy primarily support documenting OF and FOR learning opportunities. The two remaining levels, and Amplification, primarily support documenting FOR and AS learning. Advancements in technologies allow learners and documenters to rethink how to best capture the learning evidence, as well as create tasks and artifacts that are not possible in an analog environment. Likewise, the documenting process at the latter levels increases the transformative nature of both pedagogical and heutagogical documentation.

As students, teachers, and administrators embark on or continue growing in their understanding and applications of documenting learning, it is important they are aware of how technology plays a role in supporting documentation. Over time, when they have reached a point of perceiving documenting as ubiquitous with the learning process, the technologies that aid in conveying thinking, reflecting, sharing, and amplifying in purposeful and meaningful ways will simply be tools readily available in a documenting toolbox.

What Is Heutagogical Documentation?

Heutagogical documentation is learner driven and focuses on self-motivated and self-directed learning.

It can be further defined as documentation directed to aid self-awareness, fuel motivation to learn, and support decision-making concerning what wants or needs to be learned or can be learned next.

Price (2013) explains that "[Educators] will have to accommodate the social desire to shift from pedagogy to heutagogy, and support learners to become more independent and self-determined." Price also acknowledges that "Heutagogy is equally applicable to children as it is to adults. It's defined by approach, not age" (p. 208).

Self-motivated and self-directed documentation is needed for both students and teachers as learners. Educators need to ponder questions such as:

- How can I differentiate between *waiting to be taught* and *wanting to learn* in my students and myself?
- How can I make time for self-directed learning opportunities when time flies by at ever-increasing speed?
- How can I embrace passion and motivation opportunities for my students and myself when external demands seem to always take priority?

Motivation is a mindset that is often perceived as lacking in schools. Pink (2009) explains motivation from a business viewpoint:

The good news is that the scientists who've been studying motivation have given us this new approach. It's built much more around intrinsic motivation. Around the desire to do things because they matter, because we like it, they're interesting, or part of something important. And to my mind, that new operating system for our businesses revolves around three elements: autonomy, mastery, and purpose. *Autonomy*: the urge to direct our own lives. *Mastery*: the desire to get better and

DOCUMENTATION &
SAMR MODEL

HOW DOES TECHNOLOGY IMPACT DOCUMENTATION & TEACHING & LEARNING?

Transformation

Redefinition

Share Documentation | **Crowdsource** | **Act of Documenting**
Intentionally | Feedback Via | Learning Process
& Internationally | Through Experiencing | Becomes Part of Learning
| social media | Transmedia
| | **Documentation**

Modification

Share Thoughtfully | **Instantly Document** | **Make Thinking Visible** | **Curate Beyond**
Beyond Classroom | anytime/anywhere | With a variety | collecting, comment,
Walls & school | & over time | of media | categorize, present

Enhancement

Augmentation

Add explanation of | **Take a series of** | **Purposefully use slow**
What was Done | Pictures to put | mo to capture what
With annotations | together in a timeline | is invisible to the eye

Substitution

Display artifacts | **Take a Picture of** | **Video Record Long** | **Post analog Writing**
W/o interpretation | something analog | Clips W/o intention | in digital spaces

better at something that matters. *Purpose*: the yearning to do what we do in the service of something larger than ourselves. These are the building blocks of an entirely new operating system for our businesses.

In reality, these building blocks are applicable beyond business settings. They are compelling for education settings as well. Heutagogical documentation supports Pink's concepts of urging, desiring, and yearning.

Autonomy. Learning is innately self-motivated and self-directed. What young child does not curiously explore his or her surroundings, or incessantly ask, "Why?" Autonomy is defined as *freedom from external control or influence; independence.* In a classroom or professional learning environment where heutagogy is supported, learners do not rely on a specific teacher or workshop to engage meaningfully in the act of learning. Documenting opportunities that embrace autonomous perspectives are not driven by receiving a grade or fulfilling required learning hours. Motivation to begin or continue a desired learning path is encouraged. Realistically, there needs to be a balance of pedagogical-based and autonomous self-directed learning opportunities in classroom and professional settings.

Mastery. Mastery, according to Pink, does not mean obtaining perfection. It means having the desire to improve. Motivated learners naturally investigate, research, and apply what they learn to improve their understanding.

An example of this is Janet's motivation to master sketchnoting as a cognitive notetaking technique. When she first began, it was a laborious and time-consuming process. Her mind was 100% focused on the rudimentary how-tos for using a digital sketchnoting tool. Over time, this lessened and she found more of her mental energy was focused on what she wanted the sketchnote to convey to viewers based on what she read or viewed. When she occasionally paused to study and reflect on the quality of her sketches to determine if she was improving, she did recognize visual evidence of her improvement. But more important to her was the realization that her thought-process *while creating* her sketchnotes had become an important part of her creation process and was becoming more sophisticated.

Documenting provides evidence of one's acquisition of learning over time, which motivates self-directed learners in their pursuit of mastery.

Purpose. During his TED Talk, Pink stated that *purpose* is, "The yearning to do what we do in the service of something larger than ourselves." Sharing and amplifying documentation artifacts embraces this motivational element. We have seen students more excited and engaged when they are producers of knowledge and content, as well as advancing their understanding when connected with local and global learning communities. Sharing with and learning from experts beyond a traditional range of influence embraces the foundational premise of heutagogy: *self-motivation* and the desire to expand one's knowledge and understanding based on a topic of interest.

The immediacy of receiving social media responses plays a neurological motivation role that often causes learners to want to continue documenting, sharing, and amplifying their learning. Price (2013), expanding on Wise's (2004) comment, notes that, "Neuroscience suggests that every time you post a request on Twitter for a particular reference or news report you missed, and you get an immediate response, you get a little dopamine hit." For some heutagogical learners, creating artifacts is all the motivation they need to continue investigating, researching, and applying their gained knowledge to new situations. Others find the extrinsic motivation of interacting with others via social media aids in expanding or refining their thinking and learning.

Heutagogical documentation embraces the metacognition involved in documenting learning. When motivated learners capture evidence and reflect on it, what is discovered informs them of the next steps needed to further their desired learning. It also sheds light on a learner's evolving pathway of understanding, including evidence over time of successes, failures, perseverance, and persistence that is leading him or her to reach a desired learning outcome or goal.

SUMMING UP

Pedagogical and heutagogical documentation represent two different approaches for thinking about how learning takes place. These approaches can be used solo or in tandem.

For an in-tandem example, a teacher could document her students' learning process to gain insight into their abilities and approaches to tackling new information. She reflects on the documentation artifacts to determine instructional needs that will best serve her students (pedagogical documentation). Simultaneously, she uses the artifacts that represent a newly attempted instructional practice as evidence for her professional learning. By reflecting on the artifacts in comparison to student engagement and results prior to the new practice she can determine if the practice is making a positive impact and decide what she needs to do next based on her reflections (e.g., seek assistance, tweak her delivery, keep on instructing as is).

DEFINING THE DIFFERENCE BETWEEN DISPLAYING AND DOCUMENTING

As mentioned previously, simply capturing snapshots of students during a learning activity does not facilitate learning; therefore, it does not constitute pedagogical documentation. Without an attempt in meaning making, reflecting, and thinking about one's thinking in relationship to artifacts, the documentation serves no pedagogical or heutagogical purpose and creates mere display.

What Is the Difference Between Displaying and Documenting?

Displaying refers to making what has been done or happened visible to an audience. What is displayed may or may not be noticed (e.g., parents going to a school open hours may or may not stop and look at the student reports displayed on a bulletin board in the hallway outside the classroom; see Image 3.6), or may not convey students' thinking or reasoning concerning what is displayed (e.g., teacher posts a summary card next to the display of her students' illustrations of the four seasons from the viewpoint of one oak tree as it changes over a calendar year).

Displaying is documenting without a specific purpose or goal being captured *during* the learning process or over time. Traditional displays may consist of posted papers, reports, photographs, or artwork to showcase and share what students have been learning or examples of best work. Displays can also be three-dimensional, such as dioramas, prototypes created for an invention convention, or history fair display boards. Once displays are taken down, they are usually sent home where, in the best-case scenario, continued to be displayed on a refrigerator door. In the worst-case scenario, they are immediately thrown away or put into storage.

There are times when displaying from a documenting OF learning perspective is appropriate. For example, teachers are often charged with displaying samples of student work in the school's foyer, that may be educational, holiday crafts, or athletic accomplishments. Teachers often create bulletin board displays of student exemplars emulating quality work. All of these types of displays can be motivating for some students because everyone who walks by sees their work.

Image 3.6

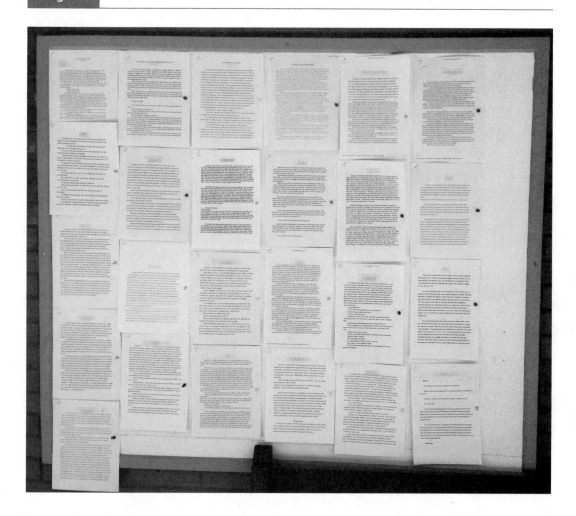

Any time a teacher displays student work outside the classroom walls, there is an opportunity to share the learning with a larger audience. Even more powerful is when what is being shared literally incorporates the students' voices. For example, an art teacher had her students create informational narratives about their soon-to-be-displayed artwork and created QR codes for the narratives to accompany the artwork. Passers-by could study the artwork and listen to each artist share his or her thinking behind the piece on display (see Images 3.7 and 3.8, and scan QR Code 3.2).

Given the array of online tools now available, it is not difficult to create displays that audiences can view and experience in a shareable and amplified way. With the ability to upload and publish instantly at little or no cost, anyone can create content that can be accessed by local and global audiences. This does not imply that students are to be given the freedom to do so at any time while in a classroom environment, nor should every artifact created be put on display. Rather, the point is that the ability to share and amplify artifacts has become much easier and provides learners with experiences in being producers beyond what was possible just a decade or so ago.

QR Code 3.2

Scan this QR code to access Jamie's explanation of her displayed artwork.

http://langwitches.me/ jamie

Image 3.7

Created by Jamie Bielski

Image 3.8

When students and teachers capture moments from an ongoing flow of learning they can freeze a moment in time or home in on significant moments to observe, study, and interpret in connection to the learning focus and goal. Whether this is done from a pedagogical or heutagogical viewpoint, the purpose is to intentionally move beyond the mere act of capturing what is taking place to contemplating and reflecting on what is taking place as evidence of moving toward understanding or application of the learning focus or goal.

For example, look at the side-by-side visuals in Image 3.9. The left-side image's white box provides a caption, but interpretation of the photograph is left up to the viewer to infer. The right-side image's white box provides a bit more detailed caption, but more importantly its annotexted photograph provides key details related to the learning. The annotexter had to first reflect, contemplate, and decide what was important information to convey in a concise, yet meaningful message.

Using documentation as display can be a first step for new documenters. If documenting for display is done strategically over a period of time, it can become a documenting FOR or AS learning opportunity. For example, an individual tweet cannot convey much about a learner. But when viewed as growth over time by studying a series of tweets, the tweets collectively reveal what the learner values or believes on a more complex level.

With this said, it is important to balance displaying with purposefully documenting opportunities wherein the act of learning *while it is taking place* is captured, reflected on, and shared with others to gain helpful insights and feedback.

What Is Acceptable as Evidence of Learning When Documenting?

Often times, educators, both teachers and administrators, assume that everyone knows and speaks the same educational language or interprets it the same way. Think about the term *learning*. Ask a few colleagues and you may be surprised at the variations of definitions shared. Whether documenting from a pedagogical or heutagogical perspective, when engaging

Image 3.9

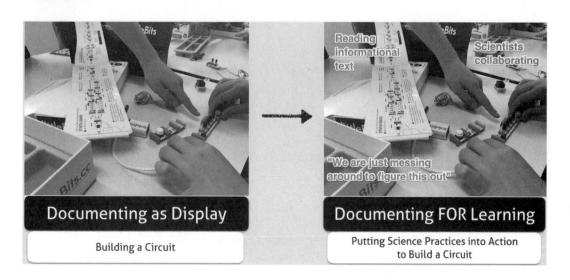

It's Time to Take Action!

Chapter 3 Action Step

Think of a moment when you captured learning taking place. Perhaps you took a photograph of your students as they were reading with their first-grade buddies or programming during coding time; or videoed them acting out a scene from *Romeo and Juliet*. Maybe you captured your own learning while attending a lecture or workshop via notetaking that included a screenshot of information you found beneficial, or videoed yourself during a classroom lesson so you could watch yourself to see if you or your students were asking the most questions.

Did you share your captured moment(s) with anyone other than yourself? Did you display your artifact somewhere for others to view? If yes, retrieve your saved display artifact as a base for this activity. If not, this is a perfect opportunity to capture a moment of learning! You can capture your students learning or your own learning, whichever you prefer.

Once you have your display selected or created, you need to determine the analog space (e.g., hallway bulletin board) or digital space (e.g., blog post, Twitter) that you will use to share and amplify.

Now it is time to turn your display into a documenting artifact, whether textual, visual, or auditory. Think metacognitively about what you selected to capture and why:

- Why did I capture this exact moment?
- What does it represent explicitly, and most importantly, what does it infer?
- How does this particular moment fit in with the same or related learning focus or goal relates over time?

Record your reflection about the captured learning and post using your selected sharing/amplifying platform (e.g., analog—stapled index card reflection, or QR code auditory reflection for bulletin board sharing platform; digital—reflective tweet with display image or video attached, or blog post with lengthier explanation and embedded image or video).

Remember to use the #documenting4learning hashtag on Twitter, Facebook, or Instagram; or by mentioning @documenting4learning on Facebook and Instagram, and @doc4learning on Twitter.

collaboratively in the documenting process, all stakeholders need to come to consensus on *answers* and *examples* to these questions:

- What does learning mean to me? Why?
- What would I consider evidence of learning in general?
- What would I consider evidence of learning for my students?
- What would I consider evidence of my own professional learning?

Here are a few more questions that can take the conversation concerning acceptable evidence even deeper:

- What does learning look like in school? Does it look different at home? In one's profession?
- How has learning and evidence of learning changed in the last 20 years? Ten years? Five years?

- What motivates learners to learn?
- Should evidence of learning look different for pedagogical documentation versus heutagogical documentation? Why or why not?
- How does reflection and sharing of learning evidence contribute to amplifying and learning growth for myself, my students, and others?

Be aware that agreement on what evidence will be, as well as what it can potentially look like, will most likely take multiple meetings to draft, plus time for iterative action research to revise, refine, and eventually reach consensus.

When agreement has been reached, be certain to inform parents and caregivers of what has been determined, given pedagogical and heutagogical practices involved in documenting FOR and AS learning can be vastly different. Another worthwhile endeavor is to conduct workshops for the local community at school or in their work-places to create and nurture learning communities. These communities can then be accessed when students are engaged in their learning processes to have authentic audiences and experts aiding in expanding or refining their knowledge, understanding, and application.

It is important that teachers as professional learners have *safe-place* opportunities to ponder and grow in their understanding of what evidence of learning looks and feels like when engaged in the documenting process. A definition of what learning is and what evidence of learning looks like will take some action research and iterative cycles before a *this is it* is reached. Networking with other educators, schools, and districts who have established or are also embarking on providing more documenting FOR and AS learning opportunities can also be helpful. By using the #documenting4learning hashtag on Twitter or Instagram, searching for @documenting4learning on Facebook post, or visiting www.documenting4learning.com, you can reach out and connect with similar teachers, schools, or districts to mutually grow in the understanding of the documenting process and its application together.

Here is an example of what a school determined would be acceptable evidence of learning for a particular documenting opportunity. On the teachers' journeys of implementing blogfolios across their K–12 school, they decided the faculty would also create learning-thinking artifacts by creating professional blogfolios.

They soon realized that everyone was not on the same page concerning what constituted evidence for their students' blog posts and their own. They knew that they had to have a schoolwide conversation about (a) what was acceptable evidence when their students, and themselves, wrote and published their blog posts, and (b) determine how to make these expectations visible and shareable. Based on their discussions, they finally reached consensus that all posts must include four components: *title, artifact, reflection,* and *categories* (see Image 3.10).

Teachers need to see and experience how artifacts can be evidence of learning that are ten times more powerful than giving a one-time summative assessment or tallying points to create a letter grade. Teachers as primary and secondary learners need ample opportunities to experience how to look for learning while the learning is happening. They also need time to learn how to recognize evidence that supports their students' learning growth over time, as well as applying the *now* literacies. This is not an easy task. It takes practice, just like any worthwhile teaching strategy.

A school or district needs to create professional learning that embeds the practice of capturing and reflecting on evidence of learning for various focuses and goals. Professional opportunities wherein teachers can select, reflect on, sharing, and amplifying their artifacts

Image 3.10

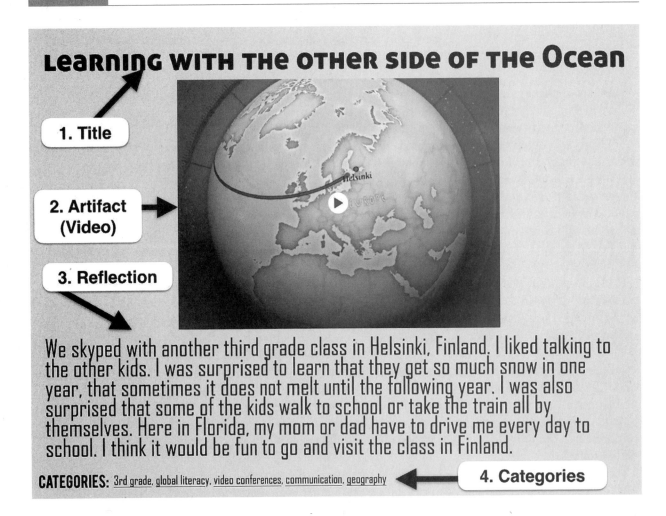

LEARNING WITH THE OTHER SIDE OF THE Ocean

1. Title

2. Artifact (Video)

3. Reflection

We skyped with another third grade class in Helsinki, Finland. I liked talking to the other kids. I was surprised to learn that they get so much snow in one year, that sometimes it does not melt until the following year. I was also surprised that some of the kids walk to school or take the train all by themselves. Here in Florida, my mom or dad have to drive me every day to school. I think it would be fun to go and visit the class in Finland.

CATEGORIES: 3rd grade, global literacy, video conferences, communication, geography

4. Categories

over time instead of relying on pre-scheduled teacher observations twice a year is so worthwhile. Consider having teachers

- Capture comments and contributions via a platform that allows users to create and curate stories and timelines using posts from bi-weekly Twitter chats throughout an academic year based on a targeted learning outcome or goal.
- Communicate with local or global colleagues through the use of blogfolios with embedded artifacts that showcase and reflect on the growth and understanding of a specific set of student-ownership strategies for a semester that are read and commented on by participant and worldwide community.
- Curate artifacts, resources, and visuals that provide evidence of understanding for a specific topic using an appropriate platform, such as Pinterest. Each image, URL, or video is not merely displayed on a board, but needs to include a curation description or explanation for each pin that serves as an annotation for the *what this pin is about . . . , how this resource can be used when learning about . . . ,* and *why this resource is important because . . .*

SUMMING UP

Fight the urge to merely display snapshots of what was done or final products, and convert display items into documentation artifacts by making the process of thinking and learning visible and meaningful. Have a clear understanding for yourself and as a classroom or school community of what learning should look like.

Similar to agreeing on what evidence of learning looks like when using a rubric or other evaluation tool, it is important for teachers and students engaged in documenting opportunities to have a clear understanding of what evidence is and what it will look like in the artifacts during the learning experience.

GOING BEYOND

To amplify your reading beyond this book's pages, we have created *discussion questions and prompts* for this chapter, which are located at *www.documenting4learning.com*. To extend your thinking, reactions, and responses, you can connect with other readers by leaving comments on individual chapter's discussion posts on our documenting4learning blog.

We also invite you to contribute and share your artifacts in other social media spaces to connect with and learn from other readers around the world using the #documenting4learning hashtag on Twitter, Facebook, or Instagram; or by mentioning @documenting4learning on Facebook and Instagram, and @doc4learning on Twitter.

Documenting Engagement and Learning Layers

If people choose to engage on a one-dimensional level, that's fine. But going beyond the surface can enrich ourselves as human beings.

—Geri Halliwell

For people to engage in learning, they need to have an intrinsic motivation, extrinsic motivation, or a combination of both. Some are motivated by passion, interest, or simply the love of learning. Others are motivated by necessity, getting a good grade, earning a living, or trying to gain a promotion. When viewing motivation from learner engagement, the layers of learning take on an interesting perspective.

DEFINING LEARNER ENGAGEMENT

Who is documenting versus who is doing the documentation? This question is not as simple as it may first appear. In any learning environment, there may be multiple learners in the room. In a classroom, it cannot be overlooked that the teacher is learning at the same time. Therefore, it is important to be aware that learner engagement is often twofold during a documenting opportunity (see Image 4.1).

The Primary Learner

When students document their own learning, they are actively engaged in the cognitive and metacognitive process involved in looking for and capturing evidence of the learning taking place. Therefore, the students are primary learners.

Image 4.1

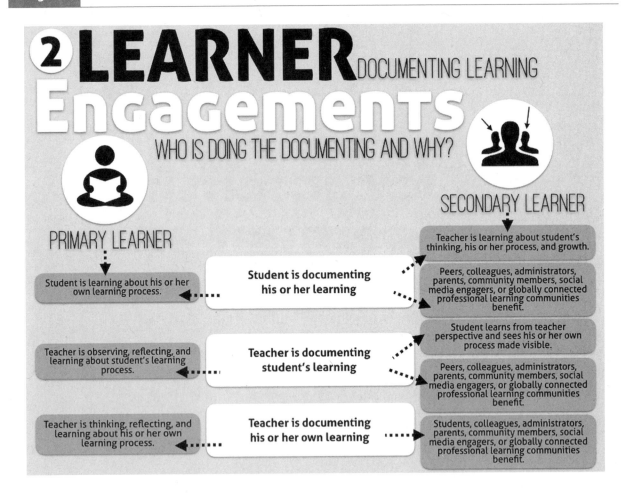

When a teacher documents her students' learning and shares artifacts with them so they can unpack the documentation by looking, reflecting on, and interpreting the artifacts, the students are the primary learners. This is especially applicable with younger students, since it is the teacher who will do the capturing and unpacking for the students to reflect on and analyze.

When teachers or administrators are documenting their own professional learning, they are the primary learners as well.

The Secondary Learner

When artifacts that have been documented and unpacked by students are then shared with the teacher, the teacher is a secondary learner because she is looking at the learning through her students' documenting perspectives. This teacher will gain valuable insights that can inform next steps in teaching, as well as deepen her own understanding about how her students personalize their acquisition of knowledge and understanding.

Any time documentation artifacts get shared or amplified, the viewers or readers automatically become secondary learners, whether fellow students, colleagues, administrators, parents, community members, social media engagers, or globally connected professional learning communities.

As Halliwell mentions in the opening quote, while being engaged on a one-dimensional level is fine, going beyond the surface level can be enriching and enlightening. Being thoughtful about who the primary learners and secondary learners are is beneficial when documenting because awareness of the two supports the ownership and sharing of learning. Likewise, when learners are conscious of their roles in a documenting opportunity, it often serves as a motivating factor.

DOCUMENTING LEARNING LAYERS

There are four documenting learning layers, each focused on a primary learner (see Image 4.2).

Students Documenting Their Own Learning

When students are documenting their own learning as primary learners, they collect, curate, and make their artifacts visible, shareable, and amplified using a variety of platforms and tools. Interacting with a local and global community of experts adds a dimension of authenticity that extends beyond brick-and-mortar classrooms. Students as primary learners can be viewed through a variety of learning perspectives (Table 4.1).

Image 4.2

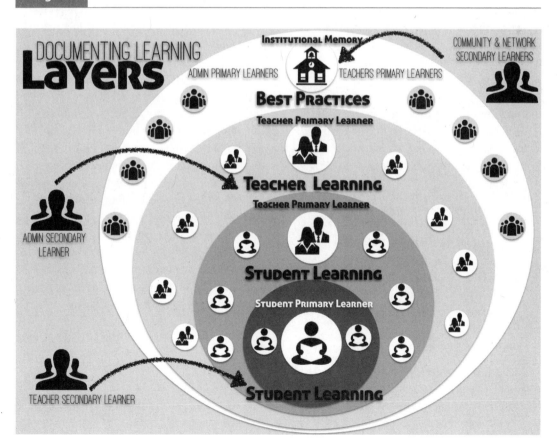

Table 4.1 Student Documenting Learning Perspectives

Heutagogy Perspective	Self-Assessment Perspective
Self-directed and self-motivated learning provide wonderful opportunities for students to choose not only what they want to learn, but the platforms and tools that will best support their learning process. When students realize that they are on a learning journey of their own choice, they find reflecting on their growth along the way and over time via their artifacts beneficial. Likewise, the decisions they make on what they need to learn next or focus on deeper is based on the evidence of their learning.	Documenting learning is not done to learners, it engages them in their own learning processes, which involves the need to self-assess one's knowledge, understanding, and application along the way. November (2017) states that, "Research clearly supports the value of self-assessment, because it helps students become independent learners. For instance, researcher John Hattie has poured over nearly 1,200 educational studies from around the world to identify the factors that most strongly correlate with student success. Of the 195 independent variables [Hattie] has identified, self-assessment ranks third on his list in terms of importance—and it's the single most effective learning strategy that students can use for themselves."
Action Research Perspective	**Gaining Understanding Perspective**
There is a need for all learners to begin seeing themselves as researchers when engaged in their learning acquisition. This involves strategically advancing one's learning by developing strategies that work well for himself or herself, as well as knowing when to discard a strategy that does not aid in furthering one's learning process. Documenting one's own learning supports the research process by asking students to • plan based on the purpose for conducting the research; • implement and revise the action plan; • reflect and report on what was done, as well as needs to be done next; • analyze and interpret the results, and retesting or re-applying when necessary; and • drawing conclusions. And, most importantly, being able to articulate what has been learned purposefully to an intended audience.	Documenting is not about showcasing perfect work. It is about embracing a growth mindset that captures, reflects on, and shares failing at and gaining understanding at specific moments in time. Mistakes, misunderstandings, and misinterpretations are important to make as they help learners grow as they grapple with correcting what is inaccurate. The learning assumptions are important to capture at various moments in the learning process as students need to able to reflect on and interpret where they are, and where they need to go as they grow in their understanding, which is enhanced when their artifacts are shared and amplified. By doing so, students naturally learn to articulate and communicate their understanding to others, as well as synthesize what is shared via feedback and apply to their learning process.

Now Literacies Perspective	Visible Thinking Perspective
As students document their own learning, the *now* literacies are naturally embedded. Students capture their learning through a variety of technology platforms and tools. They need to consider how what has been captured can best convey their learning-thinking and evidence of learning. This requires them to edit and format their selected media (*media literacy*) to best tell their narrative (*basic literacy*). Likewise, they need to consider how to best convey their evidence of learning to larger audiences to obtain their desired feedback (*network literacy, global literacy*). Students also need to make decisions concerning how to share and amplify their thoughts and evidence (*digital citizenship*), as well as how to organize, archive, and retrieve their documentation (*information literacy*).	Documenting is making thinking and learning visible to oneself and to others. Making one's thinking visible has a twofold purpose. It helps learners in clarifying their own understanding and prepares them to communicate that thinking to others. A person, regardless of age, naturally has mental models that are not necessarily accurate, although to the person they seem to be accurate. Generating artifacts aids students in articulating their mental models to themselves and others. November (2017) points out that, "Making students thinking visible is a strategy to help teachers, but making the thinking visible also helps students."
Metacognition Perspective	**Growth Over Time Perspective**
Documenting supports students in being aware of their learning, unpacking the learning, and making thinking and learning visible. When students are engaged in documenting AS learning opportunities, this type of documenting causes them to have to reflect metacognitively and deeply regarding what they determine needs to be collected, shared, and amplified to enhance their learning process.	As students document their learning, they can choose to focus on a specific topic, concept, or behavior that they want to capture and reflect on their knowledge and understanding growth over time. For clarity, here is an example of each focus type: • Content—learning specific knowledge regarding plate tectonics • Concept—designing an artificial pouch for abandon joeys • Behavior—listening well to other's ideas It takes planning and foresight to know what documentation artifacts will be needed to provide evidence of the growth, including an evolving sophistication that is visually and/or audibly recognizable.

Teachers Documenting Student Learning

When teachers are documenting their students' learning, they are not primary learners; they are documenting to help make their students learning process visible. By doing so, the students can study and analyze their learning journeys throughout a learning opportunity, as well as over time. Teachers documenting their students' learning can be viewed through a variety of learning perspectives (Table 4.2).

Table 4.2 Teachers Documenting Students' Learning Perspectives

Pedagogy Perspective	Assessing Perspective
Opportunities to home in on a specific teaching strategies in relationship to aiding or enhancing student learning can be explored. What helps one student or a group of students may hinder another. As teachers focus on understanding what learning looks like for their students, it causes them to consider how to best capture evidence of their learning so that the students can engage meaningfully and purposefully when unpacking the captured artifacts.	It is common for educators to think of documenting learning as an assessment method or tool. This is not the case when considering all the components involved in the documenting process. There is a nuanced difference between assessing (*verb: the act of evaluating the ability or quality of*) and an assessment (*noun: the product or performance that is the evaluation the ability or quality of*). Teachers are aiding their students in assessing their own learning, not administering an assessment.
Curriculum Design Perspective	**Action Research Perspective**
Teachers who provide students documenting opportunities do so with an understanding that all of the curriculum (*what students must know, be able to do, and apply in various situations independently and collaboratively*) is not created equal. Whether the teachers designed the curriculum or it was provided or purchased, it is imperative that there are systemic conversations and decision making concerning what portions of curriculum provide their students with the most leverage as current and lifelong learners. When curriculum focuses and goals have been collaboratively determined, it makes it much easier for teachers to embark on documenting opportunities that are worthy of using precious time effectively. Students grow as learners when they are provided a balance of prioritized-curriculum and passion-based learning opportunities.	How people learn is constantly evolving, including students and teachers. Today's learning environments have changed greatly since the onset of this century. New pedagogies are constantly emerging and being explored that involve new platforms, tools, and understanding of essential skills and literacies. Teachers need to have the heart of researchers to learn about, test, share, and revise their findings connected to improving student learning. A classroom makes a natural professional learning lab to answer questions such as: • How does a new method, strategy, approach, or tool positively affect or influence student learning? • Is engagement and motivation enhanced? How has it affected or increased understanding? • How does changing a variable achieve growth in learning for all students?

Teachers Documenting Their Own Professional Learning

Teachers documenting their own professional learning, whether for a pedagogical or heutagogical purpose, make their classrooms become action labs. Most educators see themselves as lifelong learners and ascribe to the notion that they need to practice what they preach, which includes embracing and applying documenting opportunities to their own learning. Teachers documenting their own professional learning can be viewed through a variety of learning perspectives (Table 4.3).

Table 4.3   Teachers Documenting Their Own Professional Learning Perspectives

Pedagogical Action Research Perspective	Self-Assessing and Accountability Perspective
Just as teachers aid students in documenting their own learning, teachers need opportunities to do the same to gain insight into the quality of their teaching practices. By combining the documenting process with action research, teachers can visually and audibly gain insights into the realities of how students are truly taking in their learning. Stockman (2015) reflects on her role as a researcher as she makes her student writers the subject of her documentation, "Teaching is all about learning, and learning is all about research. This reality fuels my curiosity and keeps me passionate about what I do." Spencer (2017) adds that teachers need opportunities to, "Identify a question or problem, test out a strategy, gather data, and determine if it works. The result is something dynamic, innovative, and tied directly to your classroom. . . . In other words, the teacher actively participates in the situation while conducting the research."	In many educational systems teachers rely on one or two formal observations an academic year conducted by an administrator as an assessment of the application of school- or district-provided professional development. Teachers are often required to write formal professional goals for which they will be held accountable. Documenting their own learning over time (throughout the year) provides teachers with ongoing assessing and evaluating opportunities. No longer do administrators need to rely on a snapshot observation of a teacher's pedagogical practice because the teacher can share and highlight his or her professional learning growth over time. Capturing, reflecting on, and applying anew via artifacts and evidence of professional learning over time is powerful, as is inviting administrators and colleagues to participate in feedback loops based on the artifacts created throughout the year.
Heutagogy Perspective	**Sharing and Amplifying Perspective**
The same holds true for teachers as learners. Providing educators with opportunities for self-directed learning aids in improving professional practices. When someone is motivated due to personalized intrinsic or extrinsic motivation, learning will take place. Just as students can see their growth over time through their artifacts, teachers are able to see themselves growing through both failures and successes, which cause them to make more meaningful and purposeful teaching decisions that positively affect their classrooms and student learning.	Just as students are asked to share and amplify their artifacts and evidence of learning to one another and the world, teachers need to be doing the same to grow and expand their understanding and practices. Moberg (2012) reflected, "I know I am not alone with my experiences with team-planning and voluntary professional development. Teachers crave other teachers' feedback and wisdom. . . . Technology has bound teachers together throughout the world. There is no limit for relationships with other teachers now! We can Facebook, Tweet, or Pin each other, not to mention just call for a long chat about our students and lessons."

It's Time to Take Action!

Chapter 4 Action Step

Choose the *Sharing and Amplifying* perspective from Table 4.3 and *one other professional-learning perspective* from the same table to create a documenting opportunity based on a professional learning goal or passion. It may be one you are currently engaged in or one that you are going to begin for this action step.

Next, determine the amount of time you will be officially engaged in your documenting opportunity (e.g., one week, one month, one semester).

Based on what you have learned thus far from reading Chapters 1 through 4, engage in a document learning opportunity that includes the two professional learning perspectives. Remember that documenting will involve sharing and amplifying your artifacts and evidence of learning, including your mistakes, failures, and successes. This process invites colleagues and experts to provide you with feedback as you grow in your understanding and application over time.

Note: If you are not comfortable with the thought of sharing and amplifying, you may want to first read Chapter 5 before beginning this action step, as well as seek someone who can aid you in the how-tos.

Remember to use the #documenting4learning hashtag on Twitter, Facebook, or Instagram; or by mentioning @documenting4learning on Facebook and Instagram, and @doc4learning on Twitter.

Schools and Districts
Documenting Learning as Institutional Memory

Institutional memory for a school or district is a collective set of facts, events, best practices, learning experiences, values, and knowledge that represents who they are and what they believe in as an educational institution at a specific moment in, as well as over time. From an administrator's school or district perspective, documenting can begin to replace traditional ways of communicating the teaching and learning taking place. When a school or district is willing to be transparent about its institutional processes and results of teaching and learning over time, all stakeholders benefit and grow.

While many institutions have embraced displaying documenting OF learning artifacts (e.g., posting photos of the Science Fair, National Honor society award winners, and banquet highlights), it is entirely different when embarking on documenting FOR and AS learning experiences. At the onset of engaging in either of these types, it will feel scary and threatening. The documenting process is not about being perfect. It is about a journey toward improvement. And the reality is that these journeys will most likely have moments of messiness that could be shared. Just as teachers are asked to be risk-takers when beginning their documenting opportunities, the same is true at an institutional level. School and districts documenting their institutional memory can be viewed through a variety of perspectives (Table 4.4).

Table 4.4 Institutional Memory Documenting Learning Perspectives

Storytelling Perspective	**Leaving a Legacy Perspective**
Great things are happening in schools. The reality is that it most likely did not start off great. Much took place to arrive at the desired destination. Providing stakeholders with artifacts as a storytelling narrative while the journey is taking place is powerful, and oftentimes evokes empathy that may not be present otherwise. And it is important to note and capture visually and/or audibly all of the journey's characters, which may involve teachers, support staff, administrators, students, and community members. When a school or district is willing to be transparent and use strategically artifacts to convey where it is in the process as it moves to where it wants to be, it allows sharing and amplifying to be a forum that embraces feedback and proves to be beneficial to all. By sharing success and failures, an institution encourages other institutions and educational organizations to also take risks and embrace their unique perspectives, challenges, and discoveries when embarking on their own learning journeys.	Schools and districts are living, breathing organisms and function as a community, which is defined as *a group of people living in the same place or having a particular characteristic in common*. Every year, new students and families, teachers and administrators, support staff, and local community members join or leave. While some institutions are more transient than others, all can benefit from strategically selecting topics or concepts to document for the sake of institutional memory. Creating and archiving artifacts provide evidence of learning and teaching that can serve to bridge the gap and connect new community members to what has been, what is now, and spark conversations concerning what needs to take place. Being able to look back and reflect on an institution's visible/audible patterns, trends, and growth over time is insightful and powerful, especially when the artifacts are from documenting FOR or AS learning experiences. Being able to view and listen to what students learned and how they are learning are powerful ways to capture and continue sharing and amplifying an institution's legacy and desires for the future.
Initiative Implementation Perspective	**Action Research Perspective**
Schools spend an incredible amount of money on initiatives to enhance and support learning and teaching practices, such as curriculum developed by teachers or purchased; soft skills, including mindsets and characteristics; technology integration; and myriad pedagogical innovations. Quite often school and district boards want to see data that prove the money has been or is being well-spent. Hattie (2011) states, "When [educational reviewers] go into schools, don't go and ask for the data because the minute you do that you've blown it. Go and ask what evidence you've got, and the same for professional development. What evidence can you produce before you do the PD, and as you do it, that you're having an impact, and what are you doing about the consequences of that. I'm suggesting that this will get away from the prescriptive notion, it opens up opportunities, it gives the communities that we work with, who are incredibly diverse, modern ways of	Price (2013) points out, "Creating a learning commons culture isn't easy, but those that have succeeded have a surprisingly consistent set of 'non-negotiables' that help to define that culture: A culture of collaborative enquiry – educators see themselves as researchers and developers. They are encouraged to look outside education for inspiration and innovation. They are required to share those enquiries, involving students, parents, and other staff. Their learning spaces welcome the disruption of visitors, because, as Stephen Harris says, 'the more students have to articulate their learning, the more they live it.'" As teachers and school administrators see themselves as researchers who are working collaboratively to improve teaching and learning practices, the closer to a positive tipping point is reached. When a critical mass of key players is willing to establish a school or district as professional research lab wherein a design-thinking process

(Continued)

Table 4.4	(Continued)
showing they're successful, but it does put the emphasis back on impact." Once teachers, support staff, and administrators have been trained and begin to exhibit a comfort level with the documenting learning process, embedding documenting opportunities into strategic plans can be a valuable method for creating meaningful and relevant data versus inconclusive or inferenced data.	involving empathy, definition, ideation, prototyping, and testing, willingness to learn and grow is valued, documented, shared, and amplified. It is risk-taking to not always appear perfect to the public and to parents, but educational institutions that are willing to say they are on a journey toward providing the best education for the students in their care oftentimes find unexpected support from boards, stakeholders, and communities.

SUMMING UP

Documenting opportunities can be experienced through various engagements and layers.

The innermost layer focuses on the student, as the primary learner becomes metacognitively aware of his or her learning process while the learning is taking place.

In the next layer, the teacher learns much by taking advantage of the artifacts produced by himself or herself or the students in terms of how they are gaining understanding and visibly thinking about what is being learned. The teacher is also able to better determine where students need support or facilitation.

In the third layer, when a teacher documents his or her professional learning, it often feels risky to share and amplify. When willing to do so, the teacher is rewarded with insights and perspectives from local and global communities of learners. This layer also provides teachers with opportunities to take personal ownership in making their professional learning visible, which can become an integral component in teacher-observation cycles or accountability requirements.

The final layer, which involves a school's or district's institutional memory, can utilize its teachers' classroom or professional learning artifacts as a way to provide stakeholders and the community with what is believed and valued. It also involves an institution's willingness to provide parents and caregivers with an awareness of new pedagogies or initiative implementations; areas in need of improvement; and making its educators and administrators' ongoing professional learning transparent.

GOING BEYOND

To amplify your reading beyond this book's pages, we have created *discussion questions and prompts* for this chapter, which are located at *www.documenting4learning.com*. To extend your thinking, reactions, and responses, you can connect with other readers by leaving comments on individual chapter's discussion posts on our documenting4learning blog.

We also invite you to contribute and share your artifacts in other social media spaces to connect with and learn from other readers around the world using the #documenting4learning hashtag on Twitter, Facebook, or Instagram; or by mentioning @documenting4learning on Facebook and Instagram, and @doc4learning on Twitter.

Documenting With Sharing and Amplifying in Mind

Social media is the greatest leadership tool ever invented. It gives you the opportunity to amplify your voice, extend your influence, and create a tribe of passionate followers who want to hear from you.

—Michael Hyatt

One perspective mentioned in the previous chapter asks students, teachers, and institutions to see themselves as action researchers. Using documenting when conducting action research includes sharing and amplifying one's learning, including both struggles and successes with local and global audiences. By doing so, audiences can engage in the learning as well by improving their knowledge and understanding, or viewing what they know from a new perspective.

Gerstein (2015) conveys her reasoning for educators sharing beyond themselves as modern learners:

On a personal level, sharing assists the educator in becoming a better educator. The act of sharing requires reflection and preparation. The educator needs to reflect on his or her own practices to identify which ones they want to share and needs to put that sharing artifact into a form (e.g. writing, images, audio, video) that will be understood by an authentic audience. This process tends to help the educator improve instructional practices. . . . On a broader, more systemic level, sharing one's experiences benefits other educators which, in turn, has the potential to advance the entire education field. It is the collective responsibility of all educators to create the change that they want to see in the education world. There really is no they in education. The *they* is really *we-us*. The we-us now have the means to have a voice.

This is true for learners of all ages. Whether adults engaged in professional learning or students engaged in academic- or passion-based learning, the need to share and amplify elevates the learning acquisition that leads to gained knowledge, understanding, and application.

SHARING AND AMPLIFYING WHEN DOCUMENTING LEARNING

Sharing and amplifying is about making one's learning visible to others with purpose and meaning, which has its rewards and benefits, as Gerstein points out. It is also about taking one's ideas, experiences, successes, challenges, questions, and resources and inviting others into the learning process.

What Are the Connections Between Sharing and Amplifying?

We find educators often have difficulty differentiating between sharing and amplifying because there are subtle distinctions between them in the documenting process. Table 5.1 explains the nuances in sharing versus amplifying.

For an ongoing example to help differentiate among the degrees of amplification when sharing (see Image 5.1), throughout this chapter we will visit Sarah, a student participating in a documenting opportunity in her sophomore English class. The class is reading a contemporary book and focusing on its two main characters. After reading sections or chapters, the students are conducting a variety of tasks, as well as meeting for small-group discussions.

One task Sarah is responsible for is publishing posts in her digital portfolio blog. Given her blog is online, her posts are technically available for the world to read. While Sarah shares her first posts pertaining to the documentation focus, there is no purposeful amplification because no one knows her blog's URL. In other words, no one knows where to find her posts. Since people are not visiting her blog and leaving comments, Sarah does not have an opportunity to interact with others about her shared learning-thinking artifacts. Likewise, she is not strategically expanding her amplification reach through additional mediums (e.g., sharing her blog with someone in person, Twitter post with hyperlink, being referenced in someone else's blog post).

When sharing takes place with a purposeful *extending the reach* to an ever-widening audience, *amplification increases*, similar to sound waves expanding and growing louder.

Image 5.1

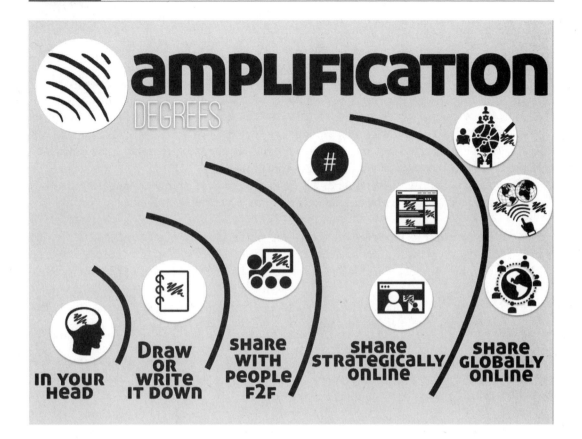

Table 5.1   Sharing and Amplifying Nuances

Sharing	Amplifying
• Share with oneself, one other person, or a small group/audience	• Amplify with larger group and wider audiences
• Allows others to take part in or benefit from what is being shared	• Strategically allows widening audiences to take part in or benefit from what is being shared
• Limits one's reach intentionally to an individual or small group/audience	• Extends one's reach intentionally (or unintentionally) beyond an initial person or small group to targeted audiences
• Views documentation as a form of learning/teaching that connects oneself with only one's sphere of influence	• Views documentation as a form of learning/teaching that connects with others who would not normally be in one's sphere of influence
• Publishes analog or digital artifacts without concern for reaching any audiences	• Publishes digital artifacts strategically to reach targeted audiences

Sharing With Oneself—Slight Degree of Amplification

Just because someone is fluent in the how-tos of riding a skateboard or driving a car, it usually takes a bit of thinking to explain the now ubiquitous actions step-by-step to others. This is also true when trying to explain one's thoughts cognitively and metacognitively while learning new information.

Learners constantly try to make sense of new facts and concepts, as well as how the new information relates to what is already known and how it applies to authentic situations. Needing to get it out of one's mind is sometimes referred to as *creating a model*. Anderson (2011) notes, "The problem with mental models is they are just yours, and yours alone. They are inside your brain. . . . They are idiosyncratic, that means they are going to be different in every individual. And also, they are oftentimes incomplete."

Therefore, taking the time while engaged in the act of learning to ponder and express one's thinking with oneself is beneficial because it involves the following:

- Requiring you to focus on what is taking place, what it means, and how it fits into your bigger picture of understanding
- Reflecting on what you think is accurate and having to articulate your thoughts and ideas
- Realizing that you may not understand as clearly as you thought *inside your head* when trying to explain or summarize key points or components

While sharing with yourself registers as only a slight degree of amplification, it does involve making what can only be heard in one's mind heard out loud and articulated—whether textually, visually, or audibly.

> Returning to Sarah's learning: While reading the book's chapters, she focuses on gaining insights into the relationship between the story's protagonist and antagonist and how their relationship continually moves the plot forward. This is a new storytelling concept for herself and her peers. Many thoughts are coming and going in her mind as she comprehends the text, while simultaneously analyzing the two characters' actions and interactions.
>
> To capture her thinking while reading she thoughtfully annotates and draws simple sketches in the margins of the chapters. This act of getting her mental-model ideas out of her head and onto paper forces her to think deeper about what she is reading and its meaning within the book's context and learning focus. Her annotations can prompt her to make further connections when she revisits them during her small-group discussions, which involves the next degree of amplification.

Sharing Face-to-Face—Low Degree of Amplification

Once someone can articulate current understanding to himself or herself via making it textually, visually, or orally visible, the next degree of amplification involves sharing the artifacts *with someone else*. This lower degree of face-to-face (F2F) amplification involves reaching out in person or digitally to someone or a small group who the learner knows well. For students, it may mean meeting during class time, later in the day at a coffee shop, or via Google Hangout. For teachers, it may be an informal discussion in the teachers' lounge, a formal faculty or professional learning community meeting, or via Skype.

To increase the face-to-face amplification degree, the learner needs to seek out people whom he or she does not intimately know. For students, it may mean meeting with students in another class or another school. For teachers, it may mean meeting with teachers in another building or district, during a conference workshop or breakout session, or meeting someone new using a virtual platform. This degree of amplification expands the ability to potentially stretch one's thinking regarding what is being learned since the ideas shared by new people may require the learner to consider perspectives never thought of or considered before, or listen to feedback provided in the form of questions or pushback.

Taking the time to textually, visually, or audibly share one's thinking with someone else or a small group is beneficial because it involves:

- Opening yourself up to instant comments and feedback regarding your ideas and concepts. Just watching a listener's facial expressions can spark questions regarding your current thinking. Comments, clarifications, resistance, and questions posed by those listening add a dimension that could not happen if talking only to yourself.
- Articulating one's thoughts beyond yourself requires the learner to generate stronger and clearer explanations and examples expressed through artifacts and accompanying conversations. Your mind will tend to assume your artifacts and thinking makes sense, when in actuality there may be gaps in your understanding's reasoning, explanations, steps, or sequences.
- Presenting your work to an audience, especially someone unfamiliar to you, tends to produce higher quality thinking and work because you are "putting yourself out there." You also tend to better articulate your reasons when wanting or needing to learn more about new information, whether intrinsically or extrinsically motivated.

When Sarah meets with her small group, one of her friends, Andrea, suggests that they meet with a study group from another class period to see what they are thinking.

When the students from both periods meet after school, Sarah has an interesting conversation with Jason, whom she has seen around school but never talked with before. They both share their annotations and Sarah shares her sketchnotes. Things get a bit heated over a disagreement concerning how the main characters' relationship moves a specific plot point forward.

After the meeting, when Sarah was walking home with Andrea, she shares in a huffy tone, "I don't like Jason." Andrea rolls her eyes and comments, "I heard the two of you talking. It's not that you don't like him. You just don't like that he didn't agree with your reasoning!" Sarah sighs and realizes Andrea is right, which causes her to want to dig deeper into her reading and thinking so that she can better defend her claim.

Sharing Online—Increased Degree of Amplification

Once a learner moves from sharing his or her ideas and thoughts with one person or a few people, moving to sharing *online* increases the amplification degree. It is important to note that simply placing documentation artifacts online does not instantly create a greater amplification, as was mentioned regarding Sarah's first blog posts.

To truly experience the power of online amplification, administrators, teachers, and stakeholders need to consider the benefits of connecting their students and their professional documentation artifacts with interested audiences and experts who can contribute to the learners' documenting opportunities that are outside a closed digital environment. It is understandable that a school or district wants to, and in some situations are obligated to, protect the students in their care. The reality is that students are getting online outside of the school day. Given the *now* literacies are so important to be learned and practiced during the school day, keeping students isolated from online interactions during school hours does not benefit students. Teachers and administrators can use these opportunities to aid students in becoming digitally literate while coaching them through participating in authentic online learning opportunities.

Due to privacy concerns, oftentimes students' online artifacts remain behind protected sites and are only accessible by a limited pre-selected audience. Private Twitter accounts, closed learning management system platforms, and password-protected digital portfolios are a few examples of limited amplification degrees, even though the artifacts are shared online. Technically, these environments are not much different from sharing face-to-face with people the students and teachers personally know.

Taking the time to share one's thinking with online audiences is beneficial because it involves the following:

- Documenting with an audience in mind (e.g., purposeful use of a #hashtag in a Twitter post) to broaden potential interactions that will positively impact your or their thinking
- Connecting with people and groups that share in your desired learning and/or interests, as well as interact when conducting research
- Being aware of the power of actively participating and building personal learning networks (e.g., Facebook groups, Twitter chats, commenting on blogs)
- Embracing the reality that you have something worthwhile to share, even when others may have shared something similar because no one else will contribute the identical perspective, idea, or interpretation
- Conveying documentation to others that can be viewed from the moment it is shared to months and years later
- Obtaining crowdsourcing feedback that will strengthen your understanding, thinking, reflections, and conclusions related to your documentation focuses
- Creating an online presence as an educator, a network connector, and branding yourself as an ongoing learner

Sarah's teacher, Mrs. Watson, coaches her class on what is meant by sharing and amplifying their artifacts beyond simply publishing a blog post. She explains it is important to invite others, including experts, to engage in their work to add to or challenge their thinking.

Sarah mentions her conversation with Jason during their after-school discussion. Her teacher asks her if it was beneficial having someone not agree with her reasoning. Sarah comments that it was frustrating at first, but then found it helpful. She mentioned that it caused her to think deeper about her reasoning and line of thinking.

Later in the lesson, Mrs. Watson challenges the class to add a degree of amplification to their next blog post by continuing to (a) include their ongoing documentation and reflection on where they currently are in their personal understanding of how the main characters' relationship is affecting the story arc, and (b) strategically

1. including the author's name, book title, and author's website as a hyperlink, as well as include strategically chosen keywords in hopes that others who might be searching for the author, book title, or associated keywords will find their post in the search results;

2. disseminating their post on Twitter by specifically mentioning the author's @username;

3. including the hashtag #comments4kids or an already established hashtag specific to the book title to attract a wider audience; and

4. creating a networking conversation by reading and thoughtfully commenting on three peers' posts from their own class, as well as three posts from another English class period.

Mrs. Watson concludes the lesson by facilitating a discussion on what quality commenting sounds like by having the class read and reflect on examples and non-examples to aid them in their understanding.

Sharing Globally—Extended Degree of Amplification

Some might say that sharing online equals sharing globally. While this may appear to be so, sharing globally cannot include only sharing in one's mother tongue or with people from one's own cultural perspective.

Documentation artifacts should not be shared with the mindset of only reaching out to those within one's country's geographic borders and regions or language. Sharing globally includes strategically reaching out to gain different and unique perspectives that can prove beneficial to a learner's research, resources, examples, and anecdotes. If the desire is to share at this amplification degree, it is not enough to have learners place their artifacts and journeys online, it needs to include a *purposeful global intention*.

Taking the time to share one's thinking globally is beneficial because it involves

- understanding that deeper learning takes place when you welcome different viewpoints and perspectives that are unique to other cultures and languages;
- taking a step back to contemplate how global learners look at the same topic, idea, or challenge with different eyes, background knowledge, experiences, interpretations, and cultural variations;
- becoming aware and acknowledging your own cultural bias regarding learning (and teaching); and
- including an openness for receiving feedback from a global perspective.

As Sarah continues with her class's novel study, she is aware that there might be something more behind the author's two main characters' relationship than what she has been thinking and hearing from her peers. She knows that the book's author grew up in China and the protagonist has a Chinese heritage. Sarah wonders if it could contribute to her understanding of this character if she could connect with someone from an Asian, or specifically Chinese, culture.

She discusses the possibilities with Mrs. Watson of creating shareable content around her cultural wonderment to engage and get input from others. Mrs. Watson suggests

(Continued)

(Continued)

Sarah speaks to a few Asian students first to aid her in her thinking. After doing so, Sarah begins to think about how she can reach a global audience and get the data she desires.

The first thing that comes to Sarah's mind is to create a Google Form survey. She picks four scenarios from the book where there is intense interaction between the two main characters and creates four corresponding open-response questions focused on how a Chinese cultural perspective may or may not influence the protagonist's behaviors and choices. She also asks the surveyors to share their age and ethnic heritage.

She asks for feedback from Mrs. Watson and the Asian students she initially approached. After making a few modifications based on their suggestions, she shares the survey strategically by

- asking some students from her class and the other class's study group to complete a printed-out survey,
- reaching out to her online network using a tweet with a link to her survey, and
- asking another teacher at her school, Mr. Phelps, who has a large professional learning network to post a tweet with the embedded survey link as well.

Sarah began to wonder if many people would complete the survey. She was pleasantly surprised when she received a large response from both the printed and Google Form surveys.

To summarize the collective survey information, she creates an infographic artifact. The infographic highlights the protagonist's significant reactions and actions when confronted by the antagonist. Sarah also includes commentary regarding the potential influence of the character's cultural heritage.

She then writes a blog post explaining her initial desire to dig deeper based on the book study's learning focus (analyze how complex characters interact and advance the plot) from a cultural lens and embeds several hyperlinks, including one to *Amazon* books, in case someone is interested in purchasing the book she is reading; as well as to the author's website. She also includes her infographic.

Once she publishes her post, she and Mr. Phelps tweet about her latest blog and include a link to her post. Sarah looks forward to reading any comments shared and begins checking her post daily to see if there are any responses so she can interact with the commenters.

It's Time to Take Action!

Chapter 5 Action Step

Look again at the *Amplification Degrees* image near the beginning of this chapter (Image 5.1). For a warm-up, think of an example for each sharing amplification degree that you have possibly done for a personal or professional learning experience.

Now think of a passion-based learning opportunity you are engaged in currently. Utilize all four degrees beyond *Sharing With Oneself* to amplify your learning-thinking artifacts and reflections.

Remember to use the #documenting4learning hashtag on Twitter, Facebook, or Instagram; or by mentioning @documenting4learning on Facebook and Instagram, and @doc4learning on Twitter.

SUMMING UP

Many educational systems still do not fully understand the value and power of sharing and networking strategically among faculties, support staff, administrators, and most importantly, students. Likewise, when the realization is there, it does take time and support investment to make it a natural component within the system versus an event or occasional experience.

In informal surveys with educators around the world, teachers have often shared reasons for not wanting to share or amplify the learning of their students or themselves:

- I don't have enough time.
- I don't have strong technology skills. I can barely use my smartphone.
- I don't want to brag.
- I don't have self-confidence in what I need to be doing.
- I don't want to deal with the potential judgment of others.
- I don't think anyone would think what I shared would be worth reading, watching, or viewing.
- I know I would have too many spelling and grammar errors. What needs to be put out there needs to be perfect.
- I don't want to have to deal with haters or bullies.

How do teachers and students overcome these fears or concerns? How can school or district administrators support a shift in their system to establish a connected sharing and amplifying community, given it is happening 24/7 outside educational walls?

A perfect way is simply *to begin*. No one has ever overcome his or her fears by avoidance. It is important to acknowledge one's fears and then figure out doable action steps to begin diving in. For some, this may mean researching and learning everything possible beforehand; while others find a reliable and trusted mentor to hold their hand and coach or mentor them on each step they take along the way.

Time constraints are real in schools and our fast-paced world. But as a popular saying goes: *Nobody is too busy; it's just a matter of priorities*. Teachers, schools, and districts who truly want to live their core values and mission, vision, or philosophy statements proclaiming support for their students must find time to practice what is being promised. It must be a priority. The more administrators and teachers, as learning leaders, are willing to model risk-taking, sharing, and highlighting learning successes, failures, and confusions by making them visible, the more students will feel comfortable, supported, and encouraged to do the same.

These actions require risk-taking, problem solving, and critical thinking regarding the how-tos. As another popular adage states, "The best way to eat an elephant is one bite at a time," simply being cognizant of what degree(s) of sharing are taking place, or can begin to take place in your classroom is a great place to begin using your current curriculum and slight modifications to your instruction, activities, and assessments.

GOING BEYOND

To amplify your reading beyond this book's pages, we have created *discussion questions and prompts* for this chapter, which are located at *www.documenting4learning.com*. To extend your thinking, reactions, and responses, you can connect with other readers by leaving comments on individual chapter's discussion posts on our documenting4learning blog.

We also invite you to contribute and share your artifacts in other social media spaces to connect with and learn from other readers around the world using the #documenting4learning hashtag on Twitter, Facebook or Instagram; or by mentioning @documenting4learning on Facebook and Instagram, and @doc4learning on Twitter.

6

Documenting Phases

There are two phases to a movie. First you shoot the movie, and then you make the movie.

Generally, post-production is longer than filming.

—Keenen Ivory Wayans

The thought processes involved in making a movie are multifaceted: *What is the purpose of the movie? How will we best capture the perfect shots, sequences, and dialogues? How will we optimally capture and edit the raw footage to transform the information into a meaningful message for our intended audience?*

There are many parallels in movie making and documenting learning. While the questions may be worded slightly different, the intent is the same: establishing purpose, capturing information, transforming information in meaningful ways for an intended audience, and sharing the message with the world.

Given the numerous facets involved when learning something new or digging deeper in understanding, it is important that the documenting learning process is viewed as a natural part of the learning experience, *not an add-on*. While at first the process may feel time-consuming, it eventually becomes a ubiquitous pedagogical and heutagogical practice. As a colleague once shared with us, "It took a while, but I think of documenting using the three phases and routine as 'learnigogy' in my classroom."

The documenting learning process is viewed as a natural part of the learning experience, *not an add-on*.

There are two components to this *learnigogy*. The first includes three *documentation phases*, similar to the phases Wayans mentions in the quote above, with the addition of a planning phase. While Wayans did not directly reference this phase, it is standard to plan when preparing for a simple or complex task.

The second component involves the *learningflow routine steps*, which are explained and explored indepth in Chapter 7. Following these steps are similar to steps in a workflow routine in the business world: each step moves the work or project through from initiation to completion.

DOCUMENTATION PHASES

To make documenting opportunities more manageable, it is important to know how the phases play a role in the overall process (see Image 6.1):

Image 6.1

1. **Pre-documentation phase**

   Thinking critically about *what* is going to be documented and *why*

2. **During-documentation phase**

   Documenting the learning moments *now* and *over time*

3. **Post-documentation phase**

   Focusing on metacognition, and *how to evaluate, use, and make meaning* of the captured media and documented artifacts

Pre-documentation Phase

While documenting learning involves collecting evidence during moments of the learning, it does not mean collecting evidence of anything and everything. Think about what most people do with their mobile devices. Since there is essentially no cost associated with snapping hundreds of images or recording multiple videos, people often will do both without deeply contemplating the value of the photo or recording taken.

When the device or a cloud storage account informs a user that space is about to run out, it is most likely the first time a decision needs to be made regarding the images or videos worth keeping and the ones that need to be deleted. The user lets out a deep sigh and begins the arduous task of looking at each photo and listening to each video in myriad collections to determine those that are worthwhile to keep. Inevitably, the user

- Is truly amazed at just how many images and recordings have been made and most importantly, *totally forgotten about*
- Begins to *thoughtfully determine* what images and videos are important and need to be saved and *why*

Image 6.2

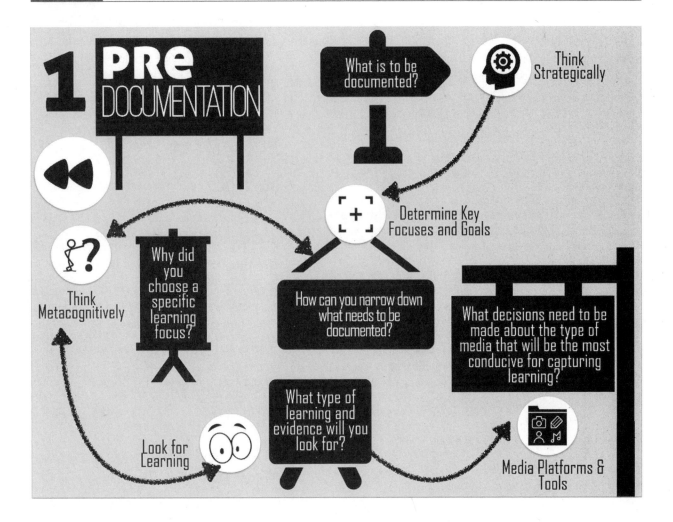

When documenting, *thoughtful determination* should happen *prior* to the documenting process begins so that learners do not end up with too many photographs or videos that can cause a paralyzed state of mind when confronted with what to do with it all (see Image 6.2).

Think Strategically: Using Guiding Questions to Aid in Preplanning

After filmmakers determine the purpose and focus of their movies, they spend a significant amount of preplanning time asking guiding questions related to their key question: *How will we best capture the perfect shots, sequences, and dialogues?* Similarly, reflecting on pre-documentation needs and guiding questions is an important step in preparing to "take the perfect shots" or "include an important conversation in the script" in the during-documentation phase that will be transformed in the post-documentation phase. Table 6.1 provides guiding questions to use during the planning process.

Table 6.1   Learners, Pre-documentation Needs, and Guiding Questions

Learners	Pre-documentation Needs	Guiding Questions

As a student learner . . .	Establish the purpose, specific focuses, and articulated goals for your learning documentation.
	
	Articulate what acceptable evidence of learning will look like to yourself and your audiences.
	
	Plan how you will collect meaningful artifacts that will provide evidence of your learning focuses and goals, which you will reflect on in the post-documentation phase.
	
	Consider the best media platforms and tools to use to capture meaningful artifacts as evidence of your learning that will be reflected on in the post-documentation phase.
	
	Think about how you can connect what you will be doing in this documenting opportunity with past learning experiences to recognize patterns or trends in how you learn and express that evidence to others.
		• What would you like to improve on or achieve related to your learning?
		  ○ Could using a KWHLAQ chart help you in deciding?
		
		QR Code 6.1
		
		Scan this QR code to learn more about the KWHLAQ strategy.
		
		  ○ Could a visible thinking routine support your brainstorming process?
		
		http://langwitches.me/kwhlaqupdate
		
		QR Code 6.2
		
		Scan this QR code to learn more about visible thinking routines.
		
		• What will be acceptable evidence of your learning based on your focuses and goals?
		• How will you make your learning and thinking visible and shareable to audiences locally and globally?
		
		http://langwitches.me/vtr

As a teacher aiding student learners . . .	Establish the purpose, specific focuses, and articulated goals for your students' learning documentation. Articulate what acceptable evidence of learning will look like to you and your students.	• What criteria, standards, or objectives do your students need to improve on or achieve? • What will you and/or your students accept as evidence of learning based on past and present learning?

Learners	Pre-documentation Needs	Guiding Questions
	Consider the best media platforms and tools to use to collect meaningful artifacts that will provide evidence of your students' learning focuses and goals, which will be reflected on in the post-documentation phase.	• What would be helpful for you to consider regarding your students' learning styles and modalities? • What evidence of learning from this documenting opportunity do you believe will be the most beneficial in guiding and informing your instruction and/or facilitation?
As a professional learner . . .	Establish the purpose, specific focuses, and articulated goals for your learning documentation. Consider if it will benefit your learning and aid in establishing your focuses and goals to seek out local or global expert advice or assistance during the pre-documentation phase. Consider the best media platforms and tools to generate artifacts that will optimally showcase your learning. Consider how action research and/or resources can aid you in improving your professional practice for your selected learning focuses or goals. Plan how you will share your learning—both successes and failures—with colleagues close by and around the world as a contributor to the collective community of professional educators.	• What would you like to improve on or achieve related to your professional learning or educational passion? • What will be acceptable evidence of your learning based on your focuses and goals? • What human, digital, or social media resources are at your disposal or you would like to seek out to aid you in establishing your understanding or deepening your learning? • How will you make your learning visible, shareable, and amplified to connect with educational audiences locally and globally? • How can your visible learning positively impact educators' and/or students' learning?

Determine a Specific Focus and Articulated Goals

What learning will be in focus and why? Like filmmakers answering the question *What is the purpose of the movie?* teachers and students need to pre-determine what learning is going to be specifically in focus (no film pun intended), as well as the articulated goals based on the focuses during the documentation process. Table 6.2 provides several examples.

Think Metacognitively

After determining the key focuses and goals, it is time to think deeper about why these areas are important to the overall learning. Look back at Image 6.2 and notice the two-way arrows connecting the two steps: *Thinking Metacognitively* and *Look for Learning.* The back-and-forth idea has been purposefully placed there to express the overlapping connections among

Table 6.2   Broad Focus, Specific Focus, and Articulated Goals

Broad Focus	Specific Focus	Articulated Goals
QR Code 6.3 **Upper Elementary, Middle, and High School Any Subject** *Being a Helpful Official Classroom Scribe* http://langwitches.me/scribe	Official scribe creates essential notes and information for students absent from class or who need to review a topic previously learned. Official scribe encourages contributors to make corrections, as well as add information or resources to his or her notes and information.	• Summarize what was learned and discussed during class time • Add images (e.g., photos, illustrations, screenshots) that support topic details • Add ancillary information, such as hyperlinks and embedded videos • Publish daily scribe information to classroom website
QR Code 6.4 **Middle School English/ Language Arts** *Participating in a Socratic Seminar* http://langwitches.me/socratic	Expand personal and collaborative thinking and conversation using a backchannel platform based on the class's established Socratic Seminar norms.	• Observe and comment on peers' Socratic Seminar norm behaviors • Observe and comment on literary discussion elements in action • Document inner circle discussion • Document parallel conversations via backchannel based on inner circle discussion • Add personal opinion commentaries in backchannel supported by reasoning and textual evidence
QR Code 6.5 **Middle School Mathematics** *Thinking Like a Mathematician* http://langwitches.me/math2	Gain insights into peers' metacognitive thinking, reflective thinking, and visible thinking during math class	• Articulate personal and collaborative thought processes orally and visually • Make fluency of personal thinking strategies audible • Provide peer feedback by listening to one another's thought processes • Annotate mathematical thinking and strategies observed in each other's videos

Broad Focus	Specific Focus	Articulated Goals
QR Code 6.6 **Elementary School Social Studies** *Learning About Communities Without Using Textbooks* http://langwitches.me/textbooks	Connect and communicate virtually with other people, cultures, and languages to learn about their communities and how they are the same and different from our communities	• Locate the people we are connecting with using maps and globes • Improve speaking and conversation skills • Ask questions that result in more detailed answers • Be aware of body language and the messages that are conveyed without words • Reflect on how and what is being learned through connections with others • Realize that questions don't stop at the end of a lesson, day, or a virtual call

thinking metacognitively *while* determining the focuses and goals *and* looking for the learning's potential visible moments.

Metacognition does not happen in isolation. It is a fluent practice that causes someone to question and be aware of his or her thinking, choices, reasons, decisions, and reflections when planning documentation:

- Why did I choose a specific learning focus?
- How are these focuses connected to potentially other areas?
- What would make more sense to document in lieu of previous or potential future documentation?
- How might an intended audience influence the documentation?
- What and how should I specifically be looking for learning?
- What will I accept as evidence of learning based on the focus and goal?
- Thinking about potential personal bias, what perceptions or preconceived notions may influence acceptable evidence? What external factors may influence acceptable evidence?

Look for Learning

While primary and secondary learners will be actively looking for learning in the during-documentation phase, it is important to already be preplanning for this step in the pre-documentation phase. *What type of learning will you need to look for to capture evidence of the learning?*

Looking for learning will have its starting points in curricular standards, objectives, and desired skills, but it is not as simple as taking a quick look at these in a teacher's guide or curriculum map. Questions that need to be considered at this time include:

- How will you recognize learning when it is happening in real time?
- How might the learning evidence over time help you look for learning in the present moment?

- How will you look for learning in individual students? How will you consider differentiating the learning?
- How will you remind yourself to look and capture learning as you are teaching, facilitating, and multitasking in the during-documentation phase?

Preparing in advance to look for learning will truly help you to remember what to look for when it comes time to document in the during-documentation phase.

Media Platform and Tool Selection
Based on Learning Focus and Articulated Goals

How will the learning be captured? Before moving on to the during-documentation phase, it is important to consider the best media platforms and tools to capture evidence of the specific learning focuses and articulated goals (see Image 6.3).

In a documenting learning context:

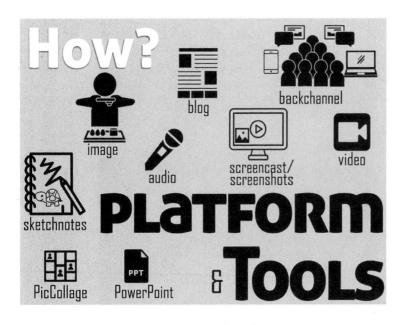

Image 6.3

- The term *platform* represents a social-media environment, as it enables a community to make friends, meet, share ideas, communicate, and learn together (e.g., Twitter, Instagram, Diigo, YouTube, Facebook, WordPress).
- The term *tools* refers to objects, devices, or apps that support and allow learners to solve a particular problem or complete a given task (e.g., PowerPoint, TodaysMeet, PicCollage).

While teachers and/or students are determining the best platforms and tools, they need to be aware that their selections may change or need to be added to in the during-documentation phase.

A filmmaker plays a critical role in the technical direction of a movie, including working with the lighting and filming crew before and during filming to ensure that the shots taken will be of the highest quality and provide the most dramatic backdrop (Sokanu.com, 2017). Likewise, the selection of the media platforms need to capture the dramatic moments of learning that will best convey meaningful evidence of the learning process. Therefore, the guiding question that needs to be posed now is

- What learning evidence are you truly looking for?

For example, a bilingual kindergarten classroom is working on phonemic exercises to improve the pronunciation of certain sounds and words in the target language: German. Given the need to hear the children speaking, taking photographs or creating sketchnotes may not be the best media to capture the intended learning.

This is not to say that images cannot capture the learning in action. The annotexted image (see Image 6.4) expresses the goal of a lesson wherein the children are working on using a strong exhaled breath at the onset of saying "Hallo!" While the teacher's annotation may convey this young girl was successful, the audience may not believe it given it looks like the pea is rolling off the child's hand due to her tilting it downward. Only by looking at the video footage (scan QR Code 6.7) can a viewer observe the evidence that she does, in fact, say "Hallo!" with a strong enough initial breath release to cause the pea to roll off her hand.

Let's take this thought concerning the selection of the best media platform or tool one step further. While recording these young learners via video did provide evidence of their breath capabilities, *what if the articulated goal requires more evidence than what can be portrayed in a video?*

The bilingual kindergarten teacher, Mariana Stürmer, is in the midst of conducting an action research project wherein one of her articulated goals is to determine if a specific set of phonemic exercises practiced over time aids her students in articulating specific target-language sounds (e.g., nuance between *Ich* and *Ach*; long German *e*, as in *wie geht's;* umlaut vowels). She decides that she needs a control group who will not receive practice opportunities based on a generated set of phonemic exercises and a second group who will receive the specific exercises. She decides to use her afternoon class as the control group (see Image 6.4).

Given her goal and instructional plans, she ponders the best media platform options and decides that audio-recording each student at the mid-mark (one month) of her action research project, and again at the end of two months will provide her with evidence of learning over time to determine if the set of phonetic exercises do improve pronunciation in the target language. She knows that an audio recording will provide the clearest-sounding evidence of proper pronunciation, or lack thereof. Mariana also realizes there could be value in periodically filming her students, possibly one or two at a time, to see if they are forming the correct mouth and tongue positions when making the specific phonemic sounds. She decides that these two media platforms will be the best: audio recordings as evidence of the specific goal, and bi-weekly video recordings to provide ongoing evidence of learning to aid her in providing immediate feedback to each student who will be observing his or her video recordings alongside Mrs. Stürmer.

Spending time thoughtfully considering the best media platforms and tools pays off later in the documenting

QR Code 6.7

Scan this QR code and watch the second video to see this child saying "hallo" in action.

http://langwitches.me/phonetics

Image 6.4

process. Capturing learning moments is a busy time wherein aspects of learning are taking place simultaneously. Students are applying their past knowledge and discovering new knowledge, and teachers are coaching and facilitating. There is not a lot of time for the documenter(s) to be introspective in the moment about deciding how to best capture the learning while it is taking place. These decisions, as well as who will be the documenter(s), need to take place in the pre-documentation phase. Think of it as applying the adage: *Measure twice, cut once.* As in life, this does not mean that everything will go picture perfect. There may be a need for additional or replacement media platforms or tools once the during-documentation phase begins.

While the application of selected media, platforms, and tools is an inherent part of capturing the learning taking place in the during-documentation phase, consideration for the choices (boldfaced titles) based on what is to be captured (bullets) belongs in the pre-documentation phase (Table 6.3).

Table 6.3 | Potential Applications for Platforms and Media

Image *Importance Placed on Visual Learning*	**Screenshot** *Importance Placed on Visual Annotexting and Learning*
• Visual support of content; someone or something taking place as part of an action or storytelling; or physical environment • Visual note-taking of moment or event • Creation of a visual timeline • Visual step-by-step instruction, how to, or explanation	• Explanation and meaning making of images through annotexting and/or highlighting various areas of an image • Pointing out subliminal or hidden meaning or action in image • Step-by-step textual directions based on screen images
Sketchnote *Importance Placed on Visual Note-Taking*	**Text** *Importance Placed on the Written Word*
• Brainstorming or mind mapping • Visual thinking • Memory triggers • Visual metaphors or analogies of content • Visual summarization • Ideation	• Summarization • Bulleted list • Extensive explanation • Narrative • Shared and collaborative word processing
Blog *Importance Placed on Reflective, Connected, and Conversational Practices*	**Mircoblogging** *Importance Placed on Concise Written Word*
• Organizing, publishing, and archiving of information, thoughts, opinions, arguments, and artifacts • Connected and hyperlinked evidence of learning artifacts • Opportunities for global dissemination • Timeline of personal learning growth over time	• Concise summarization • Backchanneling • Global networking and connections • Crowdsourcing opinions and resources • Curation

Video *Importance Placed on* *Audio, Visual, and Kinesthetic Learning*	Screencast *Importance Placed on* *Audio and Visual Learning*
• Social interactions • Subliminal messages, such as facial expression, mood, and tone • Video conference interactions and atmosphere • Sightseeing tours	• Tutorials and step-by-step guides • Explanation of something occurring on the screen • Video conference recording • Expressing subliminal evidence of learning via annotexting/subtitles
Audio *Importance Placed on* *Verbal Learning*	Backchannel *Importance Placed on* *Collaborative Writing*
• Articulation • Pronunciation • Reading fluency • Soundseeing tours • Oral summarization	• Contributions of shy students • Extension of conversation happening in the foreground • Collaborative summarization of conversation, viewed video clip, video conference, book discussion • Giving everyone a place to voice their thoughts, opinions, arguments

Summing Up

Once a teacher, student learner, or professional learner has clarity concerning the documenting purpose including the specific focuses, articulated goals, and pre-selected media platforms and tools, it becomes easier to envision the desired artifacts to capture the learning in the during-documentation phase.

During-Documentation Phase

The during-documentation phase may seem simple—document the learning while it is literally taking place—but it is much more complex than that (see Image 6.5). *How will the act of capturing learning truly transpire?*

Purpose and Perspectives When Documenting

When capturing images and videos for everyday life and learning experiences, it is important to think about purpose (*Why am I doing this?*) and perspectives (*What do I want to say? Who am I saying it to?*). This is especially true when snapping images or recording videos that will be shared via social media platforms (e.g., Facebook, Instagram, Snapchat).

The documenter metacognitively considers: *What message do I want to convey? Why is this message important to me and to those who will be viewing the image/video?* This takes on an even stronger meaning when the documenter curates what has been captured by adding a commentary during post-documentation. Learning deepens when a documenter is cognizant of both the purpose and perspectives *while the learning process is taking place.*

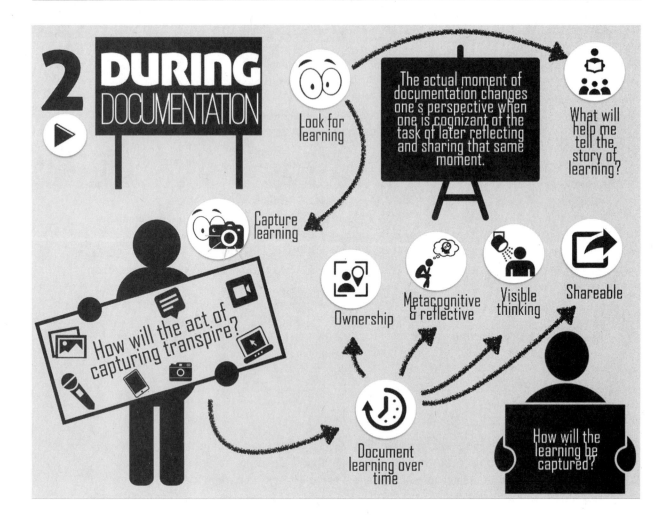

For example, a popular documentation challenge that has been circulating online for some time now is the *Photo-a-Day Challenge.* Participants are asked to take one photo a day for a predetermined timeframe. A specific challenge may be geared toward a specific group, such as travelers, photographers, fashionistas, foodies, parents, students, or educators. Challenges last for various lengths of time: a calendar year, a school year, a month, or a week (e.g., *I Love My Spouse* seven-day challenge). Some challenges last a lifetime (e.g., *My Bucket List* challenge).

The challenge may have rigid goals to be captured (e.g., on May 3rd, take a photograph of something blue; on the 1st day of each month, take a photograph of the same tree in your front yard); other times, it is open and up to the documenter's interpretation. Likewise, the challenge may be limited to a specific focus, such as *funny faces* or *finding heart images in the world around you*; to broadly defined focuses, such as *change, parenting*, or *learning*.

Exploring how the awareness level of purpose and perspective deepens by taking a color challenge. In the next day or two, plan to photograph something blue for this chapter's action step.

It's Time to Take Action!

Chapter 6 Action Step

The 1-Day Blue Color Challenge

Take time to notice all the blue hues in the world around you. As you collect your blue world, take as many photographs as you like, but remember that you can only post *one photograph* that you believe best defines *blue* in your world.

QR Code 6.8

Scan this QR code to read more about *The 1-Day Blue Photo Challenge.*

http://langwitches.me/blue

By the end of the day, upload and post your selected photograph to Twitter or Instagram using the hashtag #documenting4learningblue. Add a comment that explains why your representation of blue is important to you.

If you would like to extend your challenge experience, share your capturing-blue narrative by writing a blog post reflection about your experience of noticing all the blue you saw around you, as well as your thought process for taking the *just right* image.

Remember to use the #documenting4learning hashtag for Twitter, Facebook, or Instagram posts; or by mentioning @documenting4learning on Facebook and Instagram, and @doc4learning on Twitter.

As a documenter considering the documenting purpose and your perspective, you may be surprised at how you suddenly become hyper-aware of all that is blue around you. Remember, you are looking not only for simply the evidence of blue, but for a *meaningful representation* of blue to you. Paying attention to what is blue may cause you to also notice the intensity of non-blue colors, which creates a perspective you may not have planned. Likewise, you may begin to see shades of blue that you never noticed before in objects, gadgets, places, and natural phenomena. Which representation of blue should you photograph and why? Marcel Proust, an 1800's French novelist observed: *The real voyage of discovery consists not in seeking new landscapes, but in having new eyes.*

After completing the action step, ponder these questions:

- How did the purpose of documenting something blue add to or change your perspective about blue as you observed the world around you throughout your day?
- How did the purpose and your perspective(s) affect what you looked for and why?
- How did observing the world around you shift your thinking today?

These three questions capture the essence of what metacognitively takes place in the during-documentation phase. For example, a blue-color documenter shared on Twitter using #documenting4learningblue that participating in the challenge, "Made me aware of how we take the sky for granted, yet it is the limit for possibilities."

Taking time to participate in the action step blue-photo challenge will help you internalize documentation as a learning process. Transferring your discoveries to a classroom perspective: how will documenters (students and teachers) best capture evidence that best conveys the learning focus and goals? Being engaged in the during-documentation phase is not about simply glancing around to see what is happening. It is about being hyper-aware of opportunities that will strategically aid in conveying evidence of the specific focus and articulated goals that collectively tell a particular learning story. See Figure 6.1 for a blue-color challenge participant's reflection.

With time and practice, one's eyes and mind notice details in the moment while simultaneously filtering and discerning the best moments to capture what is being learned. Looking for what needs to be seen and later interpreted plays a key role in determining what is worthy of capturing, which makes the during-documentation process highly personalized and creates a strong sense of ownership for primary and secondary learners.

Cultivating Collaboration

Documenting opportunities are naturally collaborative. While there are times when learners will have moments of solitude, in general, documenting learning is a team sport. Just as a soccer team has individual players who have strengths they bring to the game, the team has to work collaboratively to reach its goal of winning games, and eventually, a title. To convey documented learning, it is most often based on a team effort of learners working toward reaching the same focus and goals. Even when someone is involved in a heutagogical documenting opportunity, it does not mean the learner has to *go solo*.

In the during-documentation phase, be aware of the learning that needs to be captured and conveyed when sharing and amplifying artifacts. Learners should ask themselves these questions while capturing the desired evidence of learning:

- What is the purpose—focus, goals, criteria—for capturing these moments?
- How is what I am capturing helpful in conveying the specific focus and articulated goals?
- How can I best make my/our thoughts, ideas, and thinking visible to others?
- How does my point of view affect and contribute to this learning opportunity?
- What am I thinking now when faced with later needing to select and filter the captured texts, images, and videos as evidence of learning?
- How do I perceive feedback from outside experts or persons of interest may influence the ongoing documentation when amplifying the evidence of learning?

We are often used to thinking of reflection and reflective questions occurring after the learning has taken place. As mentioned previously, reflection needs to be a part of the during- and post-documentation phases. When one becomes aware of his or her thinking during the act of documenting based on the focus, goals, and how to best capture the desired evidence, documenting AS learning is taking place.

For example, an eighth-grade class is about to participate in their first *Mystery Skype* call. Two classes, unaware of where they are geographically located in the world, will be asking each other questions with yes/no answers in a race against the clock to be the first to narrow down and finally determine the location of the other class (see Image 6.7).

Each teacher discusses the rules of participating in a Mystery Skype call and reminds his or her class what the focus and goals are for participating in the call, which are threefold in

Figure 6.1

Seeing from another perspective what we always see

During the blue challenge, I began to see blue colors that usually pass me by and never register with me. I began to look for the color blue beyond my path. I took a walk, looking not only toward the front, but to the sides and up.

Image 6.6

Photo courtesy of Florencia Gavelio

My Photo

I chose this photo above because of all the blue color that I see in my everyday life. This duck that contains the color blue is the one I always register, the one I look for every time I arrive in Mar del Plata, a popular beach city on the coast of Argentina. I connect this duck to my childhood, my family, and my friends. It represents the joy that fills me as I arrive in town and it greets me as a vacation or a weekend of relaxation is about to start. The blue colors represent new moments about to be lived, rich alfajores (a special type of Argentina cookie), the sun, the beach, the rain, chocolate, my grandparents who are no longer with us, smoothies, laughs, family, and new and old friends.

Reflection

The key is to learn, to be able to see from the other side, to see the same in a different way, or to see what is different. . . . I think that what we do in the first week has to do with looking at learning another way. If we continue doing what we have always done, we will not have changes in education. At least it is important to stop and look, or to separate ourselves a little and look from the outside in with others to be able to reflect on our practices. Why we do what we do? Was it always done like this? How else can I do it? How do others work? How do I see what I did not see during class time? As teachers, we often do not go through the same situations twice in the classroom, but through documentation we can go through the exercise of seeing what we did not see previously, finding other perspectives, rethinking, correcting, expanding, and reflecting.

Translation from Spanish to English by Silvia Rosenthal Tolisano

QR Code 6.9

Scan this QR code to access the original post in Spanish by Flor Gavelio for the #Documenting4Learning Blue Challenge.

http://langwitches.me/blue-flor

Image 6.7

Image 6.8

both schools: *content*—meaningful application of geography vocabulary and useful application of geography skills; one of the school's *missions*—global awareness; and *framework*—21st century skills and literacies, specifically critical thinking and communication.

Each teacher also predetermines the students' roles and responsibilities necessary to capture the learning during the call within each classroom. *(Note: While the collaboration for this narrative is during a Skype call, the roles and responsibilities described below can be applied to a variety of collaborative contexts.)*

During the Skype call, one student is the Photographer, armed with his cell phone, and is responsible for capturing images that best express the class's collective activity and visible thinking (see Image 6.8). He cannot do so without being reflective in the moment when contemplating the question: *How can I best make our thoughts, ideas, and thinking visible to others?*

During the post-documentation phase, the Photographer knows he will also be responsible for filtering through and selecting the photographs he captured that will best aid his class's collective evidence that reflect their articulated goals.

The Questioners are responsible for asking the other class questions pertaining to their location on behalf of the entire class. They need to synthesize the multiple forms of information being provided to them by their classmates.

The Cartographers are using a world map and Google maps to apply information gained through the other class's yes/no responses, while the Twitterers who tweet the call highlights in real time, as well as monitoring the live backchannel comments and any additional potential questions.

One student, the Notetaker, is stationed at a whiteboard and responsible for documenting the questions his or her class asks the mystery location class to narrow down their location, as well as the other class's yes or no responses (see Image 6.9). This documentation provides critical evidence of whether the class can truly apply their geography vocabulary and skills.

While documenting, a Notetaker cannot help but ask himself or herself:

How is what I am capturing helpful in conveying our focus and articulated goals?

Another important role is the Supervisor, who is responsible for observing the entire operation and taking personal notes on what appears to be working well, as well as what does not appear to be helpful. She will be leading a large-group debriefing session after the Skype call to discuss successes and her thoughts concerning areas of improvement. As she is recording her observations, she is thinking: *How does my point of view affect and contribute to this learning opportunity?*

Silvia is taking short video clips to capture the students' voices, overall atmosphere of the room, and the collaborative capabilities of the class to solve the mystery location of the other class. She is personally reflecting on the question: *What am I thinking now about what is needed later when it is time to select and filter the captured texts, images, and videos as evidence of learning?*

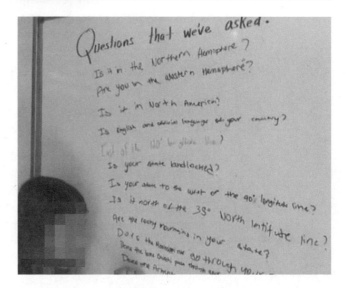

Image 6.9

Keep in mind that using a video conferencing media platform (and Skype as the tool) is *not* the goal of a Mystery Skype call. Video conferencing is simply the best media platform to connect, communicate, and raise awareness of where people are in the world, which aids in meeting the articulated goals. In addition to using a video conferencing platform, the during-documentation phase also involved capturing:

- Images and video using smartphones
- Thoughts and ideas using backchannel
- Logic and reasoning using virtual maps and physical atlases
- Search skills using search engines

The interweaving of *content learning* and *parallel goals* (e.g., one of the school's missions, global awareness, and 21st century skills and literacies) is often interwoven in documenting opportunities. For example, students in a STEM environment can be focusing on writing high-quality informational text by articulating the opportunity-cost details when creating a new iteration. While decisions about what interwoven focuses and goals will be part of a documenting opportunity are established in the pre-documentation phase, they are consistently on the primary and secondary learners' minds in the during-documentation phase.

Summing Up

The during-documentation phase allows learners to take ownership of their learning because they are involved in generating meaningful artifacts as evidence of earning.

QR Code 6.10

Scan this QR code to view *Mystery Skype*: *Roles and Collaboration* blog post.

https://langwitches.me/mysteryskype

This phase is inherently designed to support metacognitive and reflective practices while simultaneously making thinking visible and audible for, and shareable with, a widening audience. Students and teachers look for learning during this phase based on the planning in the pre-documentation phase and are now capturing evidence as potential artifacts appropriate for selecting, editing, creating, sharing, and amplifying in the post-documentation phase.

Post-documentation Phase

Documenting FOR learning focuses on the interpretation of the learning that took place thus far by the primary and secondary learners. The interpretation takes place during the post-documentation phase when the learners explore and answer the question "Where do I/ we go from here?" since the learning is still ongoing. Studying the evidence of learning captured in the during-documentation phase and analyzing the evidence (or lack thereof) as the learning progresses creates opportunities to personalize and own one's learning (see Image 6.10).

Image 6.10

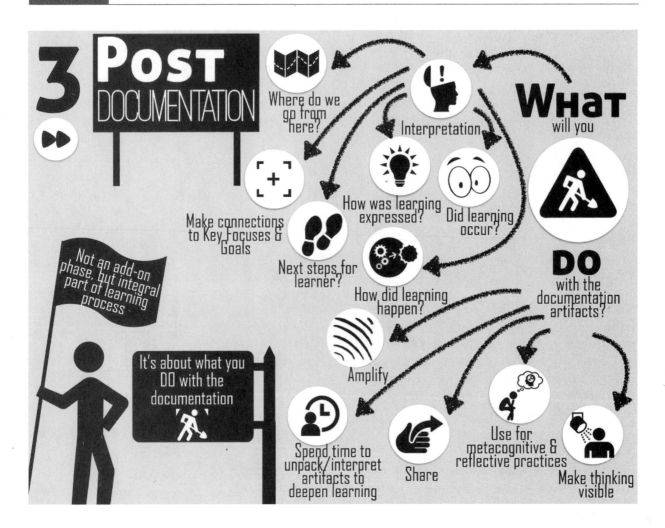

Documenting AS learning focuses on the process of learning. Metacognitively contemplating what evidence of learning looks like prior to capturing, while capturing, and after capturing is foundational to this type of documentation.

Guiding questions that aid in the post-documentation process include the following:

- What do these artifacts tell you?
- Did the articulated focuses and goals fully occur? Partially occur? Not at all? How do you know?
- What should be the learner's next step or action be and why?
- What needs to be explicitly taught? What need to be re-taught in a different way?
- What needs more application time to produce the desired evidence of learning?

The post-documentation phase is critical for both FOR and AS documenting learning because these types of documentation make meaning of the learning while the learning is taking place. Interpretation and process-focused learning zooms in and purposefully makes the learning visible and audible while the learning is taking place to inform both students and teachers. An OF learning artifact cannot convey the nuances of the learning process in action

What will be done with the captured evidence? As mentioned previously, photographs are often snapped and videos recorded in classrooms with the intent of sharing *as is*. Documenting OF learning turns into documenting FOR or AS learning when the learners *do* something with or to the artifacts captured in the during-documentation phase. For the act and art of documentation to be truly purposeful, it needs to *deepen* and *extend* the learning, which can only take place when cognitive and metacognitive actions are applied to the captured artifacts in the post-documentation phase.

The Post-documentation Phase Is Essential

It is imperative that teachers and students see the interpretations and processes involved in the post-documentation phase as essential. This is when and where the transformation truly begins. As Keenen Wayans mentioned in this chapter's opening quote: *Generally, post-production is longer than filming.* And post-production can feel overwhelming to filmmakers. Raindance.com (2014) states:

> During production, everything happens at once. The actors, lights, camera, props, schedule. . . . But you persevere. Your film is in the can. . . . What do you do now? The answer, of course, is simple. You begin post-production. Post-production, somehow, is the part of the process that intimidates people the most. Remember, it is not difficult . . . as long as you take it step by step.

There are nine steps in the post-documentation phase. Following the steps in order aids in transforming the evidence of learning into meaningful artifacts:

1. **Unpack** the artifacts to examine the extent of what has been captured and evaluate for usefulness or relevance.

2. **Filter** through and **select** the artifacts that best represent aspects of the specific focus and articulated goals.

3. **Organize** the artifacts so they can be arranged to collectively convey the evidence of learning.

4. **Reflect** on the details in the artifacts to determine and define the evidence of learning.

5. **Connect** the details in the artifacts to past or present learning or other's work or perspectives.

6. **Edit** the artifacts to best articulate details of the evidence of learning.

7. **Create** media using the edited artifacts to support the learning narrative.

8. **Share** created artifacts with an audience for engagement and to obtain feedback.

9. **Amplify** created artifacts to extend learning and reach a wider audience for engagement and to obtain feedback.

Before delving into each step, it is important to note the role cognition and metacognition play in this phase. At the onset, teachers often feel these steps are arduous and time-consuming, but they need to be embraced during this phase. Whether annotexting a video recording; reflecting textually or orally concerning a specific portion of an artifact; or creating a composite of collected text and images, the act of transforming artifacts cannot be outsourced for someone else to do.

The mental process involved in each step provides learners with opportunities to deepen their own learning and understanding. For example, Costa and Kallick's (2010) Habits of Mind are naturally embedded and nurtured during this phase, in particular:

Thinking About Thinking (Metacognition)

Metacognition, or thinking about thinking, is our ability to know what we know and what we don't know. It is our ability to plan a strategy for producing the information that is needed, to be conscious of our own steps and strategies during the act of problem solving, and to reflect on and evaluate the productiveness of our own thinking.

The post-documentation phase encourages learners to reflect on and wonder about their learning experiences, as well as evaluate the efficiency and effectiveness of their own capabilities and performances.

Thinking and Communicating With Clarity and Precision

Language and thinking are closely entwined; like either side of a coin, they are inseparable. Fuzzy, vague language is a reflection of fuzzy, vague thinking. Intelligent people strive to communicate accurately in both written and oral form, taking care to use precise language; defining terms; and using correct names, labels, and analogies. They strive to avoid overgeneralizations, deletions, and distortions. Instead, they support their statements with explanations, comparisons, quantification, and evidence.

This phase also requires learners to be articulate when conveying the evidence of their learning to others, and being able to do so in a manner that portrays the learner as having a command (or lack thereof) of the details related to the learning's articulated goals.

Applying Past Knowledge to New Situations

Intelligent humans learn from experience. When confronted with a new and perplexing problem, they will draw forth experiences from their past. They often can be heard to say, "This reminds me of . . . " or "This is just like the time when I . . . " They explain what they are doing now with analogies about or references to their experiences. They call upon their store of knowledge and experience as sources of data to support, theories to explain, or processes to solve each new challenge. They are able to abstract meaning from one experience, carry it forth, and apply it in a novel situation.

The post-documentation phase requires learners to apply their past knowledge and experiences to the current documenting opportunity. This phase encourages learners to notice patterns and trends in their learning, which deepens their own understanding of how they learn by taking new information and connecting it to what they already know and can do.

Remaining Open to Continuous Learning

Intelligent people are in a continuous learning mode. They are invigorated by the quest of lifelong learning. Their confidence, in combination with their inquisitiveness, allows them to constantly search for new and better ways. People with this Habit of Mind are always striving for improvement, growing, learning, and modifying and improving themselves. . . . [Students] have been taught to value certainty rather than doubt, to give answers rather than to inquire, to know which choice is correct rather than to explore alternatives. Unfortunately, some adults are content with what they already believe and know. Their childlike curiosity has died. They exhibit little humility because they believe they are all knowing. They do not seek out or discover the wisdom of others. They do not know how or when to leverage a love of and lust for learning. As a result, they follow a path of little value and minimal opportunity. Our wish is for creative students and people who are eager to learn.

This phase also encourages learners to see that learning is a continuous process, as well as embrace a mindset that failure is part of learning rather than a result of not knowing. Being eager to learn is nurtured when learner share and amplify their artifacts, including those that express successes and those that express failures. Gaining global insights and feedback solidifies one's realization that there are perspectives that can aid students and teachers when learning new information or deepening understanding.

The Post-production Steps

While learners' interpretations and processing of captured artifacts will vary, the post-documentation steps remain consistent (see Image 6.11). The information shared on the following pages provide a general overview of each step. Application of the steps are featured in the Chapter 11 vignette challenge.

Unpack. Unpacking is the first step in the post-production phase. Think of it as unpacking a suitcase filled with clothes you decided to take on a destination vacation. Before you left, you knew where you were going, what you would be doing, and even kept track of what the weather would be like, but now that you have arrived, *what do you really need? Which artifacts will truly aid in making the thinking and learning visible and/or audible?* Not all of the captured artifacts will end up providing the desired evidence, just like packing too many shorts or tops.

Image 6.11

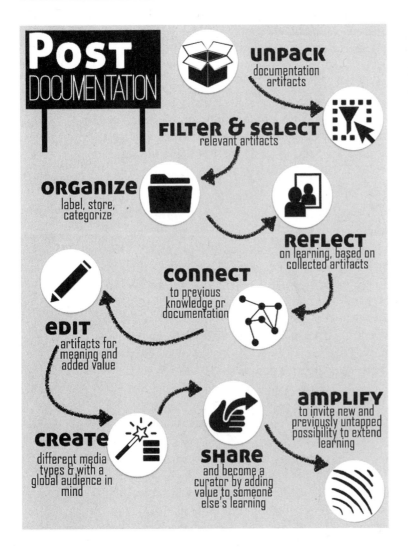

QR Code 6.11

Scan this QR code to view the bonus chapter: *Organizing and Archiving Documentation.*

http://langwitches.me/bonus-chapter

Filter and Select. The unpacked artifacts will include the *just right* evidence, but only after sifting through the inadequate evidence, such as an artifact not showing any learning evidence taking place or the image or audio is of such poor quality that it is useless.

Therefore, it is important to filter through the captured documentation and select the ones that best provide and support hearing and seeing the learners' thinking and learning based on the specific focus and articulated goals. After selecting those artifacts, discard the unhelpful ones and archive any artifacts that may prove beneficial in future documenting opportunities.

Organize. Now that the filter and selection step has been completed: *How should the artifacts be organized?* The answer to this question is twofold: one, how to name and organize the artifacts to convey the immediate evidence; and two, how to store the artifacts in the cloud or on a hard-drive for ease of retrieval and usage.

This step is especially important when documenting growth over time (e.g., weeks, months, years). Organizing the artifacts can be accomplished based on a variety of purposes, such as topic, concept, perspective, process, or timeline.

For information on the how-tos for organizing, go to www.documenting4learning.com or scan the QR Code 6.11 to access the bonus chapter, "Organizing and Archiving Documentation," which provides strategies for organizing artifacts using filters, archives, searches, and curation tips so the documentation artifacts can be easily used and accessed.

Reflect. Reflection is already happening when unpacking, filtering, selecting, and organizing the artifacts. But now it is time to plan how to formally convert the mental reflections from inside one's mind to textual or audible information (e.g., annotexting, voice over, creating a composite infographic or video, writing a blog post and embedding evidence) related to the learning focus and goals.

Guiding questions to aid in the reflection step include:

- What do I see or hear occurring? What do I not see or hear?
- What details best express the evidence of learning?

- How did the media platforms and tools used during the documentation support evidence of learning?
- How will what I have now seen or heard influence the next learning action? Next teaching action?
- What patterns or trends emerged from the evidence of learning in one or multiple documenting opportunities?

When wanting to look for patterns or trends, using a backchannel media platform tool, such as *Today's Meet*, allows learners to reflect on their learning evidence over time. Students begin by collectively contributing their thoughts and ideas in the established backchannel. This can be done synchronously, such as during a classroom discussion or interview or while watching a video clip; or asynchronously, such as during a group research project, sharing insights throughout an election campaign, or communicating opinions and claims among several classes taking the same course focused on a particular topic, problem, or issue.

Comparing the collective backchannel logs captured over time as an artifact is a powerful way to analyze trends, such as the increasing ability for a specific student or students to back up claims with relevant reasons and evidence, or the preciseness of the posts using academic vocabulary in a specific subject.

When using backchannels to study patterns, questions can be posed such as: *What is a particular student contributing, or not contributing, in the backchannel over time? Is a contributing student doing so in a purposeful manner? Another pattern study may involve analyzing backchannel logs through a digital citizenship lens: are the students consistently demonstrating respect for others views and opinions?*

Lastly, having individual students analyzing their personal contributions via studying the backchannel logs can provide insights into behavior patterns that may not be apparent to them without an introspective reflection time to study the backchannel context.

Connect. Making connections is a natural next step after reflecting on documentation artifacts. The act of connecting includes making connections to prior knowledge and experiences and the current documenting opportunity. The learning-thinking becomes more explicit during this step.

Guiding questions that can be explored when making connections include

- What occurred previously that is related to this learning?
- How is my work connected to someone else's work?
- How can I connect to other perspectives?
- How did using multiple media platforms and tools support the evidence of learning documentation?
- How does a series of artifacts demonstrate my learning growth over time?

For example, sixth graders under the facilitation of their mathematics teacher, Laurel Janewicz, had been learning how to analyze data and tell an informational story related to the collective data. The students specific focus included applying data analysis concepts to relevant school data. Two of their articulated goals involved their ability to communicate findings and conclusions visually (e.g., table or graph) and textually (e.g., script for video, blog post).

Laurel provided her students with authentic data, which was the result of a survey taken by the previous school year's sixth-grade students concerning their homework habits. By using this set of data, her current students would naturally *make connections* to their personal homework habits.

Edit. The term *edit* can be defined as prepare for publication by correcting, condensing, or otherwise modifying. In a documenting learning context, the definition that best fits is *prepare for publication by modifying.*

Consider a filmmaker being involved in editing the raw footage for a pivotal scene that was filmed from multiple angles, lightings, and dialogue exchanges. To convey the intended message to the audience, critical thinking and editorial decision making are paramount. *What footage needs to be left out? What footage needs to be merged with other footage? What needs to be rearranged?* The filmmaker may even need to call in some of the actors to do voiceovers, or a Foley artist may need to create certain sound effects.

Editing is a critical step that cannot be overlooked or left out. It is during this time that the learning narrative comes to life. Critical thinking about one's learning and the message that needs to be conveyed happens during this time. For example, when learners:

- edit a video artifact by deleting unnecessary footage,
- add annotexted explanations or spoken audio,
- create transitions,
- select a music track,
- create an appropriate title, and/or
- include any necessary credits,

a new depth to their thinking takes place because the learners need to evaluate the evidence to create a meaningful artifact.

QR Code 6.12

Scan this QR code to view the *Backchanneling-Movie Watching-Note Taking-Information Scribes* **blog post that includes the Backchannel Cleanup Role.**

http://langwitches.me/backchannel-cleanupr

A second example of editing could involve learners listening to an hour of audio recordings to summarize the key points of the learning and determine the most relevant sections to be included in a five-minute podcast they are creating.

A third example can be students who are using a backchannel platform to collaboratively take notes where one student is designated the *Backchannel Clean-Up Person* responsible for editing the post-documentation backchannel log. He removes duplicate entries, double-checks for fact accuracies, and formats the collective notes to make them visually appealing and clear, not only to his peers, but also for a wider audience once the artifacts are shared and amplified.

The editing process not only causes learners to consider the details related to the focuses and goals, it also causes them to make connections and confirm, reinforce, or disprove assumptions, which all deepen the learning. Learners need to use a critical eye or ear to ensure that an artifact's details best articulate the evidence of learning. For example, an image (e.g., photograph of two plants on a windowsill with cardboard between the window pane and one of the plants) can be edited to become an annotexted artifact by adding arrows and text that conveys a knowledge concept (e.g., student annotates on the image the scientific explanation of the effect of sun versus no sun on the two plants' growth photographed on Day 15).

How the visible and/or audible thinking is added to, placed alongside, or created anew for the selected artifacts can vary greatly. Regardless of what shape or form an artifact takes, this step coupled with the *create* step is when transformation of learning evidence takes place.

Create. *Create* is the highest level of Bloom's Taxonomy of Educational Objectives and requires producing something new or innovating what exists. During this step, learners create a new representation (e.g., annotexted screencast, infographic) or a compilation of edited artifacts or representations (e.g., a blog post that contains hyperlinked text to supportive sites, an embedded annotexted video, and a conclusion that poses a thought-provoking question to encourage comments from a targeted audience).

When creating a narrative that conveys one's learning, it is important for a learner to consider the best platforms to digitally share and amplify their learning with a global audience. Let's see this applied to Laurel's sixth-grade math students. While each student was encouraged to self-select a media platform to create a new representation that documented his or her learning—such as infographics, images, videos, presentation slides, and animations—everyone was expected to create a blog post that included their creation, which was shared and amplified globally.

It is important to note that there were two primary learners in Laurel's students' documenting opportunity—the students and Laurel, as she was documenting the difference between last year's students, who did not have documenting learning experiences, and this year's students, who have them. As part or her professional learning, she reflected on the differences she observed in the two group's capabilities to personalize their standards-based learning. By evaluating what her students created in the current year, Laurel discovered that allowing her students to be documenters gave them a greater command of the mathematics and their abilities to justify their conclusions, communicate them to others, and do so using a viable argument. Not only did her students create evidence of what they learned, but Laurel was able to use the artifacts as evidence for her professional documentation.

Share. Sharing documented learning with others adds an important dimension to the documenting process. As mentioned previously, if someone records his or her own reflections and creates artifacts as evidence of learning privately, he or she has less of an opportunity to grow as a learner. Sharing one's knowledge—or lack thereof, which is equally important—provides a learner with opportunities for personalized feedback.

Likewise, sharing one's thinking about one's learning process openly and transparently allows a learner to become a peer-colleague, expert, or role model for others. For example, to share the insights of Laurel's own learning and the students' evidence of learning, Silvia created a blog post to represent the multifaceted aspects and insights gained through the documenting opportunity. The post concluded with an invitation for readers to watch for an upcoming blog post *Blogging in Math Class*, which included student samples and a model lesson video of Laurel introducing her expectations for quality blog commenting in her math class.

QR Code 6.13

Scan this QR code to view *Telling a Story with Data* blog post.

http://langwitches.me/datastory

Amplify. When learners share their documentation with a wider public audience through amplification, they invite new and previously untapped possibilities to extend the learning both as a contributor and as a seeker of new or deeper knowledge and understanding. As mentioned previously, amplification connects beyond the limitations of a zip code or language barrier. It involves taking advantage of belonging to a global learning network (or knowing someone who does) to access experts who can provide new perspectives or new information.

For example, a third-grade class in Florida found an animal skeleton on their school campus. Naturally, they wanted to know what type of animal it was. Traditionally, they would have asked their teacher and the librarian, but the students were able to take advantage of Silvia's global professional learning network, and she amplified their investigative reach in hopes of solving the animal mystery.

| Image 6.12 |

The class composed a 280-character-limit tweet asking Silvia's network to share resources to help them figure out what type of animal they found. They also attached images of the skeleton (see Image 6.12).

Potential answers and inquiries quickly started flooding Silvia's Twitter feed. Students were asked by responders to share specific information about the geographical area and habitat the animal was found in. They were also asked questions about specific details related to their originally posted images. They placed a ruler alongside the skeleton, took a snapshot and posted the image to provide responders with an accurate length and size of the animal.

Tweet by tweet, the network responders guided the students closer and closer to a scientific conclusion (see Image 6.13). By sharing their curiosity about the animal skeleton with a global audience, the students extended their learning reach and opportunity. Their amplification created authentic accessibility to experts and researchers from around the world.

QR Code 6.14

Scan this QR code to read the full *CSI Twitter: Crime Scene Investigation* blog post.

http://langwitches.me/csitwitter

Posing Contemplative Questions

In their book, *Learning and Leading with the Habits of Mind* (2010), Costa and Kallick quoted Einstein at the onset of describing the *Questioning and Posing Problems* habit:

The formulation of a problem is often more essential than its solution, which may be merely a matter of mathematical or experimental skill. . . . To raise new questions, new possibilities, to regard old problems from a new angle, requires creative imagination and marks real advances. –*Albert Einstein* (p. 26)

Asking deeper questions, searching new possibilities, and looking for a new angle or problem to explore is at the heart of posing contemplative questions. Questions, such as these, can open possibilities for new or deeper learning.

- How did the learning process unfold for me?
- What am I struggling with in my learning? What did I struggle with during my learning?
- What are the steps I am taking, or did I take, to gain knowledge and understanding?
- What resources or strategies am I using to gain knowledge and understanding? What proved to be the most relevant or irrelevant, given my focus and goal?
- How can I best share my learning with a global audience so I can gain other's perspectives and feedback to help me grow in my knowledge and understanding?

Image 6.13

@langwitches My "bone guy" says: "Hard to tell size of whole animal, but seems to be raccoon or opossum. With the skull maybe a opossum."
cbrannon, [+] Thu 03 Dec 11:50 via web in reply to...

@langwitches I have veterinarians on the case :)
zcontreras, [+] Thu 03 Dec 11:59 via web

@langwitches I sent it to my colleagues in the Environmental Studies dept here at Antioch University New England. Maybe they can help?
CriticalSkills1, [+] Thu 03 Dec 11:52 via web

@langwitches- here with some biologists from the MN DNR- our guess is a opossum
mateslk, [+] Thu 03 Dec 12:48 via web

SUMMING UP

The post-documentation phase is paramount to the overall documenting learning process. Without it, student and teachers never reach the depth of personalizing the learning given the nine steps requirement to think cognitively and metacognitively about what learning has (and, possibly, has not) taken place.

The nine post-production steps (unpack, filter/select, organize, reflect, connect, edit, create, share, amplify) are critical for transforming the evidence of learning into meaningful learning stories based on the captured artifacts.

As the Mystery Skeleton narrative expressed, the ability to amplify the learning beyond those who are in one's physical reach, whether curiosity or passion, adds a layer to a documenting opportunity that students, and teachers, will never forget.

A final note related to all three phases: There has been contemplative questions included in each phase's section. It is important to the documenting process that cognitive and metacognitive questions need to be asked and reflected on:

- As part of the pre-documentation phase before a new documenting opportunity begins.
- Throughout the during-documentation phase, especially when considering what need to be captured in the moments the learning is taking place.
- In the post-documentation phase, and even at the conclusion of a documenting opportunity, as the responses may impact or inform the next documenting opportunity.

GOING BEYOND

To amplify your reading beyond this book's pages, we have created *discussion questions and prompts* for this chapter, which are located at *www.documenting4learning.com*. To extend your thinking, reactions, and responses, you can connect with other readers by leaving comments on individual chapter's discussion posts on our documenting4learning blog.

We also invite you to contribute and share your artifacts in other social-media spaces to connect with and learn from other readers around the world using the #documenting4learning hashtag on Twitter, Facebook, or Instagram; or by mentioning @documenting4learning on Facebook and Instagram, and @doc4learning on Twitter.

Documenting Learningflow Routine

It is not knowledge, but the act of learning; not possession, but the act of getting there, which grants the greatest enjoyment.

—Carl Friedrich Gauss

The documenting learningflow routine embraces students and teachers participating in the act of learning while the learning is taking place. Owning one's learning takes on new depths and perspectives when the five learningflow routine steps are applied to purposeful documenting opportunities.

Establishing a routine is like having a specific practice reach a point where it becomes a natural facet of whatever is being performed. For example, yoga involves building balance, increasing flexibility, and achieving mindfulness routines. Harvard's *Project Zero* visible thinking routines is founded on four practices that aid students and teachers in extending and deepening their thinking: observing, recording, interpreting, and sharing.

To ensure that a physical or mental action becomes routine, it must first become a habit. In keeping with the adage, "It takes 30 days to make a habit," it will take time and effort for the learningflow steps to become routine.

LEARNINGFLOW ROUTINE STEPS

As each step is explained in this chapter, note that there are a few terms purposefully used in both the documentation phases and the learningflow routine. For example, the action of *look* takes place in the *pre-documentation phase* when determining the focuses and goals and considering what needs to be visibly or audibly collected as evidence of learning. *Look* also

Image 7.1

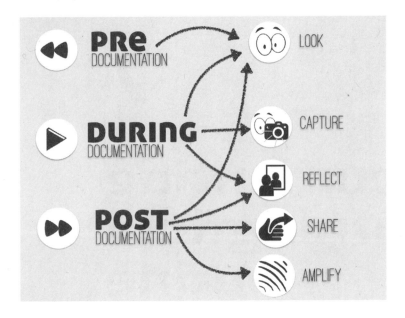

Image 7.2

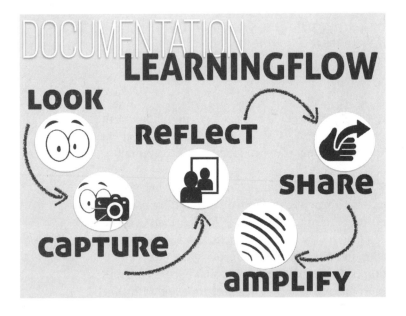

takes place when a learner is hyper-aware of what needs to be captured in the *during-documentation phase* (Image 7.1).

Another example is the duality of *reflection*. This term often evokes an *it's already happened* feeling, as in reflecting on a summer vacation's highlights or low points, or reflecting on when a child was young who is now full grown.

While these two examples evoke a post-documentation phase and learningflow routine's act of reflection, there are often *in-the-moment* reflections taking place in the during-documentation phase. For example, while on a SCUBA diving trip on the island of Little Cayman, Janet and her husband, Johnny, were sitting on a boat's bow while speeding through the ocean's waves toward a morning dive site. A warm breeze was blowing, the sun was shining brightly, and flying fish were soaring above the waterline in tandem with the boat. Janet thought to herself: *Remember everything about this moment. It may never happen again.* This was a *during* reflection, not a post-reflection moment. Janet was hyperaware of every aspect of what was taking place around her and reflecting on what was important *in the moment* to capture or remember.

The routine steps create a fluidity within the three documentation phases and are designed to create a flow from documenting initiation to completion based on the selected focuses and goals (Image 7.2).

Look for Learning

Teachers often feel overwhelmed with daily workloads, paperwork, and ever-increasing demands imposed on them. Many times, the covering of curriculum overshadows the much-needed uncovering of knowledge and understanding that promotes deeper learning and thinking (Image 7.3).

Look for learning means actively seeking the learning that will be taking place (pre-documentation phase) or is taking place (during-documentation phase). It is important to think of the term *learning* in this context as a verb (act of), rather than a noun (result of).

For many, evidence of learning may be perceived as the result of a test, quiz, or final product, such as an engineering diagram, oration, or narrative essay. While there is a place and time for these examples of learning evidence, the foundation to the documenting process is perceiving evidence of learning as the *act* of learning. *What is taking place that leads to a final outcome, whether product or performance? Is it final, or just a moment in time to capture, reflect, share, and amplify where a learner is in his or her learning journey?*

Specific focuses with articulated goals born from standards, objectives, and desired skills are a good starting

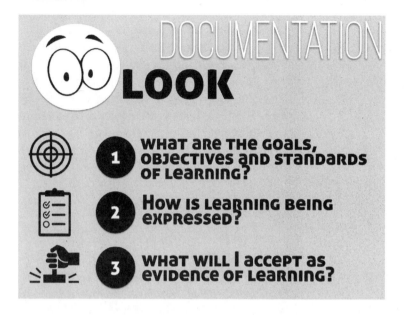

Image 7.3

point to look for learning. Equally important is to plan how to best gather evidence of learning that makes a learner's systemic growth visible over time (e.g., over weeks, months, years). Capturing and reflecting on evidence over a length of time allows a learner to analyze how he or she learns, as well as see trends and patterns in others' learning.

Look for learning has learners incorporating multiple media platforms and tools through authentic applications. Considering the speed that technology changes in society and education, it is imperative that traditional teaching and learning methods evolve. The reality for many teachers continues to be time constraints and a feeling of overwhelmness caused by a cacophony of media platform and tool choices, which causes many to fall prey to, "I'll use what I know." This mindset can cripple the documenting learning dynamics.

Look for opportunities to try out and showcase new media platforms and tools is essential to providing authentic documenting opportunities. This is where *orbits of ability* can play a significant and purposeful role. Hale and Fisher (2013) explain:

An *orbit of ability* is a given person's knowledge and talent, or expertise. When one person moves into another person's orbit of ability, his or her knowledge and capabilities grow. Every teacher has his or her own orbit or orbits of ability that others can learn from. Accessing orbits of ability can take place during any interaction with colleagues, friends, family members, or even a new acquaintance. (p. 10)

Teachers and students need to actively look for expertise and people of interest in their orbits of ability who can aid them with new or unfamiliar media platforms and tools. It is not uncommon for teachers to work on a documenting opportunity in teams of two to four where one or two teachers have stronger content knowledge and the other teachers have a greater comfort level with the chosen media platforms and tools.

Another important practice in the *look for learning* routine step is to be conscious and respectful of how learners prefer to learn, access, and process information. When determining what is acceptable evidence when documenting, it does not have to be the same for all learners.

Documenters will find these questions helpful to ask during this routine step and throughout the documentation phases:

- What are the standards, focuses, and goals involved in the learning? What are the connections among them? How could they be made visible in documentation artifacts?
- How could you be sensitive to or aware of potential unrelated learning taking place?
- What will be accepted as evidence of learning? How could the evidence include moving beyond traditional forms of evidence? How is learning begin expressed?
- How well can you connect or translate different learning expressions to previously imagined learning outcomes?
- What can you do to ensure you are prepared to capture learning once you found what you were looking for?

Capture Learning

The second routine step involves considering how to best capture the learning *in the moment* that has been determined and planned for during the pre-documentation phase.

It is important to remember that the *look for learning* step is naturally embedded in the *capture learning* step. What was determined to be acceptable evidence in the pre-documentation phase is now happening *live*, which means whoever is capturing the learning needs to be hypervigilant regarding how the learning is taking place, especially when considering that all the learners may not be displaying evidence of the learning in identical or similar ways (Image 7.4).

Documenters need to make these questions a common practice while engaged in the during-documentation phase and this routine step:

Image 7.4

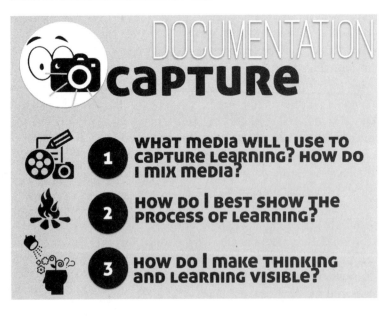

- How can I best capture evidence of learning with the articulated goals in mind that makes the learning visible and audible to myself, other learners, and a wider audience?
- How can I best capture evidence of my/the learners' thinking processes, not just the end results?
- Am I using the best media platforms and tools to capture my/the learners' learning and thinking?

One of the goals of the three documentation phases and learningflow routine is to transform educational teaching and learning practices, including the authentic use of media platforms and tools to capture the learning and thinking as it is taking place over time. Technology provides the ability to record experiences, moments, and events involving multiple senses, going beyond the capabilities of depending on just our own eyes and ears.

Likewise, using a mix of media enables learners to gain insights and evidence from multiple locations and perspectives simultaneously. Technology also allows learners to capture a moment in time now that can be unpacked sooner or later. Captured artifacts can serve as memory triggers regarding what happened at a given moment in time or took place in a sequence of learning events.

Tasked with the responsibility of capturing learning while it is taking place, documenters need to practice and develop skills to look for learning with a strong critical eye to make better decisions about how the captured artifacts will best represent the desired learning evidence. In essence, they become more strategic in their planning by:

- Having capturing devices readily available. For example, a smartphone often proves the most handy and versatile device to document and create artifacts. Having a cache of digital options and knowing how the devices can be best utilized is beneficial in the during-documentation phase.
- Delegating and assigning tasks to collaborators with varying capture responsibilities (e.g., Photographer, Videographer, Microblogger, Backchanneler) to multi-capture the evidence of learning.
- Embedding capture-oriented tasks as a natural component of a learner's thinking process to deepen her or his learning experiences.

Reflect on Learning

A famous John Dewey quote, "We don't learn from experience, we learn from reflecting on the experience," is timeless and true. It is not by accident that the third routine step involves reflecting on the learning experience that took place in the during-documentation phase.

What distinguishes this step from the captured documentation in the previous step is that it now moves beyond *display* to begin conveying a *learning narrative through a reflection process* (Image 7.5).

As Krechevsky, Mardell, Rivard, and Wilson (2013) point out, "Interpreting documentation is essential to the practice of documentation and what distinguishes it from display" (p. 82). The reflection practice is an integral part of the documenting process as it opens further possibilities to make thinking, and consequently learning, more visible and/or audible.

Since reflecting on and interpreting the selected artifacts takes learners beyond a display of the learning, this routine is a critical value-added practice that aids primary and secondary learners in making connections to previous learning, other learners, and outside perspectives.

When reflecting in the after-documentation phase, taking time to

Image 7.5

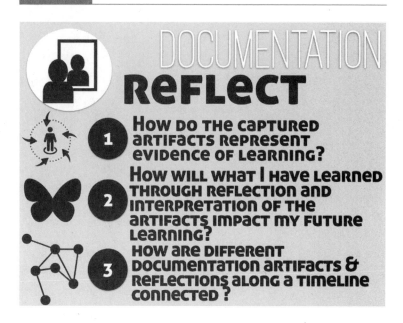

DOCUMENTATION

REFLECT

1 HOW DO THE CAPTURED ARTIFACTS REPRESENT EVIDENCE OF LEARNING?

2 HOW WILL WHAT I HAVE LEARNED THROUGH REFLECTION AND INTERPRETATION OF THE ARTIFACTS IMPACT MY FUTURE LEARNING?

3 HOW ARE DIFFERENT DOCUMENTATION ARTIFACTS & REFLECTIONS ALONG A TIMELINE CONNECTED?

ponder the responses to these types of questions adds a layer of *going deeper* as introspective learners:

- How do the captured artifacts represent evidence of learning?
- What is the meaning or significance of the artifacts in terms of my learning focuses and goals?
- What are the connections I can make among different artifacts that have been taken over time, from different perspectives, or using different media?
- What can I see or hear that surprises me? What did I *not* see or hear, but anticipated I would?
- How will what I have learned through my reflection and interpretation of the artifacts impact my future learning?

Krechevsky et al. (2013) also note that,

> It is critical that teachers and students go through the process of interpreting—making meaning—before moving onto the next practice—sharing.
>
> The documentation we share should be selective—identified through the process of interpretation as having the potential to serve specific learning purposes for various audiences. (p. 87)

This step involves cognitive thinking, and metacognitive thinking, especially when a teacher as a secondary learner is reflecting on the reflections of his or her students. There is an important connection between student reflection and taking it one step further and using it for professional reflection regarding instructional practice and content. It is meant to be about students reflecting deeply, and their teacher reflecting deeply as well. For example, during a student-led conference some teachers asked their students to "go and reflect," but never read their reflective blog posts intentionally or intently to learn from them and inform their own professional practice, while others dug deeply and were truly reflective about their students' reflections.

QR Code 7.1

Scan this QR code to read a reflection blog based on the reflections students made while preparing for their student-led conferences.

http://langwitches.me/slc

It's Time to Take Action!

Chapter 7 Action Step

For an upcoming learning experience (e.g., lesson, authentic task) where you will be a secondary learner, plan how your students will include a reflection for a text, image, audio, or video artifact based on their learning focuses and goals.

As you are planning, consider your responses to these questions:

- What do I want my students specifically reflecting on related to this learning?
- How can this reflection best be captured (e.g., analog or digital exit ticket, reflective audio or video response, visible thinking routine sketchnote)?
- How will I capture my professional reflection as an artifact that summarizes my analysis and synthesis of their reflections?

The point of this action step is for you to take the time to look deeper at your students' abilities to be meaningful and insightful self-reflectors, as well as deepening your own reflecting process when analyzing your student's reflections.

The next routine step is *share*, which you need to do with your reflection artifact. Share your documentation with a colleague at school or a mentor.

The last routine step is *amplify*. If or when you are ready to share this artifact digitally beyond one or two people, remember to use the #documenting4learning hashtag on Twitter, Facebook, or Instagram; or by mentioning @documenting4learning on Facebook and Instagram, and @doc4learning on Twitter.

QR 7.2

Scan this QR code to read a blog post by Silvia that may give you some ideas for how to beat capture your students' reflections to prepare for creating your reflection artifact.

http://langwitches.me/amplify-reflection

Share Learning

Students and teachers benefit from others who are willing to share their teaching and learning practices and evidence of learning in person and online; therefore, it is imperative that this action is reciprocated.

The shift from a culture of consumers to producers is an important practice in sharing and disseminating one's learning progress with others, including successes, failures, and lessons learned, with others.

Students embrace a digital culture of sharing. Educators need to acknowledge that this behavior is their *normal* outside of classrooms and take advantage of their desire to share with others when learning new information or exploring deeper what has been learned.

Therefore, learning in classrooms need to be social and collaborative (Image 7.6).

Having and growing professional learning networks is built on the concept of sharing. For an exchange to take place, someone must step up to the plate and first *share*. Without sharing, there is no network.

Image 7.6

DOCUMENTATION
SHARE

1 WHO IS YOUR INTENDED AUDIENCE?

2 WHAT PLATFORM WOULD LEND ITSELF THE BEST FOR SHARING?

3 HOW CAN I BEST DISSEMINATE MY WORK?

Someone needs to give, and someone needs to take. If there are not enough givers, then there would not be takers, and the network would no longer function. In the Information Age where information is being generated at exponential speed, learners often rely on a network to filter quality and relevant information. It is imperative that students learn how to responsibly access, filter, and curate what is being shared, as well as think critically about what they will share.

While sharing commonly takes place using digital tools, learners can share their thinking using a mind map or sketchnote created with paper and pencil. The point is that the act of sharing takes one's thinking and moves it from his or her mind to a visible and/or audible format so that others can see and/or hear the learner's thoughts. There are three critical questions to consider when preparing to share:

- **Who is your audience?**

  What and how a learner shares his or her edited or created artifacts, including reflections and interpretations, will depend on the intended audience.
  - From students as learners: *Is the documentation intended for my peers? Experts in a field to aid me in gaining more knowledge or specific feedback?*
  - For teachers as professional learners: *Is the documentation intended for my colleagues in my school? My students' parents and caregivers? Stakeholders? School community? My professional learning network?*
- **What media platforms and tools are the best choices for sharing?**

  Choosing media platforms and tools will depend on the intended audiences. Sometimes sharing proves best when using several platforms and tools to reach a maximum amount of people. The selected tools may alter who is reached and how many are reached (e.g., personal blog post versus Twitter with an intentional hashtag).
- **How can I best disseminate my evidence of learning?**

  The ability to disseminate information is an increasingly important capability in today's world. Network literacy does not necessarily mean having to know how the technology behind a network works, or knowing how to code. As mentioned in Chapter 2, according to Hellweg (2012), network literacy is about obtaining, "At least a basic understanding of network technology, crafting a network identity, understanding network intelligence, and knowing about network capabilities." Hellweg states that network savvy users, as we do for learners who are preparing to share their documentation, need to understand that, "The capabilities of services, like social networks, and the differences and similarities between them." This understanding contributes to making intentional decisions about how, when, and through what media platforms and tools will best disseminate the work and gain the desired interaction with the intended audience.

Amplify Learning

When thinking about the word *amplify* in a traditional sense, one might think of turning up the volume or increasing an intensity. For this routine step, it means *creating a ripple effect of potential learning extensions*.

By reaching out to a wider audience than oneself or a classroom, it opens the door to possibilities for network connections, multiple perspectives, expert feedback, and additional resources (see Image 7.7).

Image 7.7

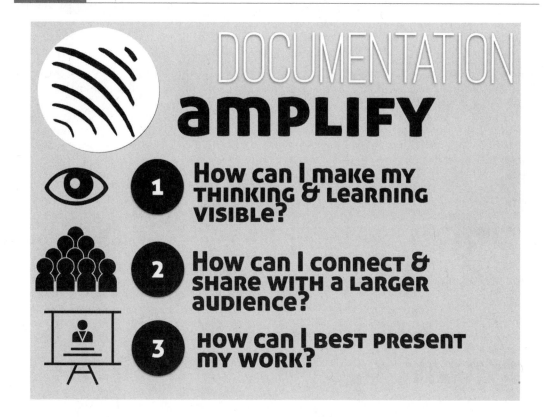

Amplifying often boosts the learning opportunity in ways that could not be planned for in the pre-documentation phase. It is oftentimes organic.

As with the other routine steps, posing questions aid in determining how the amplification's intentional purpose could extend the learning related to the specific focus and articulated goals.

It is important to encourage students to share and amplify their learning with others beyond their teacher. Couros (2016) mentions an observation made by Rushton Hurley, "When students are sharing their work with the world, they want it to be good. If they're just sharing it with you, they want it to be good enough."

The four amplification degrees explained in Chapter 5 do not need to be followed in a sequential order. The key is that the amplification increasingly widens once a person's initial thought, idea, or concept has been moved from his or her mind to a textual, auditory, or pictorial representation. A learner can skip from a slight degree to a greater degree of amplification simply by being strategic.

In this chapter's opening quote, Carl Friedrich Gauss, a famous mathematician, observed, "It is not knowledge, but the act of learning; not possession, but the act of getting there, which grants the greatest enjoyment." For learners, the greatest joy is when their amplified learning gets noticed by people locally and globally. It is the action of getting there—the personal investment of participating in the phases and routine that is affirmed when those from the great beyond care enough to respond and/or interact. This is true for student learners and educators as professional learners.

SUMMING UP

The purpose and intent of the documentation phases and learningflow routine steps is to be the heartbeat of the documenting learning framework. When learners are engaged in documenting OF learning, the learning involves the *look* and *capture* steps. When learners are engaged in documenting FOR or AS learning, all five steps: *look, capture, reflect, share,* and *amplify* are interwoven throughout the phases in a documenting opportunity (Image 7.8).

Image 7.8

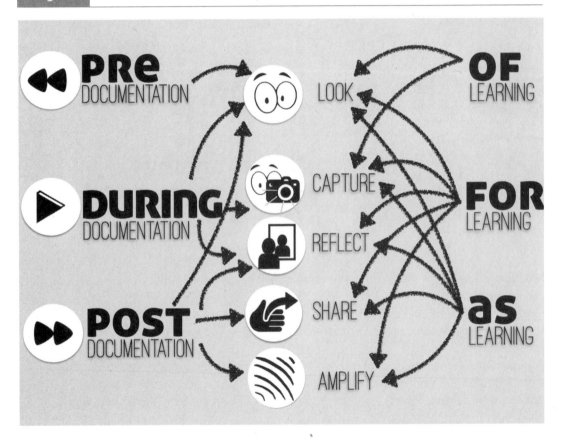

GOING BEYOND

To amplify your reading beyond this book's pages, we have created *discussion questions and prompts* for this chapter, which are located at *www.documenting4learning.com*. To extend your thinking, reactions, and responses, you can connect with other readers by leaving comments on individual chapter's discussion posts on our documenting4learning blog.

We also invite you to contribute and share your artifacts in other social media spaces to connect with and learn from other readers around the world using the #documenting4learning hashtag on Twitter, Facebook, or Instagram; or by mentioning @documenting4learning on Facebook and Instagram, and @doc4learning on Twitter.

8

Documenting With Textual and Visual Platforms and Tools in Mind

Social media is the ultimate equalizer. It gives a voice and a platform to anyone willing to engage.

—Amy Jo Martin

Technopedia (2017) explains that "From a user's perspective, a social platform enables communities, sharing of content, adding friends, setting privacy controls, and other native social media network features." Examples include Twitter, Instagram, Diigo, YouTube, Facebook, and WordPress. Social media platforms are sub-grouped into categories, such as backchanneling sites, photo-sharing sites, social bookmarking sites, video-sharing sites, and blogging sites.

The Oxford Dictionary (2017b) defines *tool* as a, "Device or implement . . . used to carry out a particular function." Given its function is to accomplish a task or solve a problem, a digital tool is never viewed as a learning focus or goal. For example, such tools as PowerPoint, TodaysMeet, WordSwag, and PicCollage can be helpful tools to convey learning-thinking artifacts.

TEXT AND VISUAL PLATFORMS AND TOOLS

Educators who are unfamiliar with these two terms in a social media context often express confusion when trying to differentiate between digital platforms and digital tools. Analogies aid in clearing up misunderstandings, and several are provided in Image 8.1. It is important to remember that the goal is never *the* platform or tool. It is about authentically using platforms and tools in documenting opportunities.

While examining the SAMR taxonomy in Chapter 2, it was mentioned that it is the use of technology, not the technology itself, that enables students and teachers to document learning and take their learning process to new levels, especially in documenting FOR and AS learning opportunities. The wide range of pedagogical teaching and learning that can now take place at the *Modification* and *Redefinition* levels were previously inconceivable because the necessary technology platforms and tools had not yet been invented or developed.

Digital tools and platforms aid in acquiring and disseminating evidence of learning. Sharing and amplifying artifacts aid in reaching audiences for local and global opportunities in order to contribute to the learning process. This adds value in new and exciting ways. Platforms and tools serve as conduits to support attaining the learning focuses and goals. They aid primary and secondary learners in

- Capturing a moment in time
- Sharing synchronously and asynchronously

Image 8.1

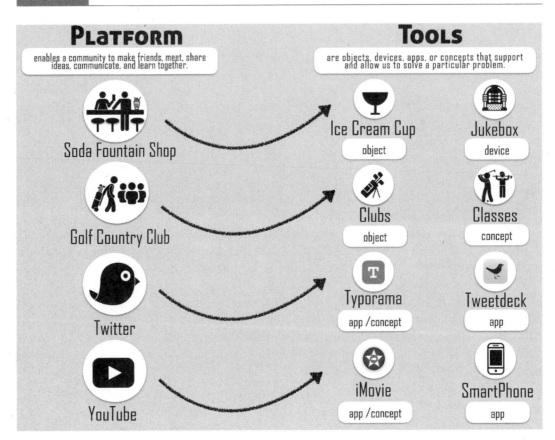

- Slowing down time
- Making invisible visible and tangible
- Making what has been captured editable
- Making what has been captured and unpacked shareable and amplifiable with others

Schoolware and Worldware Considerations

There are many digital platforms and tools available, and more are being invented and innovated every day. Developing the best framework for documenting in a classroom, school, or district through the strategic use of available platforms and tools saves time in the long run because when a tool is no longer available, it does not affect the learning focuses or goals. It simply involves finding a new, and often improved, platform or tool to meet the needs of the documenting opportunities and tasks.

It is worth taking a moment to think about and reflect on the trend of using education-specific platforms and tools, purchased through a vendor or online educational company. There are concerns associated with allowing students to only experience social media and sharing through the use of schoolware.

Before addressing the concerns, it is important to know the difference between *schoolware* and *worldware*. Ehrmann (1995) coined the term worldware to, "denote materials that are created and marketed mainly for purposes other than teaching and learning, but which are also used for teaching and learning." For example, WordPress was not invented for education, but myriad teachers and schools use this platform for creating classroom blogs. Students (at home and in school) often use YouTube to share and amplify their learning.

The first concern is that schoolware creates a digital wall that does not allow students and teachers to access the real world to amplify and invite local and global authentic audiences to participate in their learning. While it is understood that learning institutions have obligations, and often legal mandates, to protect those in their care, the reality is that when students are not in school, there are no protective walls or barriers. Therefore, it is wiser to teach students the *now* literacies and coach them on what it means to navigate in a worldware-world authentically while in school, rather than trying to shield them from it.

It is wiser to teach students the *now* literacies and coach them on what it means to navigate in a worldware-world authentically while in school, rather than trying to shield them from it.

Janet likes to use an analogy about teaching swimming lessons to children to express this concern. When she was a swimming instructor years ago, one of the first cautions she shared with parents, grandparents, and caregivers on the first day of swim class was,

Please do not put floaties on your child and let them jump in the water and play around. The floaties become a potentially deadly crutch. One reason you are here today is that you are worried about your child falling into a pool when you are not around. If that happens and all your child has ever known is depending on a pair of floaties to keep him or her on the surface, it is highly likely that he or she will panic and not be able to make it to the edge.

It is the same with thinking that a school or district is protecting its students by providing schoolware floaties.

Schoolware often has benefits for educators, such as streamlining the recording of student information, uploading certain types of documents, sharing with others inside the schoolware's digital walls, and providing a protective and controlled environment. While schoolware does provide basic social media capabilities, the second concern is that it usually does not provide a full range of platforms and tools that allow students and teachers to fully capture, unpack, share, and amplify their documentation artifacts with local and global communities as primary or secondary learners. The older the students are, the more concerning this becomes.

In all fairness to the reality that some educators do have the ability to use any worldware platform and tool they desire, others are limited to using schoolware platforms and tools. The good news is that sometimes the two *wares* can be combined. For example, *Skitch*, a screenshot editing and sharing utility for iOS, OSX, Windows, and Android platforms, is a worldware tool that can be used to annotext an image. That image can then be saved and uploaded to an approved schoolware platform.

Text and Backchannel Documentation

Text documentation is probably the most commonly used by learners when wanting to capture their thoughts or convey information. Whether they are equipped with paper and pen, laptop or tablet, learners are often asked to

- take notes by writing annotations on the side of a page or record them digitally in a nearby text box;
- provide handwritten or digital feedback to others at the bottom of a page or paper, or composing a post in a backchannel; or
- write and attach a sticky note comment or post a comment in a shared-writing digital document.

Using digital platforms and tools that allow multiple voices to take notes, add perspectives to the writing, ask and answer questions, provide thought-provoking insights, summarize and synthesize, create new content, and recognize patterns and trends are a necessity in a collaborative learning environment.

Asking learners to be conscious and look for opportunities to capture, reflect on, share, and amplify their learning is at the heart of purposeful documentation. All of these actions can happen using a backchannel platform. As the information enters a backchannel and is captured in real time, the text-based log or transcript provides evidence of the collaborative conversation taking place or which took place. The need to engage in the act of writing can be centered around a learning focus or goal based on a topic, theme, phenomenon, mathematical situation, or information in a film clip, podcast, blog post, book, or poem, to name a few.

Receptive and expressive words, phrases, and sentences are being processed by those participating in backchannels. Backchannel-conversation feeds provide evidence of learning that is prime for unpacking, which is explained in detail in Chapter 10. For the purpose of this section, backchanneling is being viewed as a platform to capture a *secondary* conversation supporting a *primary* learning topic based on a learning focuses and goals. While there is a variety of backchannel platforms available, Twitter, TodaysMeet, and Google Docs are featured below.

Twitter

Twitter is a popular worldware backchannel. It originated as a social platform to connect friends and colleagues. Over time, it has evolved into being a significant worldwide information system. Lapowsky (2013) quoted one of Twitter's creator's comment on its evolution:

With Twitter, it wasn't clear what it was. They called it a social network, they called it microblogging, but it was hard to define, because it didn't replace anything. There was this path of discovery with something like that, where over time you figure out what it is. Twitter actually changed from what we thought it was in the beginning, which we described as status updates and a social utility. It is that, in part, but the insight we eventually came to was Twitter was really more of an information network than it is a social network.

Because Twitter is both social and informational, it is a perfect platform for students to not only interact and share with one another, but also share and strategically amplify to reach experts during their learning opportunities. A powerful way to reach out to specific experts and audiences is through the purposeful use of hashtags.

Hashtags are words or phrases spelled in a continuous string of letters that begin with a pound sign # to identify and connect tweets on a specific topic. The value of hashtags lies in their repeated and continued use by Twitterers who are interested in collaboratively participating and contributing to a string of conversation tweets about a given topic, which is an example of crowdsourcing.

Scheduled Twitter chats for synchronous backchannel conversations are based on a specific hashtag. They usually last an hour and take place at a consistent designated date and time (e.g., every Tuesday, once a month on the 15th). Hashtag chats are designed to be open to all. They create an ongoing backchannel conversation focused on an overarching theme. Each chat meeting focuses on a specific topic around the theme wherein the attendees contribute their thoughts, ideas, perspectives, and resources. The hashtagged contributions provide a documentation timeline of participation because each tweet is timestamped.

The two Twitter hashtag chat activities explained in the next few pages can be used in the classroom or for professional learning. They require learners to concisely synthesize, summarize, and connect their thoughts, ideas, conversations, and crowdsourced content using 280 characters or less.

The first activity is a Twitter simulation that can be conducted as an introduction to engaging in a hashtag chat as a foundational learning experience, or can be used in lieu of online Twitter backchanneling if a classroom, school, or district has limited access to computers or devices that allow access to the Internet. The second activity provides the basics for students and educators to participate in live hashtag chats using chat etiquette when responding to officially posed questions and contributors' tweets.

Paper Tweeting. This simulation provides the context of a Twitter chat. For the basic how-to, there is purposefully no mention or requirement for using a hashtag, since the process can feel overwhelming if new to a hashtag chat environment. The inclusion of a hashtag is one of the suggestions for more advanced paper tweeting, which is provided following the directions.

Set up the Twittersphere chatroom simulation space:

- Place several sheets of large chart paper side-by-side or a long length of bulletin-board paper hanging horizontally on a wall that is easily accessible by the participants.
- Provide each participant (Twitterer) with a small stack of larger-sized sticky notes and dark-colored markers so that the text can be seen easily from a distance.

Before officially beginning the paper tweeting conversation (rounds)

- Ask each person to write his or her real or made-up Twitter handle (e.g., @janet_hale, @langwitches) at the bottom of each provided sticky note, large enough to be seen from a few feet away, but not so large that there is no room to write up-to-280-characters posts on the sticky notes.
- Provide a short tutorial on common Twitter abbreviations to allow for more characters being used in a post (e.g., Ss—students; Ts—teachers; U— you; R—are; w/—with; ?— I have a question; number quantity under 10 written as a numeral—2).

Follow the steps below for each round:

- **Round One**—Each Twitterer initially enters the chatroom by posting one sticky note that contains his or her @username and a greeting of choice (e.g., @ronnyg Hello!, @lovelearning Howdy from Houston).

  Make certain for conducting Round Two that participants add their posts on the chart or bulletin-board paper in a continuous one-post-under-the-other, vertical fashion from the top of the paper to bottom (and top again) in a column pattern to simulate a continuous Twitter stream.

- **Round Two**—Put up a thought-provoking question, written large enough for everyone to see (e.g., on a separate sheet of chart paper from the rounds sheets, projected onto a whiteboard or screen). Each Twitterer reads and contemplates a response to the question. When ready, he or she writes the response on one of the prepared sticky notes following the 280-characters-or-less requirement. He or she then adds it to the wall, taking turns, so that the collective sticky notes are listed vertically to represent a chronologically tweeted order.

  Now pause to allow time for each participant to read through the collective posted tweets and reflect on which tweet or two he or she would like to respond to its contributor in the next round.

- **Round Three**—Each Twitterer responds in 280 characters or less to the selected contributors' tweets using the prepared sticky notes and places the new tweet sticky notes in close proximity to (but not on top of) the responding-to contributors' original sticky notes from Round One.

  Pause to allow time for each participant to read through the newly posted tweets in connection to the already posted tweets, which may be personal in that a Twitterer responded specifically to his or her post. Regardless, all participants need time to read through and reflect on the collective new tweets.

  In Round Four, each contributor will again create one or two tweets. He or she can do so by responding to a particular contributor, or by simply sharing a reflective thought or important point regarding the overall message growing from the ongoing tweets.

- **Round Four**—Each Twitterer posts a reflection and/or responds to one of his or her selected contributor's tweet(s) following the 280-characters-or-less requirement using the prepared sticky notes and places this post's sticky note (a) at the bottom of the vertical flow of continuing tweets, if sharing a reflective thought or important point; or (b) in close proximity to the responding-to contributor's post(s).

  If this paper tweeting activity is the first time the learners have ever engaged in tweeting and/or a hashtag chat backchannel, it is recommended that some time is now spent debriefing both the cognitive and actionable skills required to engage in the chat conversation.

If using digital tools is accessible after the paper simulation is concluded, use the Post-It Plus app to take an image of the collective posted sticky notes. This image can then be unpacked by moving the sticky note images around to organize and categorize the notes' content, as well as export, archive, and share the crowdsourced contributions with those who participated in the tweeting simulation, and possibly reaching a wider audience as well.

The sticky notes on the wall at this activity's conclusion are artifacts that can be unpacked by the participants as primary learners or secondary learners. Learners can reflect on the thinking that was taking place throughout the backchannel chat based on the evidence visible in the tweets, as well as the interactive tweets among the contributors.

For more advanced paper tweeting, consider adding one or more of the following options to the first or later paper tweeting activities:

- Instead of using one color of sticky notes for the simulation, provide each participant with three different color of sticky notes for Rounds Two through Four. During each round, a different color is used so that when the contributors get up to add their next tweet, they will not place that sticky note in close proximity of the one to which they are responding. Instead, all contributions will continue in one vertical posting stream, as this is the way tweets visually appear in the Twittersphere. This will also provide a simulated timestamp of the chronological order of the postings, which can play an important role when reflecting on and interpreting the posts during the unpacking process of the collective Twitter-stream artifact.
- Ask contributors to include a required hashtag (e.g., #elephants, #guidedreading) that counts as characters, so participants need to be even more concise in what they convey in their tweets.
- Provide some time in-between Round Two and Round Three (as well as Round Three and Round Four, if desired) to allow participants to access readily available paper or digital resources to research the question prompt or #topic to enhance the quality of the tweet responses in the next round.
- When responding to a particular contributor, begin the tweet by stating *Replying to @handle.*
- Use two or three questions over the course of the rounds (there would need to be more rounds), so that the participants can get used to using the question-and-answer conventions, which is explained in more detail for the second activity (below).

Twitter Hashtag Chat—Questions and Answers. As mentioned previously, Twitterers can choose to participate in a synchronous Twitter chat's conversation about a given topic at a predetermined time. During that time, minds and messages are moving at a whirlwind pace. For some, it is way too fast; for others, it is invigorating.

If a student or educator has not participated in a hashtag chat before, focusing on the chat topic is often lost because the contributor gets confused in the midst of the busyness. A learner needs to first get past an initial whelmed feeling of the speedy tweeting process so that he or she can truly concentrate on responding to the topic, questions, and the other contributors' responses being posted.

Therefore, it is worthwhile to do the following, in either order, in a classroom or professional learning environment prior to contributing to an online non-publicized or publicized Twitter hashtag chat:

- Participating in one or more increasingly difficult paper tweeting simulation
- Observing an online Twitter chat taking place live on a personal or classroom screen
- Lurking in real time and reviewing the archived chat at a later time

During an online Twitter chat, a moderator will begin by welcoming the arriving contributors, as well as throughout if new contributors join in. The moderator will pose thought-provoking questions one at a time, usually up to seven questions over the course of chat time. The questions are oftentimes announced prior to the scheduled chat so that contributors have time to reflect on the questions, conduct research, and/or prepare resources to share when the questions are posed during the live hashtag chat.

Contributing to a Twitter hashtag chat requires knowing chat etiquette. While there are online resources that explain the protocols involved, here is one of the most important to be aware of:

- Knowing how to post and respond to questions and follow-up responses properly

Given the speediness of the flow of the tweets, contributors' answers and ongoing responses can easily get lost in the flow once the first question tweet has been posted. When the moderator posts the first question, he or she will indicate that it is the first by using the capital letter Q and the number 1 prior to the question, as well as including the chat's hashtag after the question (as well as other hashtags, if appropriate to the topic or question posed). For example:

- Q1: How do your questions challenge students to think deeply? #CDeduchat #DOK

As contributors respond to this hashtag chat question, they begin their responses with a capital letter A and the corresponding number. For example, here are two different contributor's responses to the question just posed:

- A1: Questions can help students to make connections between current and past information #CDeduchat
- A1: by pushing them to uncover how they know what they know and/or why they think something. open-ended #CDeduchat

Later in this hashtag chat feed, a contributor posted a reflective thought and connected her tweet back to the first question by indicating A1, even though the second question, Q2, had already been posted and responded to by many of the contributors in the hashtag chat stream:

- A1: a good question also makes you question your assumptions, preconceived ideas and makes you catch a glimpse of other perspectives #CDeduchat

While the action of including A1 in the post was important in the context of this contributor applying hashtag chat etiquette, this skill is imperative when wanting to capture learners' posts in Twitter feeds for documenting purposes because it enables the primary and secondary learners to follow and unpack a specific learner's thoughts and responses throughout a hashtag chat stream.

At the conclusion of the hashtag chat the moderator will thank all of the contributors and remind them that the chat stream (conversation) can be kept going using the hashtag. He or she will often mention that the hashtag chat's archive will be available soon using a social media platform tool.

Once students or professional learners have participated in Twitter chats enough to move beyond the basic protocols and procedures and are ready to focus on a topic, the learning doors are opened wide for creating crowdsourced documenting opportunities that engage learners in meaningful and purposeful chat conversations with their peers, and most importantly, with experts who are invited to contribute during a hashtag chat conversation. When a hashtag chat conversation has concluded, the Twitter feed can be collected using a capturing tool as evidence of learning and archived. When the time comes for the documentation to be unpacked, the primary or secondary learners can reflect on the Twitter feed's content based on a specific focus or goal and annotext the images using annotating tools, such as Skitch or Jing, to transform the image into a learning-thinking artifact.

For example, eighth-grade students were trying to figure out a video phenomenon they had been observing: the release action of the venom when a rattlesnake was biting into a venom-catching tube and the relationship between the action and the snake's sensory receptors responding to stimuli. The teacher, Mrs. Searle, had contacted herpetologists at a local university and asked them to participate in her class's upcoming hashtag chat that would be taking place during the school day the following week. Two of the professors had a comfort level with tweeting and being involved in Twitter chats and volunteered to attend. The students were not told about the special guests who would be joining in. The class had been announcing their upcoming Twitter #rattlesnakevenom hashtag chat using Mrs. Searle's and another teacher's professional learning network. Mrs. Searle had her students brainstorm and select the three questions they wanted to pose to the contributors in their half-hour hashtag chat after doing research based on their current scientific knowledge and understanding.

During their #rattlesnakevenom hashtag chat, the students were also responsible for collaboratively hosting and monitoring the chat feed. They were ecstatic when the two professors joined in! The half-hour flew by, and at the conclusion the two class moderators thanked all of the contributors for participating. After the chat, the students instantly wanted to review their hashtag chat feed. Mrs. Searle coached them on how to go through the process of creating a curated feed for their #rattlesnakevenom chat, which they would be unpacking tomorrow.

The next day the students worked in quad-teams to unpack the Twitter story by opening the feed on their iPads. Each team selected a section of the feed to take a photo of the tweets and upload the image into Skitch. They collaboratively discussed in their mini-teams what evidence in their feed section helped them continue their quest to fully explain the venom-releasing stimulus-response phenomenon. They unpacked their document sections and annotexted the images to create artifacts. Then they shared the collective sections by displaying them in turn on the classroom's whiteboard screen and discussed the new learning and insights gained from their Twitter chat.

The next day, each student was asked to illustrate a new iteration model that visually expressed and textually labeled and summarized the bone, muscle, and duct structures' roles and actions involved in the stimuli-response behavior of a rattlesnake's fangs releasing venom. The models were shared as a starting point for their continued conversation leading to a consensus model for the stimulus-response phenomenon.

It's Time to Take Action!

Chapter 8 Action Step

You may be new to the world of Twitter backchanneling and hashtag conversations. Maybe you have heard of them, but you have never actively participated in an educationally oriented hashtag conversation. Now is your chance!

Note: If you are a frequent hashtag chat Twitterer, how about coming alongside a colleague who is not and coaching him or her through the engagement process?

You can either begin by conducting the *Paper Tweet's* initial activity, as well as the additional complexities, with some colleagues or friends, or go right to the Twittersphere to begin.

When or if you are ready to enter the real world of hashtag chats, scan the QR code to the left to view an extensive list of possible hashtag chats, as well as a link to chat meeting schedules.

Remember to use #documenting4learning along with the Twitter hashtag for the chat you decide to join in, as a way to extend the amplification during your backchanneling experience.

When your hashtag chat conversation is over, send out two reflection posts about your experience: the first post focused on what you found most enjoyable, and the second post sharing what you found most frustrating. Post your two reflection tweets using the chat's hashtag and #documenting4learning.

QR Code 8.1

Scan this QR code to view list of *Cybrary Man's Educational Hashtags.*

http://langwitches.me/edu-hashtags

TodaysMeet

This backchanneling platform is a private chatroom, whereas Twitter is an open-chat environment. In TodaysMeet, the first step is to create a private area in the cloud that only those who know the customized URL can enter the room. Be aware, it is easy to invite others to collaborate simply by sharing the custom link for the room once it is created.

When creating a chat room, TodaysMeet will also ask how long the room will be kept open; in other words, how long can contributors continue to post in the private room's backchannel feed.

Once contributors are logged into the created chatroom, they can share their thoughts and ideas with a 280-characters-or-less limitation. Unlike Twitter, the ability to attach images, videos, GIFs; create polls; or add locations is not available. It is a straight-forward, text-based tool.

Backchannel moderators can strategically place guiding questions, reflective prompts, or cues during a backchannel session, similar to a moderator doing so in a Twitter hashtag chat.

One of the strongest advantages for using a TodaysMeet chatroom for documenting learning is that a room can stay open beyond classroom hours or the timeframe of a unit or series of lessons. This means that learners and external contributors, if invited by sharing the URL, can go beyond synchronous contributions and provide asynchronous posts over time. The transcript for a specific range of time can be downloaded and unpacked immediately or archived for later use. If the transcripts are captured periodically (e.g., every week for a month), growth over time can be looked for by unpacking the transcripts based on a specific focus or goal.

Paper TodaysMeet Posting. If students or educators have not experienced a TodaysMeet or similar private-room chat, a simulation can be conducted using the same overall guidelines and directions for paper tweeting with a few exceptions:

- Before officially beginning the paper posting conversation (rounds)
  - Ask each person to write his or her first name and last initial as a nickname (e.g., Janet H, Silvia T) at the bottom of each provided sticky note, large enough to been seen from a distance, but not so large that there is no room to write an up-to-280-characters post on the sticky notes.
- During the simulation
  - **Round One**—Each contributor initially enters the closed chatroom by posting one sticky note that contains his or her *first name* and *last name's first initial*, and a greeting of choice (e.g., Ronny G Hello!, Pete H Howdy from Houston).
- When conducting the more advanced simulations
  - The last suggestion for paper tweeting needs to be modified slightly regarding usernames:
    - ❖ When responding to a particular contributor, begin the post by stating *the* contributors (Ronny G, Pete H), and all of the characters in the person's count against the 280-characters limitation.

Google Docs

Google Docs is another platform that invites and encourages collaborative writing. To use it as a backchannel documentation tool, the document creator/moderator (or the learners once they have accessed and opened the document) creates a table with the appropriate number of columns and/or rows for the writing purpose.

To create or add information to the table, the backchannel participants not only need access to the document, but need to be given editing privilege as well. This can be accomplished by

- **Invitational Collaboration**
  - Clicking on *Share* and add the collaborators' email addresses. When done adding, click *Save*. Google Docs will automatically send a notification to each contributor inviting him or her to access the Google Doc. Once the person clicks on the link in his or her email, the document will open. It will be accessible via the contributor's Google Drive for future access, assuming he or she has a Gmail account.
  - Sharing the unique URL generated when a new Google Doc is created. It can be shared with any desired contributors via email, text, or text-communication platform. If the URL is long and convoluted, the creator/moderator can use a Bit.ly to

make it easier to remember for contributors to access the document (e.g., during a workshop the facilitator includes a Bitly.com-shortened URL in his opening slide and waits a few moments to allow attendees to type in the URL in their tab screens and enter the collaborative writing Google Doc).

- **Automatic Collaboration**
    - ○ Knowing if a contributor's email address is already associated with the Google Drive folder where the newly created document is being placed. If yes, he or she can contribute, but be aware that the contributor will *not* be notified via email that a new document has been added to the folder. The new document will be accessible via the contributor's Google Drive and in the shared folder, assuming he or she has a Gmail account. It can also be located in the *Shared with me* Google Drive folder.
    - ○ Knowing if the new document created is a *copy* of an original document. If it is, all of the contributors associated with the original document should be given the same sharing rights in the new document. Be aware that the contributors will *not* be notified of the new document's creation. It will be accessible via the contributor's Google Drive and in the shared folder, assuming he or she has a Gmail account. It can also be located in the *Shared with me* Google Drive folder.

When it is time for the learner-contributors to actively engage in writing in the backchannel Google Doc, they can be directed to write in a particular cell or use a specific color to differentiate the contributors. The moderator could assign specific backchannel contributors to filter, summarize, or capture resources.

There is no end to what can be collected in a collaborative Google Doc backchannel. Learners can, for example

- Take collective notes highlighting key points based on the learning focus, such as summarizing information shared during a presentation, discussion, or virtual conversation
- Note the subtle actions of the protagonist and/or antagonist in a pivotal chapter of a book
- Highlight connections between cause-and-effect events in a historical article
- Determine how dialogue moves a major plot point forward in a film or television show
- Analyze whether an algorithm tutorial is easy to follow and mathematically accurate

Another example of using a Google Doc backchannel is having learners complete an exit ticket and using the visible thinking routine: *I see, I think, I wonder . . .*

For his professional learning workshop, Mr. Hicksman chose to use this visible thinking routine for a backchannel exit-ticket. He created a Google Doc and added a table with four labeled columns: *Name / I See / I Think / I Wonder*, and a fifth column labeled: *Support Needed*. Above the graphic organizer, he wrote the name of the workshop focus: Digital Portfolios.

Near the conclusion of the workshop, Mr. Hicksman briefly explained the concept of visible thinking routines, and specifically the purpose of this routine. He provided reflection time for the participants and then asked each participant to record his or her comments using a different color font in the created table.

While unpacking documents is addressed in Chapter 10, it is important to note here that there are times when artifacts can be unpacked in more than one way and more than one time. For this example, the workshop participants are cognitively recording their reflective responses *while simultaneously metacognitively thinking about the collective comments being shared* and thinking about whether the learning of others was the same for him or herself. This means that each participant, as a primary learner, is unpacking while the documenting is still taking place. This action would not be possible if the exit ticket reflections were written on slips of paper and left on a front table for only Mr. Hickman's eyes to see. Since the reflections were recorded openly and collectively, the participants instantly sharing their thoughts with everyone in the workshop created a slight degree of amplification. The attendees were able to glean and grow by reading one other's reflections.

As for Mr. Hicksman, unpacking the exit-ticket documentation was not to be done solo, which is oftentimes the case for a presenter or facilitator. When two or more are included in reflectively unpacking, the degree of amplification increases, as well as the benefit of working with others to make better decisions. As Helen Keller said, "Alone we can do so little; together we can do so much." Mr. Hicksman had the school principal, Mr. Hillman, open the Google Doc on his computer, and together they unpacked the reflective responses and analyzed them to determine what appeared to have the largest to smallest impact on the teachers regarding the recent implementation of digital portfolios. Most importantly, they discussed how the teachers' recorded reflective perceptions may impact transfer of the workshop learning into their classroom practices. Lastly, they read through the *Support Needed* comments and began to brainstorm differentiated next steps based on the needs indicated.

The goals for using a co-writing Google Doc backchannel strategy include

- Allowing the learners time for reflection
- Giving the learners confidence that they will be personally supported
- Seeing the power of collaborative writing in real time
- Increasing the take-aways for the learners, due to being able to read what others are sharing

Image/Photograph Documentation

Documenting life, history, knowledge, and stories via images is the oldest form of documentation. Cave drawings are the earliest form of documented documentation (pun intended). *Although an image can speak a thousand words, how insightful would it have been if those cave drawings had annotations? In other words, what are the details that the drawings cannot reveal?*

Current societies are image-rich. There are no lack of visuals playing important roles in telling the story of the times, families, and communities. It is amazing to see the youngest and oldest possessing devices that allow them to instantaneously snap, store, and send thousands of images. No longer are people held back by location, and even wealth, from having a smartphone that allows images to be shared and amplified worldwide within moments of capturing people, places, and perspectives.

Using images as part of capturing artifacts is a powerful tool when documenting FOR and AS learning. Here are six strategies, which are by no means exhaustive, to aid in using images effectively.

QR Code 8.2

Scan this QR code to watch a screencast on how to create a Google Doc backchannel exit ticket based on the Visible Thinking Routine: *I See, I Think, I Wonder.*

http://langwitches.me/backchannel-exit

Strategy 1: Annotexting

Annotexting is annotating an image. An arrow points a viewer's eye to a specific area of the image; frames highlight and point out specific details; and concise text provides context. Most annotating tools have a blurring feature so that students' faces can be pixelated for security reasons, when necessary. An image can be uploaded to a slide and annotexted using the shape, arrow, and text box features.

Annotexting is an essential strategy for documenting learning, especially when unpacking and reflecting in the after-documentation phase. It is a cognitive, and oftentimes metacognitive, process that requires thoughtful consideration for what the artifact is revealing as evidence of learning. Without an explanation of or reflection about what is being observed in an image, the image is merely a display.

There are a variety of tools that can be used for annotexting. Some are specifically for overlaying purposes, such as Skitch (which is what was used for annotexting Image 8.2), Preview (the native image and PDF viewer for iOS), Annotate, and Notability. Applications, such as PowerPoint, Keynote, and Google Presentation, can also be used for annotexting.

Image 8.2

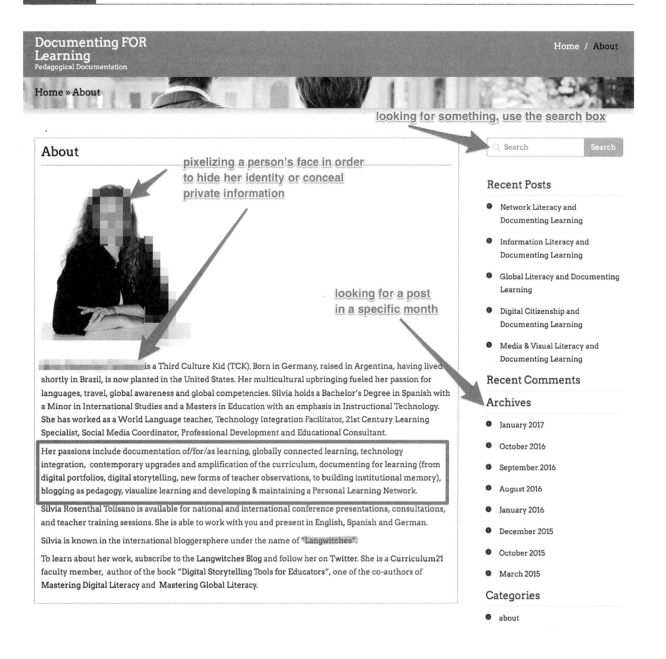

Strategy 2: Screenshooting

A *screenshot* is an image taken to capture a specific moment on a digital screen, such as a laptop, tablet, or smartphone. The purpose for taking a screenshot for documentation purposes can vary, such as capturing an image that will change in a few moments (e.g., the first draft of a correspondence), over time (e.g., series of daily screenshots of weather forecasts for a city or town), or where only certain parts or sections of the screen are needed (e.g., creating a tutorial and taking a screenshot of a small section of the images on the screen to use in the explanation sequence).

Screenshooting is the act of taking a screenshot. Planning for this action is often a part of the pre-documentation phase planning, as it is the time for primary or secondary learners to consider what needs to be captured and the specifics concerning what shots will best convey the desired details or message. For example, a series of sectional screenshots would be best for creating a blog post that will include a how-to tutorial for podcast versus a single shot of a close-up of an insect taken on an iPad in preparation for a younger learner to label its body parts as a documentation artifact.

Oftentimes, there is confusion between screenshooting and screencasting. Screenshooting produces a still image, while screencasting produces a video. There may or may not be audio narration involved when screencasting. Screencasting documentation is addressed later in this chapter.

Screenshooting features are usually included in annotexting tools, such as Skitch, Preview, and Snagit.

Strategy 3: Sketchnoting

Sketchnoting is a form of taking notes wherein the sketchnoter visually represents his or her thoughts and ideas. Lee (2017) comments that, "[Sketchnoting] must be seen as a way to communicate and document one's thinking as opposed to a way to draw."

Through purposeful placement of titles, subtitles, icons, frames, containers, arrows, connectors, and typography, a sketchnoter visually conveys the key points or details of something being read, listened to, viewed, or simply thought about for one moment in time or over period of time.

Sketchnoting is useful when wanting or needing to get a mental model out of one's head in order to share with oneself and others. Regardless of the reason for sketchnoting, the sketchnoter provides visual evidence of his or her thinking in terms of the content's importance, relationships, hierarchy, sequences, timelines, and/or metaphors. This supports documenting FOR and AS learning opportunities because it requires the process of reflection and interpretation of the content the learner is processing, while tapping into one's cognitive and metacognitive thinking.

There are eight strategic documenting purposes that sketchnoting can support, which are represented in the sketchnote (see Image 8.3).

There are a variety of sketchnoting tools available, including Procreate, Adobe Draw, Brushes, Explain Everything, and Flipink. Image 8.3 was created using Paper by FiftyThree.

Strategy 4: Comic Strips

Drawings or images in panels (single frames) placed in sequential tiers (rows), as well as overlaid narrator captions (rectangular boxes) and speech bubbles or dialogue balloons compose a comic strip.

Image 8.3

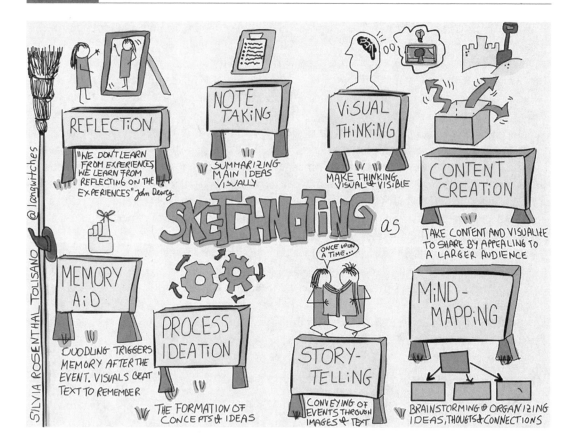

When the panels are read collectively or in a sequential order, a "story" is formed, which is not meant or required to be comical. This term is simply referring to the visual format and layout, rather than the strip's content and message.

While comic strips usually have the name of the strip included, for documenting purposes the title reflects the topic or theme the strip is representing. Creating strips is a helpful documenting strategy for primary learners in that they need to first determine what set of photographs and/or screenshots that have collected will be thoughtfully placed in a strip's panels to convey an experience, such as a science inquiry lab or mathematical task.

Then the learners need to determine what needs to be added regarding captions, dialogue balloons, and appropriate title to become a learning narrative.

As a secondary learner, a teacher can use the comic strip strategy as an artifact to convey to his or her students what they are orally expressing during a collaborative project or task. In the during-documentation phase, while students are actively engaged in the learning experience, the teacher needs to multitask to

- Gather visual evidence by taking photos and/or screenshots
- Jot down written anecdotes or capture audio recordings

Image 8.4

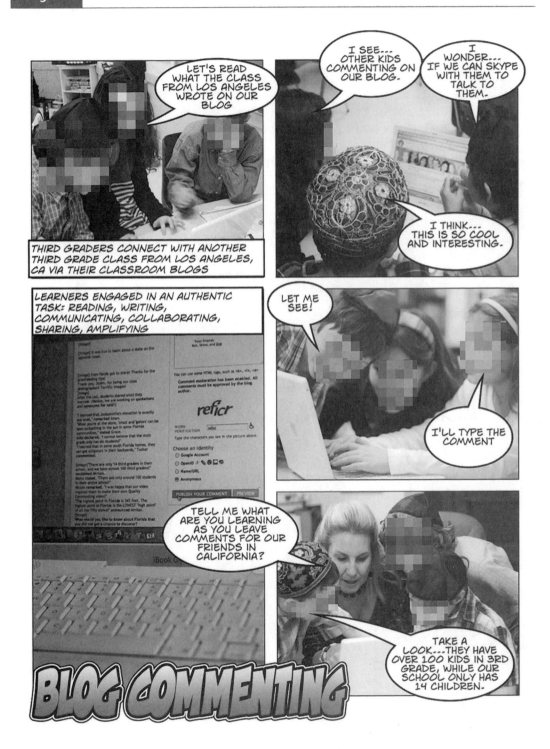

In the post-documentation phase, the teacher will select the desired images and anecdotes that best convey evidence of learning and create one class strip, or one strip per collaborative team, highlighting the learning focus or goal.

The cognitive reflections the teacher needs to incorporate when selecting the photo images for the panels, narrator captions, and speech bubbles are a form of unpacking that leads to creating the artifact or artifacts.

When the teacher shares the strips with his or her students, amplification begins because the sharing extends beyond the teacher's personal thinking, interpretation, and learning. The comic strip artifact(s) can also be amplified to a larger audience by including in a blog post, posting to Instagram, or adding to a Twitter post.

Image 8.4 strip was made with Comic Life. Other strip-creation tools include Strip Designer, Comic Book!, and Make Believe Comix.

Strategy 5: Infographics and Visual Quote Cards

While photographs alone play a significant role in documenting, there are two additional types of visuals that can also prove meaningful: *infographics* and *visual quote cards*.

Just as with sketchnotes, infographics use titles, shapes, figures, icons, containers, frames, arrows, connectors, and typography to make one's thinking visible. A key difference between sketchnotes and infographics is purpose: Sketchnotes aid the creator in getting his or her ideas out of his or her head and onto paper or screen to convey a mental model, whereas an infographic's foremost purpose is to express a concept, idea, or topic to an audience.

A component of the documenting learningflow routine is focused on sharing the learning with an audience greater than oneself (degrees of sharing amplification). At times, this will authentically involve conveying a message to a target audience. When doing so, it is important for the learners to consider how the message can best be conveyed visually and concisely. Watson (2015) shared evidence that, "According to scientists, the age of smartphones has left humans with such a short attention span, [which] has fallen from 12 seconds in 2000, or around the time the mobile revolution began, to eight seconds."

This is one reason why infographics have become such an effective way to communicate. For example, look at Images 8.5 and 8.6. Image 8.5 is an artifact of a learner's expression of why heutagogy is an important approach to learning written as a textual passage. Image 8.6 is the same learner's expression conveyed in an infographic wherein the important points to support her reasoning uses a

Image 8.5

Heutagogy is not a thing or a fad; it is about possessing a certain mindset and being self-motivated to learn. Learning how to learn is about seeing yourself as a researcher in the topic of your interest, as well as being at center of your own learning, pushing yourself outside of your comfort zone and letting learning happen in a nonlinear way by not being a passive participant, but actively being involved.

Image 8.6

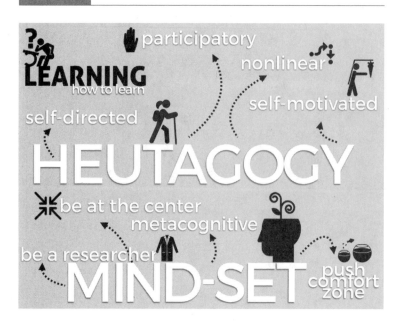

title and short word or phrases paired with images. *Which one catches the attention of a reader quickest and holds interest the longest? When scanning the two images, which one stimulates the brain to wonder about what is being conveyed?*

Infographics create visually appealing and easily understandable artifacts that can

- highlight sequential or chronological events;
- summarize key points and concepts of something read, listened to, or viewed;
- explain a relationship between or among large sums of numbers or statistics; or
- represent a social pattern or trend.

Creating infographics is an excellent strategy for educators' professional learning opportunities, especially when they are expected to share or amplify what they have gleaned from text read, video viewed, or audio heard.

A few infographic creation tools include Piktochart, Canva, Visme, and easel.ly.

QR Code 8.3

Scan this QR code to view the infographic Janet created to summarize key points after reading an article for a project-based learning coaching institute she was attending.

http://langwitches.me/what-good-coaches-do

Visual Quote Cards

On the surface, it may appear to be a simple task to create a visual quote card: choose a background and place a quote and attributor on the foreground. This is not the case when using this form as thoughtful visual documentation.

Here are two examples that express why visual quote cards are perfect for creating learning-thinking artifacts.

Conference/Workshop or Classroom Highlights. When attending a conference or workshop, there are often hours and hours of receptive information coming into the brain. Attendees can oftentimes be heard saying, "I can't take any more information in . . . I am on overload!"

For professional learning opportunities, it is important to plan what photographs or images will be used as backgrounds for the visual quote cards that will aid or enhance the capture-worthy quotes shared during the attended sessions or workshops.

There are three options for conducting background planning: (1) during the pre-documentation phase; (2) at the onset of the during-documentation phase; or (3) a combination of both.

Image 8.7

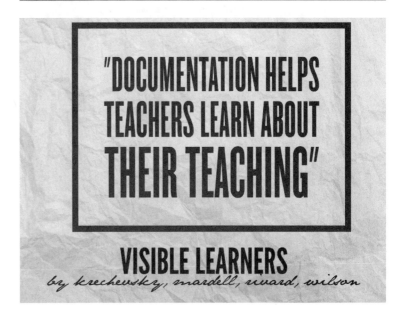

"DOCUMENTATION HELPS TEACHERS LEARN ABOUT THEIR TEACHING"

VISIBLE LEARNERS
by krechevsky, mardell, rivard, wilson

Whichever option is selected, here are option considerations for creating the visual quote cards:

1. Pick the sessions or workshops you plan on attending and immediately begin taking photographs that pertain to the session or workshop topic or theme in your classroom or school. For example, if you are attending a session on the Next Generation Science Standards (NGSS) iterative model-making concept, take photos of your students creating models or presenting arguments about their generated models. If you will be attending a Writer's Workshop training, have someone be your photographer and take photographs of you working with your students during various moments during your class's Writer's Workshop time.

   If you prefer, or would simply like to have more background options—without infringing on copyright you can search for appropriate photographs or images using free or subscription services, such as Flickr, FreeImages.com, 123RFStock Images, or iStock.

   As the conference, workshop, or training date approaches or arrives, organize and have ready your pre-taken and/or pre-selected photographs or images to be imported into your desired typography designer tool, often referred to as a word swag app (e.g., Typorama, WordSwag, Kwote, Quotes Creator); or to a tool that has a slide feature, wherein a slide will become a visual quote card (e.g., PowerPoint, Keynote, Google Slides).

2. At the onset of the session, workshop, or training you are now attending, have your desired tool up and running on your mobile device (e.g., smartphone or tablet). To prepare for capturing worthwhile quotes, take photographs of the presenter or presenters getting the session started, as well as the venue. If using Google Slides, for example, upload the various photographs, one image per slide, so you will have a series of backgrounds ready to use. If using Typorama or similar app, chose a just-taken image from your photo gallery to upload to the app and prepare to overlay it with the desired text quote.

   When a presenter shares a worth-capturing quote, use the text overlay feature in your selected tool and type in the quote. Depending on the tool and text layout capabilities, add the attributor's name and save image to your device. Continue capturing worthwhile quotes and attributions throughout the conference, workshop, or training.

Important Note: Be certain you are cognizant of *leaving an adequate amount of open space* in a background photograph so that the added quote and attribution will not interfere with the image's focal point or points. For example, look at Images 8.8 and 8.9. Technically, they are the same image of Alan November, but notice the difference in the open (negative) space in Image 8.9. This is what is visually meant by leaving enough open space to overlay with text, as you can see in the visual quote card (see Image 8.10). An open space can be anywhere within the frame: top, bottom, side, or in the middle, as varying the openness provides unique perspectives when creating a relationship between the background image and the overlaid quote.

Lastly, do not forget to share the visual quote cards you created during the presentation. A small degree of amplification would be printing them out and sharing copies with a few colleagues or sending them digitally via an email. A greater degree of amplification would be sharing your cards using social media, such as Twitter, Instagram, Facebook, on a website, or in a blog post. The greatest amplification would be to also strategically include a #hashtag or

@username, such as #writersworkshop or @doc4learning, to reach a specific social-media audience.

Remember that visual quote cards are an excellent strategy to use in the classroom as well. It is eye-opening to see the visual quote cards students have generated based on what they perceive to be worthy of noting that a teacher or peer has stated.

Visual quote cards can be used by learners when reading text or listening to orations (see Image 8.7).

Image 8.8

Image 8.9

Image 8.10

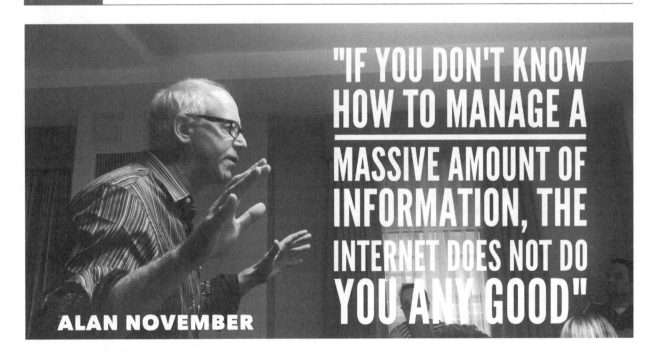

For example, Mrs. Seinhart's second graders were about to begin reading a self-selected chapter book from five book options and meeting in literature-circle discussion groups to discuss each chapter. She knew having her students create visual quote cards per chapter for their selected books would be a perfect documenting opportunity.

She decided on three learning focuses:

- Making text-to-self connections
- Supporting media literacy
- Communicating beyond text using a visual medium

She posted the focuses and discussed her reasoning for selecting each one with her students. Mrs. Seinhart then told her students they needed to not only visualize connections between what they are reading and themselves, but also, "Be able to get the mental picture of what you are seeing in your mind's eye out and share that mental image with others in a different way than just writing sentences or paragraphs."

Mrs. Seinhart shared that instead of writing sentences or paragraphs, they would be creating visual quote cards to make their thinking visible as they read each chapter. She told them the quote could not tap into just any thought. It needed to, "Make a connection that left an emotional mental impression." She then showed them the two tools they could choose from to create their visual quote cards: PicCollage or Google Slides.

She continued by explaining that after choosing a quote from a chapter, they needed to take a photograph at home (or the appropriate location for the connection) that aids in conveying the personal connection to the selected chapter quote. Each student will then upload the photograph to his or her selected tool and use it as a full-frame background or as a smaller image within the final image.

She concluded the task explanation by conducting a model lesson that demonstrated what needed to take place from start to finish:

- Read the chapter.
- Select a text-to-self quote.
- Take a complimentary photo (she had one ready for the lesson).
- Upload the photograph to the selected tool and place onto or in quote card frame.
- Overlay the image with the quote and the chapter title, book title, and author information.
- Save the file.
- Print out a copy of the visual quote card to take to literature-circle discussion time.
- Upload saved file appropriately to the class portfolio platform.

Sophia found a quote that made her giggle in Chapter 1 of her selected chapter book: *Junie B. Jones Smells Something Fishy*. When she read a particular passage, she immediately made a connection to her dog, Dax, and pictured Junie B. Jones lugging him to school in a very large cage for Pet Day. Sophia thought to herself that would be very funny to watch happen.

When she went home that day, she took a photograph of Dax in his crate. She then followed the directions provided by Mrs. Seinhart and created a visual quote card for Chapter 1 that included her photograph, the quote using quotation marks, and the required attribution. She saved her quote card and uploaded the file to her account in the class portfolio platform (see Image 8.11).

During her literature-circle Chapter 1 discussion time, she shared her visual quote card and provided details about her quote selection based on her peers asking her questions related to her visual image and quoted text.

Image 8.11

Image 8.12

A few tools to create visual quote cards include PicCollage, Typorama, Word Swag, Powerpoint, Keynote, Google Slides, Canva, Piktochart, and Book Creator.

Strategy 6: Collages

The last image/photo documentation strategy focuses on using collage creation as an artifact.

A *collage* is a digital collection of images purposely selected to convey a message on one page or one slide (see Image 8.12). The visual message is supported using concise text. A collage's images can be grouped in predefined layouts provided by the collage tool (e.g., PicCollage) or arranged freehand (e.g., PowerPoint slide).

Students as primary learners or teachers as secondary learners cluster the connected images and annotate with appropriate information or commentary. Once created, it is saved as one image file, which makes filing, organizing, and retrieving the artifact easier than having to keep track of the independent image files included in the collage.

The possibilities for creating artifact collages are endless with a little imagination. For example:

- When studying the life cycle of insects in a primary grade, instead of filling out a pre-printed worksheet or hand-drawing illustrations or diagrams of the different life stages, the students can begin by locating online copyright-friendly images (or take their own photographs, if possible). Next, with or without adult assistance, they will unpack the images to create a collage artifact starting with combining and arranging the images and then adding the annotations to convey their key learning points about the insect's life cycle.

- Middle schoolers and high schoolers can use collages to enhance lab reports by collecting their own observations via photographs and screenshots they believe have brought them closer to confirming or disproving a current claim for an iterative phenomenon model.
- World language students can create photographic collages to share cultural folk-tales they have adapted to modern times.
- Music students can visualize the emotional trajectory of a melody or song by creating photo-collage interpretations of the music and/or lyrics.
- Math students can find real-world examples of mathematical concepts they are studying and create collages to capture and document the authentic situations.
- Each educator observing a model lesson by a teacher can arrange some of the photographs captured during the observation and create a collage with annotations as evidence of learning to use during the post-lesson debriefing session with colleagues, principal, and facilitator.

A few collage tools include PicCollage, PicStitch, and Diptic, PowerPoint, Keynote, and Google Slides.

SUMMING UP

It is important to realize that text and visual platforms and tools are being invented and/or upgraded continuously. For example, while it was not featured in the visual-documentation section, an emerging platform is Pinterest.

This social-network worldware platform has steadily increased in popularity outside and inside education. Its key draw is that users can go window shopping by searching and scanning like-category images (and videos) based on a topic, idea, or concept. Users can upload their own images (pins) and pin others' pins to their boards in a customizable, organized fashion.

Given Pinterest's capabilities to upload, organize, share, and amplify the reach of images coupled with providing descriptions and links to further information (increasing the sharing degree of amplification), educators are using this platform as a way in which to curate their classroom and professional learning opportunities. It is what a student or teacher titles his or her documentation boards and what description he or she adds to each pin that makes this platform a powerful documentation hub. Given Pinterest is designed to socially link its users by meaningfully connecting and suggesting similar pins and boards, the ability to share and amplify increases.

It is important to remember that in all the examples and narratives shared in this chapter, it was never meant to be about the platforms and tools. It is always about using the appropriate technology to support the actions involved in a learner's documenting opportunity. Always at the forefront of the documentation phases and learningflow routine steps is thinking about how the primary and secondary learners will look for, capture, unpack, reflect on, share, and amplify their evidence of learning based on the pre-determined focuses and goals.

GOING BEYOND

To amplify your reading beyond this book's pages, we have created *discussion questions and prompts* for this chapter, which are located at *www.documenting4learning.com*. To extend your thinking, reactions, and responses, you can connect with other readers by leaving comments on individual chapter's discussion posts on our documenting4learning blog.

We also invite you to contribute and share your artifacts in other social media spaces to connect with and learn from other readers around the world using the #documenting4learning hashtag on Twitter, Facebook, or Instagram; or by mentioning @documenting4learning on Facebook and Instagram, and @doc4learning on Twitter.

9

Documenting With Audio, Video, and Blogging Platforms and Tools in Mind

When the wind of change blows, some people build walls, others build windmills.

—Chinese Proverb

As mentioned in Chapter 8, the purpose of digital tools and platforms is to aid in acquiring and disseminating evidence of learning to evaluate, share, and amplify artifacts with local and global audiences, as well as having those audiences contributing and adding value in new and exciting ways. In this chapter, the use of platforms and tools to create and connect with authentic audiences continues.

The first section involves audio and video documentation; followed by blogging documentation, which serves as a hub for multimedia integration (text, image, audio, video); and the third section focuses on a digital-writing genre, *hyperlinked writing*, which is an essential genre to understand and engage in as a *now* form of communication.

AUDIO AND VIDEO PLATFORMS AND TOOLS

Audio Documentation

Audio documentation focuses on words, phrases, and sound effects that support the learning content. Just as *making thinking visible* contributes to creating artifacts, *making thinking audible* does the same. For example, audio-documentation artifacts can capture conversations, concerns, reflections, thoughts, impressions, connections, and predictions.

Being able to communicate is a cornerstone of both traditional reading and writing, as well as the *now* literacies. In today's world, being literate involves conveying meaning through textual, visual, and audible communication. In certain situations, the combination of static images (e.g., photograph, infographic) or video (e.g., film, animation) and meaningful audio (e.g., podcast) can be a powerful method to convey learning-thinking. Other times, this combination may be too much to ask of primary or secondary learners, due to their lack of experience or comfort level with capturing and unpacking audio recordings.

Therefore, a wise place to begin may be pure audio documentation, as it is a powerful moment when the communication of ideas, thoughts, and beliefs has to depend solely on sound to convey, reflect upon, and interpret one's evidence of learning. Also, there are times when an image or video can steal the limelight from what is at the heart of being aurally conveyed.

Audio is well-suited for emerging readers and writers, as well as second-language learners. Audio-only documentation can also protect a learner's identity in situations when privacy is needed. This may be an excellent documenting alternative in a school or district where photographs are not permitted on school-related websites or social media. Also, some learners do not like being photographed or filmed, but do not mind having their voices recorded and heard by peers or local or global audiences.

Speaking out loud to explain one's thinking or articulating one's reasoning can be a complex communication process that involves both cognitive and metacognitive processes. This is especially true when learners are expected to unpack and reflect on the captured recordings.

Take into consideration a time when you have heard your own voice recording. If it is beyond singing a song or reciting a poem, usually a specific word or phrase becomes a favorite (e.g., whereas . . . whereas . . .), *ahhs* and *umms* abound, or your rate changes to lightning speed.

In during-documentation recordings, a speaker needs to be cognizant of not only what he or she is trying to convey to an intended audience, but how it is being conveyed as well. In the post-documentation phase when unpacking the recording, editing to clean-up dead air time or vocalized pauses (e.g., *uhhs*) needs to take place, as well as the application of two higher-level thinking skills-based purpose and intended message:

- Removing (cutting away) unimportant or unrelated-to-purpose clips
- Remixing based on finding common threads or related sections

Putting these skills into action coupled with the content-learning focus to create podcasts and other audio formats (e.g., public service announcements, audio storytelling) provide documenting opportunities that learners often say are some of their favorites.

For example, second graders at a Jewish Day School were learning the historical and religious context of Purim, which is told in the book of Esther. Their Jewish Studies teacher, Rivka, and Silvia as her documenting coach, collaborated to plan a documenting opportunity for her class that included three learning focuses: writing a script that conveys an event-sequence; collaborating on a project; and working on their speaking fluency in the target language, Hebrew. To amplify sharing, they planned on having the students record their informational podcast, as well as share them with their parents via the second-grade class blog.

Given the students had experience with podcasting the previous year as they produced *Flat Stanley* and *Magic Tree House* podcasts as first graders, the learning curve for editing and remixing the audio clips would not be great, except for a new student who the teacher and Silvia knew would quickly catch on with the help and support of her peers.

The pre-documentation phase included Rivka working with her class to figure out how to break apart the Purim story into key-event sections. She worked with each student to write his or her designated section of the story in Hebrew to create a collective script. The class then collaboratively made certain the entire sequence of events in Esther's story was conveyed accurately and in order and by practice-reading their orated sentences. Lastly, they discussed and made decisions regarding the sound of their voices and sound effects needed to enhance their oration and engage a listening audience.

The during-documentation phase involved the students recording their sections in GarageBand. Silvia facilitated this process. While she made certain that each student's sentence was recorded clearly, she purposefully had each student come to the microphone and record his or her sentence out of the sequential order of the story in preparation for the students to apply one of the learning focuses during post-production. The students loved listening to their sentence recordings over and over again. Some of them asked if they could re-record their sentences as they were trying to perfect their Hebrew articulation.

In the post-documentation phase, it was time for the students to edit the podcast file and re-mix each student's sentence clip so that the collective clips were in the correct sequence of the Purim narrative. To make certain all students could be engaged in the decision-making process simultaneously, the teacher connected the computer to the classroom's interactive whiteboard.

The students took turns coming up to the whiteboard and using their fingertips to highlight an audio snippet and drag and drop it into the recording track (see Image 9.1).

Image 9.1

QR Code 9.1

Scan this QR code to listen to the class's *Purim* podcast episode.

http://langwitches.me/purim

They also took turns performing the editing process. They needed to listen, pause, decide where to position or reposition a clip, and listen once again to the entire track, assembling a giant audio puzzle. Eventually, they decided their Purim story was in the correct sequence.

Next, it was time to intersperse sound effects throughout the recording to add to the meaning and support the story being told. This part especially engaged students and heightened their enthusiasm to continue listening and sharing their story with their parents and families at home (scan QR Code 9.1).

While coaching Rivka and modeling the documenting phases and learningflow routine for her, Silvia created a collaborative Google Doc that served as a brainstorming tool, as well as a constant reminder of the opportunity's learning focuses and goal for the podcasting project. Capturing the audio was inherent, as the podcast itself produced an audio recording with the student voices. The photographed images that were captured while students were working on the various stages of creating the audio recording served as visual evidence of what was being learned and how it authentically applied in the moment versus afterward.

Silvia was also mindful of her plans to share this class's documenting opportunity beyond this classroom. Silvia's blog was the platform she used to convey the artifacts of the class as primary learners, as well as her own professional learning as a secondary learner, and as amplification inspiration for her blog readers to try the same or similar documenting opportunity with their classes. Silvia believes that evidence FOR and AS learning artifacts are the best motivating change agent for students and educators, which she continually advocates by curating, sharing, and amplifying her experiences with educators from around the world in-person at workshops and conferences, as well as digitally through her blog and professional learning network (PLN).

Table 9.1 provides several more activities that may spark ideas for audio-documentation opportunities.

A few audio-recording tools include GarageBand, AudioMemo, and Voice Memos.

Video Documentation

Video recording and sharing using varying degrees of amplification are a daily occurrence. The amount of videos uploaded and viewed on social media platforms each day is astounding. And the numbers are only increasing. Therefore, it should not be a surprise that using video is an important aspect for capturing and conveying documenting FOR and AS learning.

There are several reasons why using video to capture learning and share reflections is beneficial:

- Viewers feel present when physically unable to be where the learning is taking place.
- Viewers can play back moments in time, as many times as desired.
- Changes over time can be seen due to stringing together related videos or segments.
- Learners can annotext what is taking place for the purposes of reflection, commentary, and feedback.

One documentation bonus is that video provides the capability for capturing slow-motion and time-lapse video to convey a different perspective than the human eye is capable of capturing.

Table 9.1 Audio Documentation Activities

In the News Podcast	**Soundhearing Tour Podcast**	**Interview Podcast**
Student focused on history (or any discipline) become two sets of radio-news announcers and report on a particular event. In preparation for creating the podcasts, they need to research and apply what they learn when researching the question: *How would two radio stations from different regions or countries report the same news?*	Create an auditory-only field trip by having each learner or team of learners begin by collecting location sounds and voices (e.g., zoo, museum, courtroom) that will be edited and remixed to create a podcast. *Note: Can be done in professional-learning environments as well (e.g., conference session, after-school training).*	Create a collaborative podcast by strategically sharing the responsibility for interviewing a group of people who have varying perspectives, points of view, and information regarding a specific topic, theme, problem, or issue that has a local or global focus.
Mixed-Up Timelines	**Professional Podcast**	**Two-Sentence Reflections**
Have world language or English-as-second-language learners break up a story or informational narrative into small or medium-sized passages depending on their language-level capabilities. Each learner records one (or more) of the passages as audio clips. Mix up the timeline clips by renaming them so the sequence is not apparent when reading the file names. Have them work collaboratively to listen to the audio passages and put the clips in the correct timeline sequence. *Note: To increase the complexity, include a few outlier audio clips that the learners will eventually realize are not part of the story or narrative.*	Connect with up to four colleagues and/or field experts *(five people total counting you, who will be the podcast host or moderator)* who are willing to meet in an online discussion forum for a half-hour to an hour. The focus can be on a particular topic or passion pursuit. Record the conversation to later turn it into a podcast and amplify via social media. Be certain you are thinking about the target audience as you all share so that you can frame the discussion at the onset by first stating the focus, as well as the participants' names. When you begin, be certain to give each participant time to share the context for why he or she is joining in the conversation and sharing the thought or insight.	Record two sentences each month for the school year (and summer, if appropriate) based on a professional learning focus. The short commentary is based on answering each question per sentence: 1. *What is most important this month about what I am learning or realizing about my curriculum design or instructional practice?* 2. *What am I wondering about?* Combine the audio clips in sequence at the conclusion of the school year. Add an introduction to set the purpose of the audio reflection series, as well as a one-minute final audio reflection focused on these two questions: 1. *What do I notice about my thoughts over time?* 2. *What patterns or trends do I hear being conveyed?*

A common mistake when first beginning to capture learning evidence using video is trying to record everything, or letting the camera keep recording for long periods of time. As previously mentioned, learners as documenters do not want to have to wade through countless hours of raw collected footage to find a learning moment nugget. With experience, documenters develop a feel for what type of video needs to be captured, as well as how long a scene needs to be recorded in order to best capture the desired learning evidence. To minimize frustrations, be very clear on what and how to look for learning before documenters start recording the learning in action.

The following section provides several examples of video activities.

Video Scavenger Hunt. When participating in a traditional scavenger hunt, the goal is to find discrete items. The same is true for a video scavenger hunt.

On a professional level, it is not uncommon for teachers and administrators to participate in classroom observations or walkthroughs. Instead of entering with a textual-recording source, enter with a camera in hand. Based on predetermined one or two discrete focuses, purposefully hunt for and capture video clips that express the desired learning moment (or possibly lack thereof) so the educator being observed can be included in the unpacking and reflection process in the post-documentation phase. Do not collect tons of footage. Only record what is necessary to adequately capture the pre-determined focuses. During the post-observation meeting, the footage can be unpacked by both the observer and the observee. If desired, the video clips can then be annotexted and included in the teacher's professional digital portfolio.

For a collaborative professional learning scavenger hunt, have a documenting team pre-select the scavenger-hunt skill or behavior "items" that need to be collected based on a specific discipline's learning specifics, or soft-skill habits or temperaments (e.g., a student providing two reasons for evidence related to a claim; student displaying self-control), which will be shared at the next professional-meeting time.

The rules are simple:

- No video clips can be no longer than 30 seconds.
- All of the pre-selected skill or behavior items must be captured.

Once a participant has collected all of the required items, he or she imports the video clips into a preferred video-editing tool (e.g., iMovie, Movie Maker, Apple Clips, Adobe Spark Video) and places them in order of the agreed-upon scavenger-hunt item list. He or she then annotexts the clips using reflective subtitles and text boxes, or adds reflective audio commentary to create a video documentation artifact.

When the team reconvenes, each person plays his or her video on a screen or whiteboard while the rest of the team watches and takes mental or written notes. After all the videos have been viewed, the group collaboratively discusses the videos' highlights, reflects on the documenting opportunity in general, and if appropriate, plans for the next professional-learning scavenger hunt.

As with adult learners, a video scavenger hunt can heighten students' awareness for particular topics, learning objectives, or making personal connections. For example, two fifth-grade classrooms traditionally end the school year by visiting a local science and history museum near their school. Mrs. Heavener and the other fifth-grade teacher wanted their classes to experience this year's field trip through the lens of a collaborative documenting opportunity. While they worked with their respective class regarding the documentation phases and learningflow routine, the culminating experience would be to share their scavenger hunt–based videos to the other class, as well as guest docents from the museum.

Mrs. Heavener began by providing context for her students. She shared, "You have learned so much this year, both in science and history. Given we will be going to a museum focused on these two subjects soon, you need to decide what you would like to focus on while there and participate in a video scavenger hunt for information." Her class was excited, but unclear about what she meant by a video scavenger hunt in this context. She asked them to be patient, and continued, "First, as a class you need to come to a consensus on what you will be researching and conveying information about based on the topics we focused on in science or history this past school year." After brainstorming topics, she had them facilitate their own decision-making process (with a little bit of coaching, when needed) to narrow down their topics, and then refine the selected topic to be more specific and actionable. The class's final selection was: *healthy eating equals healthy minds and bodies.*

She then facilitated a brainstorming session on possible video-based collecting and capturing scavenger-hunt item options while at the museum that will collectively convey to an audience of peers and guests how the museum provides information concerning their selected science-health idea. By the conclusion of the brainstorming process, Mrs. Heavener's class had five video requirements that made up their scavenger-hunt item list:

- A video that explains what nutrition means and its importance for staying healthy
- A video interview with a museum curator about one of the exhibits that supports having healthy minds or bodies
- A video that explains important facts to persuade viewers to eat and drink healthy foods
- A sightseeing tour through one of the interactive exhibits with an explanation that aids viewers in understanding why it is important to eat healthy every day
- A 30-second Public Service Announcement to encourage viewers to stay healthy now, so it will help them stay healthy as they grow older

Lastly, each student selected which one of the five scavenger-hunt items he or she wanted to work on as a mini-team to capture the needed information while at the museum. The class ended up being in groups of either four or five per item.

Mrs. Heavener then modeled and coached her students through the *Look for Learning* step in the pre-documentation phase before going on their field trip. Each team researched the museum's website to get a feeling for the exhibits that would best aid them in their video scavenger-hunt item during their visit. She met with each team and discussed their roles and overall goals for each team's item. For example, she reviewed the attributes of good interview questions for the museum-curator interview item. For all the teams, she provided three questions and a visible thinking routine to consider when filming at the museum to support their team's learning evidence and address the scavenger-hunt item requirements:

- What do I notice?
- Why do I think that?
- How do I know?
- Visible Thinking Routine: *I see, I think, I wonder*

She reminded them to

- Bring a recording device: either your own smartphone, or check out a tablet from the school library.
- Do not take any video clips longer than 30 seconds.

- Be aware of the lighting and noise level in the area you are choosing to record.
- Make connections by asking yourselves questions, such as: *What did I encounter that I already knew something about? What have I learned that is brand new? How does this help me understand what we need to express to our audience in our video?*
- Be ready to share with your audience: *What surprised you? What was most interesting to you? Will this information keep your video viewers interested too?*
- Film your team responding to the following reflective statements at the conclusion of our time at the museum: *I used to think . . . Now I think . . .*

Mrs. Heavener and her colleague were impressed with the excitement, teamwork, and tenacity their students displayed while at the museum. The next day during the post-documentation phase, Mrs. Heavener's student teams began to unpack, edit, and annotext their captured video clips to create their video artifacts that addressed their team's item focus. Two teams forgot to record themselves responding to the final reflective statements at the museum, so she gave each team the choice of using the voice-over function in their movie-tool's editing program, or annotexting their reflections by adding text frames to their movie.

As a class, the students watched each team's draft movie and collectively used a video-media rubric to determine if each team met or exceeded their scavenger-hunt item requirements. If a team did not reach the desired level concerning a specific rubric specification, the class and Mrs. Heavener provided thoughtful feedback to aid them in improving the quality of their video.

Finally, the day came for the two classes to present their videos to each other and the museum guests. The other class of fifth graders had selected a history focus, which made it a perfect match for the museum's twofold purpose. After presenting their videos, the students asked for improvement feedback concerning their videos' messages and appreciated what the docents suggested. One of the docents mentioned that she was going to speak to the curators of both wings (history and science) and see if they could use the videos at the museum in some capacity, with their parents' or guardians' permission. This was an unexpected amplification degree that the fifth graders were thrilled to hear!

Notecard Confession Video. Notecard confession videos are a technique for telling a short narrative that elicits emotions and encourages continued reflection from viewers. In essence, the confession is a message the creator wants to share but has never had the confidence to do so before publicly.

QR Code 9.2

Scan this QR code to experience an index-card narrative *Hi my name is Brittany.*

http://langwitches.me/index-cards

If you viewed Brittany's confession video (scan QR Code 9.2), you can see that she tapped deeply into her personal emotions concerning her mother's debilitating disease and how it is affecting her life. Through her simple, yet powerful, statements she clearly provided evidence of her metacognition, reflection, and understanding. One important note: If you are a teacher, you noticed Brittany's misspellings and grammar errors. This is one of those documenting experiences where that does not matter! It is about connecting with oneself and connecting with viewers, which Brittany does by asking foreshadowing questions: *Do you have a mom? Does she know your middle name? or your birthday? Can she spell your NAME? Can she read?*

In the pre-documentation phase, the confession-creator (learner-documenter) begins by reflecting introspectively on the message he, she, or they want to convey by developing a string of short phrases that become sentences. Each sentence segment is written on an index card using a thick, dark marker. The cards are stacked so they cumulatively create the completed sentences. During this time, the background music is also determined. The learner needs to make certain there is no copyright infringement by using the audio selection.

During documentation, the learner/character sits in front of a camera and recording begins. While the original intent of the confession-video concept is for the confessor to be the one filming him or herself; for adaption to a classroom setting, the recording could be done by a peer or adult. When the learner/character is revealing the index cards, he or she needs to remember to place the displaying of each card so that the audience has time to take in and reflect on each card, as well as the collective cards.

Therefore, there may need to be a few "takes" before the documenter is satisfied with the flow.

In the post-documentation phase, the raw footage is uploaded to a movie-creation tool, such as Movie Maker. The documenter either simply adds an introduction segment and exit segment (including music attribution) to the favorite takes, or does some editing or remixing of individual clips, plus adding intro and exit segments to create the final video production. The video can then be uploaded to the desired platform and shared with the amplification degree desired.

While using the concept of emotional-based notecard confession videos provides opportunities to convey worthwhile messages and experiment with a powerful communication strategy, adapting the confession concept to specific classroom learning is also worthwhile and engaging. Examples of notecard confession videos that provide evidence of learning could include researching

- An historical character and taking on his or her persona and revealing a confession (including dressing like the character when filming, if possible)
- Statistics related to a local or global problem to convey the magnitude of a particular statistic or statistics as the researcher or by taking on a character that is affected by the static (e.g., a sea turtle who is upset because fellow turtles are being killed due to the ingestion of plastics being thrown into the ocean)
- A cause or issue to be advocated through promoting awareness and encouraging action steps

Bitesize Learning. Gutierrez (2014) quotes Cohen's (director at a creative agency that specializes in social-media strategies and data visualization) definition of *bitesize information*:

> Bite-sized nuggets of content that are easy to consume, sometimes they're images or image based, whose meaning can be grasped quickly, and often create deeper meaning by referencing shared experiences or stories. And essentially, it's faster than reading an explanation of the same information.

Couros (2015b), an educational advocate for innovative change, expanded on Gutierrez's bitesize-learning concept to the video feature available in the Twittersphere, "Knowing that Twitter has recently created an option to share videos up to 30 seconds, I thought about creating a new project to get people to share ideas and things that they are doing, going beyond the 280 characters." Couros provided a hashtag to aid in his project's crowdsourcing and amplification: #EDUin30.

The point of creating bitesize 30-second learning moments is not to create a Hollywood-quality production. Instead, the intent is to capture

QR Code 9.3

Scan this QR code to read Couros's blog post *New Project: #EDUin30.*

http://langwitches.me/couros

thoughtful anecdotes through conversational-style snippets that can be crowdsourced and accessed easily over time.

Think about the positive impacts sharing and amplifying in a global-learning community could have if every educator recorded an #EDUin30 video once a month. He or she could share his or her thoughts about any topic related to becoming an increasingly effective teacher, administrator, or professional learner. And, as Couros recommends, include a few more hashtags that relate to that month's video's topic, which contributes to amplifying one's sharing.

To adapt Couros' #EDUin30 concept for student-learner use, one suggestion is to use the Visible Thinking Routines prompts from ProjectZero.com and have students create 30-second bitesize documentation artifacts that they can unpack and reflect on over time to see if there are patterns or trends to what they are saying or conveying.

In the post-documentation phase, given the 30-second video is not meant to be polished, it simply needs to be uploaded to a classroom, school, local, or global networking community using two of the following hashtags: #LearnIn30, #StudentVoices, #ReflectionTime, as well as a hashtag appropriate to the topic or idea being shared, such as #StopWastingWater, #WrinkleInTime, #NoMorePlastic, #DanceForLife. And do not forget to include #documenting4learning.

If a teacher decides that deeper reflection or a specific learning goal should be focused on in post-production, the video footage can be annotexted by the learners using an appropriate tool, such as iMovie.

Interviews. Video interviews provide viewers with an opportunity to experience someone's unique perspective through his or her voice, tone, facial expressions, and personality. Digitally enhanced communication involving interviewing for personal and educational purposes has expanded in recent years thanks to the immediacy of video cameras in smartphones, tablets, and platforms, such as Skype, FaceTime, and Google Hangout.

When recording an interview conducted via one of these video conferencing platforms, one has to keep in mind that they do not natively support a recording feature to capture the interview taking place as a stand-alone video file. For Google Hangouts, an alternative is using Google Hangout *on Air,* which broadcasts the interview live and publicly; then automatically saves the recording to the person's YouTube account. For Skype and FaceTime, the alternative is recording the interview using a third-party app (tool), or choosing to use a screencasting tool to record the screen and audio while conducting the video conference.

As mentioned previously, when conducting *Mystery Skype Call* interviews, both classes work to narrow down each other's geographic locations. While there is excitement when the locations are eventually determined, the true power of the connecting begins when each class asks two or three data-based questions about the everyday life or culture of their new-found friends and discover similarities and differences among the collective groups interviewed *by adding a degree of amplification by sharing the cumulative data with each new set of friends they encounter.*

For example, Mr. Frederick's third-grade class asked their newest Mystery Skype Call friends in Mrs. Isaac's third-grade class their first data collection question, "What was the main food each person in your class ate for breakfast today?" After conducting their data collection and calculating, Mrs. Isaac's class's interviewer shares, "Fifteen people ate cereal, five people ate pancakes, two people ate grapefruit, and one person ate oatmeal."

Mr. Frederick's class quickly adds the latest data to their data collection chart. In a few moments, Mr. Frederick's class's interviewer shares fill-in-the-blank sentences that the data-collectors had just completed,

With your data, the most common breakfast food is still _cereal_. From _125_ people surveyed, _68_ ate _cereal_ for breakfast on the days we have skyped. No other breakfast food has that high of a number for a subtotal." You could hear the chatter among Mrs. Isaac's students. Soon their interviewer asks, "What about pancakes?"

The data collectors and a few other students in Mt. Fredericks' class quickly scan their data collection and confer with the interviewer who responds,

That is sort of a tricky question because we have a subtotal of 35 pancakes, but also a subtotal of five people who ate crêpes for breakfast. Crêpes are kind of like pancakes, just not exactly like the ones we make here in the United States. We decided that to answer your question, we are counting both foods as pancakes, so out of 125 people surveyed, 40 people ate pancakes on the days we have skyped.

In this Skype-call exchange, the amplification was increased because Mr. Frederick's class not only asked their data-collection questions, but they also _shared their cumulative results_ with each interviewed class: San Diego, California, in the United States; Montreal, Quebec, and Wood Buffalo, Alberta, in Canada; Nassau, Bahamas, which now included a fifth location: Syracuse, New York.

To add a meaningful documenting learning purpose to conducting Mystery Skype calls, the purposeful documentation requires strategically planning the learning focuses and goals involved, which commonly includes communication skills being practiced, as well as the sophistication of geography or mathematical terminology being applied authentically. For example, in Mr. Frederick's class, the dialogue conveyed above was near the beginning of the school year. Later in the year, his students will not be using cloze-reading sentences to convey their cumulative data responses. They will also grow in their independent command of the geography and mathematical language needed during the Skype calls. One of Mr. Frederick's year-long patterns and trends documenting opportunities involves having his students review the series of archived interview calls to unpack their improvement-over-time skills related to oral communication and use of precise academic vocabulary. Each student will share the unpacked evidence of their learning with his or her parents or caregivers during the end-of-the-school-year student-led progress conference time.

Traditional video interviews focused solely on the person or persons being interviewed also offer learners with meaningful opportunities. This is especially true when connected to an authentic purpose, such as adding human-interest stories to a local history organization or museum, or passion-based beliefs and values to a local group or agency website. Likewise, capturing family stories from grandparents, aunts, and uncles; or eye-witness accounts of historical events before they are incapable of sharing or have passed on is invaluable to capturing meaningful information pertaining to the heartbeats of nuclear and extended families or the local community.

Given the rate of exponential change in human lives and behaviors, it is not frivolity, it is a necessity, to capture life today and past memories where learners can meaningfully engage with interviewees. While unpacking the interview documentation, thoughtfully reflecting on what was particularly moving or most important is critical. Create informational and/or emotional video artifacts that can be shared and strategically amplified serve as anchors of time for generations to come both locally and globally.

Video Documentaries. Another opportunity that involves the recording interviews is video documentaries. One of the documenting team members "becomes" the person being interviewed. For example, the interview may involve a university professor who has made a scientific breakthrough; a world-famous athlete sharing insights on a given topic; famous archeologists who have made a new discovery; biographers who researched a current or past famous person; or the concerns of a past or current politician.

Whether set in the past, present, or future, the video documentary could be simple with introduction and exit video clips; objective narration (narrator can be visually seen by viewers or only heard via voice-over); and cut-aways to the interview clips at appropriate times. To create a more complex product, as seen in many television or film documentaries, extend the simple version to include additional strategic multimedia, such as interview clips from others who provide different perspectives and context; photographs; panoramic views of landscapes or cityscapes; close-ups of man-made or natural objects; and background music to aid in conveying the documentary's overall tone or mood. This involves learners needing to capture and unpack multiple forms of media that visibly and audibly convey the learning focuses and goals that will be evident in the individual artifacts, as well as the final synthesized video documentary artifact.

And last, but not humorously least, consider having older learners who understand the concept of parody and its use in various forms of media create a video documentary parody from an historical living museum perspective, similar to one created by *The Onion News Network.* (Note: While some of the videos on this website are appropriate for younger ages, there is a disclaimer on the site that states: *The Onion is not intended for readers under 18 years of age.*) Scan QR code 9.4 to experience a student-friendly blast-from-the-past moment that some readers may remember personally experiencing, given it was not that long ago when *Blockbuster* was *the* place to go to access movies.

Several video/movie-making platforms and tools include: iMovie, Movie Maker, 1 Second Everyday, Vine, Periscope, Instagram, Twitter, YouTube, Vimeo, and Snapchat.

Screencasting. Screencasts record and produce a video of what is transpiring on a digital screen. A screencast's audio can consist of the audio playing on the screen while recording or as a voice-over through the device's microphone.

QR Code 9.4

Scan this QR code to view the humorous parody on historical living museums: *Historic 'Blockbuster' Store Offers Glimpse of How Movies Were Rented in The Past.*

http://langwitches.me/blockbuster

Screencasting is a beneficial form of documenting in the during-documentation phase, but also plays a powerful unpacking role in the post-documentation phase. Whether the screencast is focused on a captured action or an imported screenshot image or photograph, unpacking begins through reflecting and analyzing what is on the screen while recording the screencast. When the learner conveys the thinking behind what is visible via annotexting and/or voice-over, the screencast artifact informs the learner if he or she is moving toward, has met, or exceeds the learning focuses or goals.

For example, Mrs. Yegelwel, a kindergarten teacher, set up several number set-comparison scenarios where the learning focus was on differentiating mathematically among three set comparisons: *fewer*, *more*, and *equal to.* She took photographs of her students working on solving the different scenarios via triad teams. She then sent each team's set of photographs to an iPad and saved the photographs in a classroom Photo Album.

To promotes student choice, each student looked at the captured images and selected the scenario he or she wanted to unpack for audience viewers. Mrs. Yegelwel and a classroom volunteer assisted her students when necessary in using a screencasting tool, Explain Everything, to import the selected image. The student recorded his or her voice explaining what the photograph mathematically represented concerning the two visible sets. While recording, he or she added drawing features (e.g., dots) appropriately to visually support his or her reasoning. Some students were able to pause and draw, which demonstrated media fluency as well, which Mrs. Yegelwel made digital anecdote of on her iPad.

Each student's' project was saved in the Explain Everything app and then sent to Mrs. Yegelwel's email. She then uploaded the screencast videos to the classroom's Vimeo account and embedded the appropriate video in each student's blogfolio. When she published each blog post, she included three categories: *Kindergarten, Math,* and *Oral Language.* By publishing her students' screencast videos to their public blogfolios, she added an amplification degree in two ways:

1. By the act of publishing online posts, Mrs. Yegelwel is able to link her students' work in tweets. By using hashtags, she not only connected to her professional learning network, but also invited anyone in the Twittersphere interested in one or more of the hashtag topics to visit her students' learning.

2. Mrs. Yegelwel will continue to archive video and other types of documentation artifacts in the blogfolios throughout the year using one or more of the same terms to tag and categorize appropriate artifacts to an amplification of learning evidence over time. By strategically using tags and categories, she will be able to locate and retrieve collective evidence that conveys a student's mathematical knowledge and understanding growth. Archiving evidence of learning that extends beyond simply displaying learning allows her students, their families, and herself to gain deeper insights into their cognition and metacognition learning processes by reflecting and analyzing similar-topic artifacts. This is a major reason why blogging documentation is so beneficial to classrooms and professional environments.

Metacognition Mission. Being aware of one's personal thought process and having the ability to articulate those thoughts to oneself and to others is not a natural skill for many. Metacognition involves thinking deeply and introspectively, which takes time to develop as a self-directed learner. Creating metacognitive videos can help learners talk through their thinking, as it aids a learner to hear his or her own thinking while speaking, as well as when unpacking captured documentation.

Laurel Janewicz, the middle-school mathematics teacher featured previously, is passionately piloting metacognitive thinking and reflection in her sixth-grade classes. She starts out by laying a foundation of the purposes and procedures at the onset of the school year, and then coaches her students in metacognitive strategies applied to themselves as mathematicians throughout the academic year. As the year progresses, her students create short videos that become a personalized video series titled *Why, How, and What Next?* that captures each student's metacognitive reflections about various math topics the class focuses on throughout the year.

Using a screencasting tool to produce their videos, each student records himself or herself as voice-over and/or annotexting to explain his or her process, thinking, and reasoning for solving a given mathematical problem or situation, which is the first degree of amplification: sharing with oneself.

A second amplification degree takes place during this unpacking process. The initial screencast gets the mental model out of the learner's head and makes it visible to himself or herself via the voice-over or annotexted video. When the student shares the visible/audible screencast artifact with a peer, the next amplification degree begins: sharing face-to-face. The peer

QR Code 9.5

Scan this QR code to read a metacognitive-focused blog post *Kindergarten using Explain Everything app to explain Math Scenarios.*

http://langwitches.me/math-scissors

partner now annotexts the partner's video with his or her observations, noting where and when a math strategy or strategies are being or not being used, which adds an additional layer of thinking to the original artifact.

Technically, the sharing degree of amplification increases the minute the video was viewed by another person, whether a peer, Laurel, or a mathematician guest who visits the classroom to engage with them and their metacognitive videos. The benefit to having her students sharing face-to-face with a peer who adds observations and feedback is that the evidence of the meeting is preserved within the screencasting artifact. The peer's shared thoughts would be lost if the two students only had an oral discussion about how the one student solved the math problem or situation.

To round out the school year, Laurel uses five questions as reflective prompts that have evolved over time by getting feedback from her students on their effectiveness in further aiding them in developing their metacognitive thinking. (Note: While Laurel uses these prompts toward the end of her year-long documenting opportunity, the questions could be used periodically throughout the school year.)

What does metacognition, *thinking about your thinking*, mean to you and how has it helped you in math?
To me, metacognition means . . . And it helps me in math . . .

What does your *inner voice* say to you, or what questions does it ask you, as you solve a particular problem or situation?
My inner voice is saying . . .

How has reflecting on your thinking *while solving a problem or situation* helped your mathematical thinking?
Reflecting on my thinking and listening to my inner voice while solving . . .

What are you learning about yourself as a mathematician from this ongoing project?
I am learning that . . .

What are you realizing about yourself as a mathematician based on the entire year's reflection project?
This project has made me realize that I . . .

Laurel ends the school year with her students celebrating their cumulative visible and audible evidence-of-learning growth over time as mathematicians and introspective thinkers.

Tutorial Designers. November (2012) mentions four types of jobs students need to be responsible for on what he calls the *digital learning farm,* "*Tutorial Designers, Students Scribes, Student Researchers,* and *Global Communicators and Collaborators.*" These jobs help students participate and contribute to the whole, much like children did centuries ago on a family farm. The first job, *Tutorial Designers,* is a perfect fit for capturing evidence of learning through video documentation.

Creating screencasting tutorials provides authentic purpose for the designer by having to break down the steps of a procedure or task into small learning pieces or steps for the end user. The designer needs to think deeply about the cognitive capabilities of the viewing learner, including:

- At what points should I divide the steps or process into manageable information segments?
- How should I explain the information within each divided step?
- What visuals will support the explanation of each step? What will be necessary to point out?
- How can I make sure I am aware of not assuming pre-existing knowledge of the learner?
- How can I avoid falling into the trap of assuming a detail might be too obvious to mention?
- Should I explain what is needed the same way throughout the entire tutorial or change it as needed to keep the learner engaged, address different learning style preferences, or help make what is being explained easier to comprehend?
- Will I be using voice-over for the entire tutorial, or will I be including annotexted information as well?

QR Code 9.6

Scan this QR code to read a metacognitive-focused blog post *Visible Thinking in Math – Part 2.*

http://langwitches.me/math2

Most important to all tutorial designers is constantly thinking about the target audience and not skipping important pieces of information or steps in the explanation process. While some of the above questions may appear sophisticated, even young learners think about similar wonderments when designing tutorials, even if on a simplistic level.

While this section is dedicated to screencasting tutorials, take a moment to watch *The Lily Show—Holiday Craft Edition* snowflake-making tutorial (scan QR code 9.7). Nine-year-old Lily (with assistance from her younger sister, Charlie) is the tutor appearing on the screen. She moves through the step-by-step procedure to create paper snowflakes, and she includes coaching points to support and encourage her audience to be successful in making their snowflakes.

Mrs. Villard is a middle-school computer teacher in a K–12 school. She noticed that more and more staff, teachers, and students were coming to her to request assistance in using popular programs, apps, and websites. She realized that these problems offered a perfect, and authentic, screencast tutorial opportunity for her students. Her learning focuses included her students' abilities to

- Articulate the features and functions involved in the selected program, app, or website
- Convey a step-by-step procedure or process concisely
- Explain orally or in writing using accurate tool or platform-specific vocabulary
- Constantly keep the audience viewer in mind when speaking (voice-over) and pointing out various locations on the screen

QR Code 9.7

Scan this QR code to view *The Lily Show – Holiday Craft Edition* **tutorial.**

http://langwitches.me/lily-show

Her learning goal was for her students to use foresight and apply empathic understanding regarding the common problems or frustrations that a viewer may be encountering and wants to resolve by viewing the tutorial video. The finalized screencast tutorials will serve as her students' artifacts. She would have them reflect and analyze them to see if viewer empathy is present explicitly or inferred based on voice-over and image directions.

QR Code 9.8

Scan this QR code to view the *Tutorial Design Checklist*.

http://langwitches.me/tutorial-designer-checklist

Her students were enthusiastic about getting started. Before they began planning and creating their screencasts, they surveyed their fellow students from first grade to twelfth grade, all of the K–12 teachers, and the school staff using a Google Form they had collaboratively developed. After the collected survey data were compiled, the results showed a wide variety of tutorial needs, including basic tasks using word-processing tools to in-depth help with creating, navigating, or commenting on classroom blogs.

One of the major challenges that became quickly apparent was the need for considering age-level appropriateness for the tutorial's topic. In other words, designing a tutorial for a second grader on how to create a shareable DropBox folder would sound and look quite different than one designed for an eighth grader. Each student determined what specific task he or she wanted to focus on for creating a tutorial, including the age-range of the tutorial viewer, which sometimes affected a student's tutorial choice (e.g., kindergartners would not be independently creating Google Sheets).

Mrs. Villard provided each tutorial-designer with a reminder sheet including

- Answering pre-planning reflective questions, similar to those mentioned on page 161.
- Using age-appropriate and platform-specific vocabulary when conducting voice-overs
- Keeping track of tasks included on a screencasting tutorial design checklist (scan QR code 9.8)

As part of the pre-documentation phase, her students were responsible for viewing several screencast tutorials available on YouTube to reflect on the effective, or not so effective, design methods and techniques they observed. She included these reflective tutorial-observation questions on their reminder sheet:

- What type(s) of tutorial design did I learn from the best? Why?
- Which tutorial(s) did I find the most engaging? Why?
- What specific actions (e.g., voice-over, directional arrows, framing) enhanced your watching of a favorite tutorial? Why?
- What was it about the tutorial(s) that caused you to lose interest and discontinue watching? Why?
- When specific actions distracted you while watching the tutorial? Why?

She met with any students who were not familiar with creating screencasts or screencasting terminology or techniques, such as using voice-over, text boxes or frames, directional arrows, opacity factor, and cursor or mouse visibility used to draw attention to a specific spot or area on the screen. She also provided them with step-by-step visuals and a screencast how-to tutorial to watch while practice-using the screencasting tool. (For example, Image 9.2 is a screenshot of the screen as someone is annotating a video recorded in ScreenFlow. The information arrows indicate the various features terminology found throughout the editing screen.)

Image 9.2

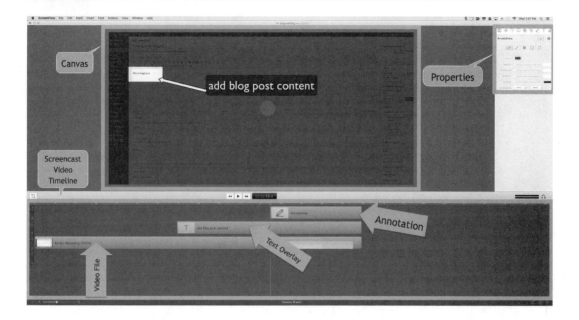

Students used peer-review and peer-feedback cycles through the three documentation phases, which included the storyboarding, recording, revising, and editing their screencast tutorials. Mrs. Villard noticed that their cognitive and metacognitive processes played critical roles in being tutorial designers. When they were unpacking and reflecting on their drafted and finalized tutorials, the insights they shared regarding their learning were evident as she listened in on their review-feedback discussions.

Once the tutorials were finalized, the students saved and uploaded them to the cloud via YouTube. The students then emailed the survey participants to let them know that their requested tutorials were now available for viewing. They also digitally designed posters and flyers with QR codes announcing their online-tutorial video bank, which they printed out and hung in the school hallways, as well as placed in the faculty lounge and the school's front office.

While Mrs. Villard did not do so for this documenting opportunity, she made a note in her professional learning journal that the next time she has students creating screencasts or other types of tutorials, she would ask them to save their first-attempt tutorial and make a copy to make any revision or edit changes based on that review-feedback cycle. She would also ask them to continue creating new iterations of the tutorial based on review-feedback until it is finalized. By doing so, she and her students will have growth-over-time evidence of learning artifacts that visibly and audibly convey nuances in how they grew as tutorial designers and gaining understanding of what constitutes quality, effective screencasting tutorial design.

Several screencasting platforms and tools include: ScreenFlow, Screen-cast-o-matic, Explain Everything, Jing, CamStudio, and Quicktime.

QR Code 9.9

Scan this QR code to experience student-created screencasting tutorials.

http://langwitches.me/tutorials

It's Time to Take Action!

Chapter 9 Action Step

Now that you have read through a wide variety of audio and video documentation explanations and narratives since the first page of this chapter, it is time for you to take action and create an audio or video artifact using one of the highlighted features.

Whichever one you select, be certain that what you create reflects a

- Personal learning focus with your target audience being your family or friends (e.g., hobby, favorite book or movie highlights, family event, holiday tradition)
- Professional learning focus with your target audience being colleagues, administrators, or professors
- Classroom learning focus where you and your students are co-learners with your target audience to be determined as a collaborative team.

Given there is a variety of video, movie-making, and screencasting platforms and tools to choose from, rather than stay in your tool-and-platform comfort zone, find someone (possibly even a student) or YouTube video that can help you learn a new platform or tool that is a perfect fit for your action step's focus and goal.

Be aware of your learning curve when using the new platform or tool to create your artifact:

- What skills are you developing or expanding as a documenter-learner while using the selected platform or tool?

Share your reflections and audience reactions to your audio or video recording digitally. Don't forget to link, attach, or embed your audio- or video-based artifact to your selected social media platform.

Remember to use the #documenting4learning hashtag on Twitter, Facebook, or Instagram; or by mentioning @documenting4learning on Facebook and Instagram, and @doc4learning on Twitter.

BLOGGING PLATFORMS AND TOOLS

Blogging Documentation

Clark (2007) observes, "Don't focus on having a great blog. Focus on producing a blog that's great for your readers." What he conveys is that people want to read a blogger's latest posts because of the interest and mental engagement the posts generate. Interests could be based on thought-provoking points, helpful hints, or information presented from unique or unusual perspectives that create a collective narrative shared over time.

A blogging platform, such as WordPress, allows a blogger, as a primary or secondary learner, to create documentation in a variety of formats. This leads to blogging that serves as a hub for multimedia artifacts and a wide range of evidence of learning. Blogs allow learners to

- tag and categorize posts based on content;
- automatically archive the documentation, due to the platform saving the posts in reverse chronological order;

- embed textual, visual, audio, and video artifacts to aid in expressing thoughts or sharing narratives;
- hyperlink to previous posts, as well as resources and references on the Internet; and
- encourage commenting as a form of reflection and conversation with an audience.

A blog provides a documenter-learner with a platform hub to voice his or her thoughts, ideas, and information with a global audience that promotes sharing and amplify in visible, purposeful, and meaningful ways.

The following section provides examples of blogging documentation activities.

Blogging Challenge. There are many blogging challenges available online for educators and students to participate in individually or collaboratively. These challenges range from a task that teaches the blogger the logistics of blogging to connecting bloggers with like interests to share and discuss topics to write about in future posts. Participating in a challenge gives learners documenting opportunities that provide visible patterns, trends, and growth over time.

As a professional learning or student documenter-blogger, participating in a formal blogging challenge project from *Edublogs Teacher Challenges* may prove beneficial, especially if new to this platform. The Edublogs website provides four challenge categories to choose from:

- Blogging with Students (for Educators)
- Blogging Boot Camp (for Students)
- Personal (or Professional) Blogging (for Educators)
- Building your PLN (which includes some blogging aspects)

For educators and students who already have a comfort level with blogging, there have been numerous examples throughout this book that have incorporated the use of blog posts as an avenue for sharing and amplifying evidence of learning artifacts. Beyond thinking about how to use blog posts strategically in future documenting opportunities, designing or participating in more advanced challenges can be an excellent way to crowdsource learning moments and document a variety of learning focuses and goals.

Conduct a search for *blogging challenge*, and myriad hits will appear. Narrowing down the search by adding a descriptor may prove beneficial (e.g., *blogging challenge for elementary students*). Remember that one of the key purposes for participating in blogging challenges is to capture evidence of one's thinking at that particular time. It is not about being perfect in conveying thoughts, grammar, or punctuation; or being an expert in a topic or concept. It is about being transparent in what someone is learning or discovering and how that is affecting him or her at that moment.

For blogging inspiration, Image 9.3 contains a *Documentation & Blogging Challenge* that blends some of the documentation activities and examples shared in this book with classic blogging topics. While growth over time is limited in this challenge versus a year's worth of posts to reflect on or analyze based on a consistent topic or theme, it is often surprising to discover nuances in one's posting practices that become visible in just a short period of time. For a full explanation of each of the 18 challenges, scan QR code 9.11 or go directly to www.documenting4learning.com.

QR Code 9.10

Scan this QR code to read a how-to guide for *Edublogs Teacher Challenges.*

http://langwitches.me/teacherchallenge

QR Code 9.11

Scan this QR code to go to the Documenting4Learning website and access the *Documentation & Blogging Challenge* details.

http://langwitches.me/blogging-challenge

Image 9.3

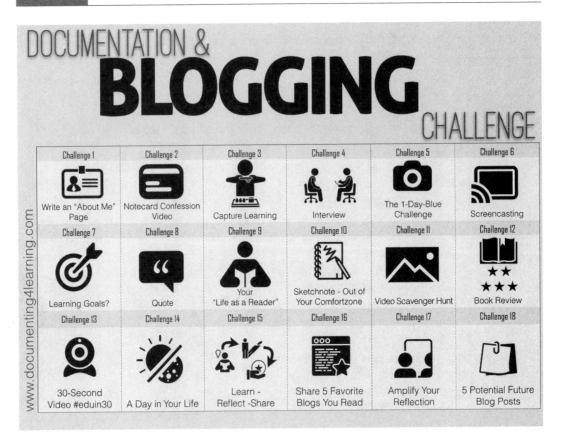

Team Blogging. Blogging can be lonely and frustrating, especially in the beginning when it is just the learner-blogger's thoughts while sitting at his or her keyboard. Although the blogger is writing and publishing with an audience in mind, first-time visitors and commenters might take a while to find their way to a newbie's blog. Therefore, participating in team blogging may be an answer.

This concept creates a formal partnership with at least one other learner-blogger or fellow blogging classroom. The alliance between or among the bloggers consists of a commitment to alternatively read and comment on one another's blog posts. An example of buddy learner-blogging could be between two biology teachers, one living in the United States and the other living in Argentina, who commit for one school year to read each other's blog posts on a consistent basis and provide each another thoughts and feedback using the blog's comment feature.

A student example of learner-blogging can involve three classrooms. A benefit to a team blogging challenge is that it can be conducted asynchronously. For the example explained here, the classrooms are located in the United States, Switzerland, and Thailand. Their team blogging challenge will last three weeks (see Image 9.4):

- **First week**: The United States classroom is responsible for writing blog posts on their classroom blog, while the Switzerland and Thailand classrooms take on the role of readers and commenters.

- **Second week**: The Switzerland classroom is responsible for writing blog posts on their classroom blog, while the Thailand and United States classrooms take on the role of readers and commenters.
- **Third week**: The Thailand classroom is responsible for writing blog posts on their classroom blog, while the United States and Switzerland classrooms take on the role of readers and commenters.

The number of team blogging classrooms or participants can be increased, but if there are too many the challenge loses its intimacy, which a smaller number of participants provide. Whether buddy or team blogging, thinking of a theme, concept, or topic to use throughout the blogging challenge's series of exchanges helps determine the desired evidence of learning in the blog posts. Learning focuses and goals are endless. They can be related to curriculum content, global awareness connections, digital citizenship, metacognition, or communication skills to name a few. Regardless of what is selected, team blogging provides authentic and meaningful documenting opportunities for all those involved.

Hyperlinked Writing

Hyperlinked writing is an often overlooked and misunderstood genre, which is detrimental to digital-age learners and society as a whole. It is sometimes referred to as *multilayered writing, non-linear writing,* or *amplified writing* because the original layer of text has

Image 9.4

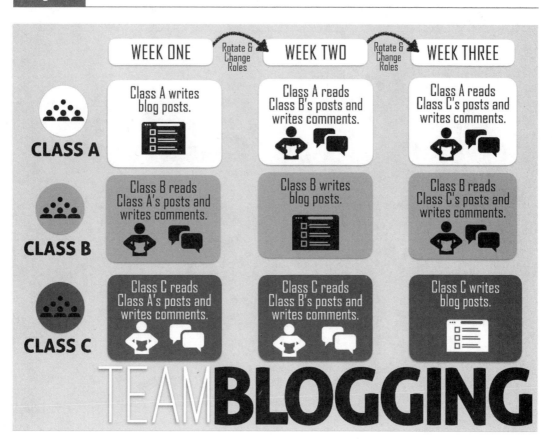

purposefully been extended—linked—with text, image, or video to additional resources, making the author's thinking about the content's relationships and connections visible.

Unfortunately, educational digital writing (e.g., blogs, websites, wikis, social media platforms, shared documents) oftentimes merely substitutes analog writing for digital versions, which is the lowest level of the SAMR taxonomy. While a simple transfer from analog to digital is possible, the majority of current learning does not require learners to *think hyperlinked* when writing. This is unfortunately true for many professional writers as well who have their books or materials on digital devices. Who has not clicked on a challenging word or phrase in an article or book in hopes of being taken to its definition or further explanation, *and it does not happen.*

Hunt (2011) reflected on his concern from a digital writer's perspective when students and teachers merely use substitution of traditional writing on a digital tool or platform:

> [What is] the kind of writing that's being asked of students in these spaces? Well, it's interesting—I can break it down into three types—daily summaries, written collectively by elementary school classes; reflective essays about various topics; and responses to teacher questions. Lots of it is writing that doesn't require a blog. And it's writing that involves very, very, very little source material. Very few quotes. Very few links. And the links, when they're present, are not embedded in the text. They lie naked and open in the text. And that seems problematic to me.

It is therefore imperative that contemporary learners have an awareness and ability to apply hyperlinked-writing characteristics to their digital writing artifacts, including reaching the higher levels of the Hyperlinked Writing Taxonomy (see Image 9.5).

Image 9.5

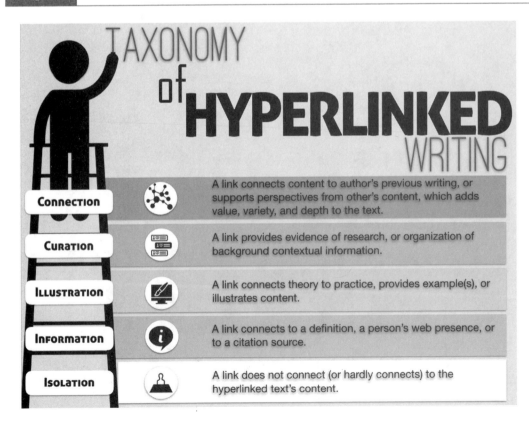

To aid in understanding the nuance among the five hyperlinked-writing levels, here is a sentence that can be used to convey each level's hyperlinked functionality from *greatest impact to least impact.*

Documenting learning supports critical thinking and sharing with others.

Connection: <u>**Documenting learning**</u> supports critical thinking and sharing with others.

- The boldfaced and underlined phrase *documenting learning* links to a previous blog post the writer published. The link provides evidence of the blogger's learning over time, as well as a different lens and an additional layer of content, given her understanding and perspective was most likely different at that time.

Curation: Documenting learning <u>**supports critical thinking**</u> and sharing with others.

- The boldfaced and underlined phrase *supports critical thinking* links to a non-subscription professional journal article that curates current research on how critical thinking supports learning.

Illustration: Documenting learning supports critical thinking and <u>**sharing with others**</u>.

- The boldfaced and underlined phrase *sharing with others* links to a blog post that illustrates a real-world example of how sharing amplified the blogger's learning.

Information: Documenting learning supports <u>**critical thinking**</u> and sharing with others.

- The boldfaced and underlined term *critical thinking* links to a website that defines the term.

Isolation: Documenting learning <u>**supports**</u> critical thinking and sharing with others.

- The boldfaced and underlined word *supports* links to an online fundraising announcement, which has nothing to do with the sentence or overall content.

Creating content using digital writing tools and platforms requires writers to reflect on their digital reading experiences based on the importance of hyperlinking as conveyed in the Hyperlinked Writing Taxonomy.

To do so accurately enables documenter-learners to be cognizant of the necessary choice-making in ensuring they are effective hyperlinking writers. Fryer (2008) shares, "Hyperlinked writing is the most powerful form of writing, and provides one of the most important aspects of complexity in writing for a global audience. There is great power as well as responsibility when you link to the ideas of another."

As learners create digital writing artifacts, it is important to require them to embed relevant links to individual words or phrases to extend readers' experience. Doing so adds a depth to the digital writing that aids readers in making stronger connections with the writer's message, and not just satisfying the teacher or completing a task.

Hyperlinked writing goes beyond simply adding clickable words to otherwise static, one-dimensional text. Critical thinking and strategizing are necessary to be functioning at a *higher-order hyperlinking* ability. A digital writer must be able to

- Emphasize and purposefully point readers to a virtual resource or website to connect them to a specific idea or concept that supports the writing content and context
- Provide a framework and content-background context based on target audience's needs and/or expertise
- Ensure credibility of being a quality researcher by allowing readers to verify his or her claims, opinions, or shared information by accessing and analyzing hyperlinked sources

- Incorporate specific resources and citations as a form of filtering and refining relevant content for the readers
- Use hyperlinks effectively as a medium to convey her or his personal train of thought
- Create a larger meaning making picture for readers that may have otherwise been disconnected content or context

Rosen (2008) explains the critical connection linking causes among hyperlinked writing, one's thinking, and one of the key reasons the Internet was developed:

The link, which is the idea that you're interested in this, but did you know about that. Or here's what I'm saying, but you should see what they're saying. Or you're here, but you know there is also this over here, is actually building out the potential of the web to link people, which is what Timothy Berners-Lee [inventor of the World Wide Web] put into it in the first place. So, when we link, we are expressing the ethic of the web, which is to connect people and knowledge. And the reason you link doesn't have anything to do with copywriting and property, it has to do it that's how we make the web into a web of connections, and that's how we connect knowledge to people.

Hyperlinked writing is a complex genre that all readers and writers need to realize is part of the *now* literacies. If someone cannot see how hyperlinked writing can be considered a genre, it is important to think outside the traditional box of when paper-pen and typewriter writing was the norm. While learners need to be introduced to and sharpen their skills in writing established genres, including argument, persuasion, informational, and narrative, the hyperlinked writing genre adds a new critical-thinking depth and dimension to writing and reading any established genre in a digital form. Basic literacy, as mentioned in Chapter 2, is the ability to read and write many text types. In today's world, the amount of text read digitally via smartphones, tablets, and eReaders outweighs what is read in analog form (e.g., paper books, newspapers, magazines), especially when not in school.

The thought processes and actions involved in quality hyperlinked writing to ensure quality digital reading experiences are a natural fit for blog writing, as well as other content-creation writing (e.g., website page, wiki page), which students and educators are involved in creating with increasing frequency.

Higher-level thinking takes place when writers are strategically reflecting on potential web-based sources to meaningfully connect to their selected hyperlinked words and phrases in their digital text. It is important to note that this contemporary writing genre does not come naturally for most learners, and will not happen consistently as a ubiquitous behavior after just a lesson or two, or a few hyperlinked writing attempts.

During a pre-writing time, a hyperlinking writer needs to consider what and how to convey his or her intended message using higher hyperlinked taxonomy levels. The writer needs to consider *what to link* and *when best to link it* to convey the desired connection, curation, illustration, or information source. Here are examples of potential *hypertext* and hyperlinks:

- *Person's name* > URL of hub (e.g., website, blog, Twitter, Facebook profile)
- *Brand name* > URL of company's website
- *Term* > URL of definition
- *Quote* > URL of original source

- *Word or phrase* > URL of content context/background
- *Word or phrase* > URL of someone else's perspective
- *Conversation* > URL of Twitter hashtag
- *Example* > URL of explanation, demonstration, or action
- *Theory* > URL of recognized practice
- *Theme / topic / concept* > URL of previous writing by self, a collaboration, or another

The writer also needs to consider how to strategically use the to-be-hyperlinked text to create purposeful connections for readers, such as

- Being responsible for previewing prospective URL links for quality and relevance before linking
- Using descriptive text with meaningful keywords or key phrases in preparation to link
- Keeping the amount of underlined words or phrases to a minimum; do not create links where the linked text is a full sentence or an entire paragraph

Krochmal (2010) uses a helpful analogy regarding the purpose of a strategically hyperlinked word or phrase in the context of the included content, "Link[ed] text must telegraph the destination. 'Click here' is completely meaningless." In other words, let readers know descriptively what content to expect before they click on the link.

Lastly, there are logistical skills needed to support a writer's hyperlinked writing fluency:

- Selecting a link in a browser
- Copying a link in a browser
- Creating a link on your digital page, either with HTML code or WYSIWYG editor
- Pasting the URL into the link code
- Opening up a new tab in your browser to switch easily back and forth between digital writing page and pages to be linked

Given all that is involved in the learning curve for becoming a fluent hyperlinking writer, using documenting OF and FOR learning opportunities provides an excellent avenue for creating and unpacking the visible evidence of a digital writer's learning growth over time concerning his or her hyperlinked writing capabilities.

Hunt (2008) reminds educators and learners alike, "Digital texts have the potential to make a big, juicy mess of a linear experience. Or to turn a so-so piece of writing into a masterful collection of references, linktributions, and pointers to other good stuff."

Levine (2006) defines a *linktribution* as, "An attribution via a web link or offering a 'linktribute.'" This term and its definition leads to a final point about hyperlinked writing or any contemporary reading or writing genres: *new forms require new terms and phrases to communicate meaning and understanding* about the genre's characteristics and elements.

For additional insights concerning how to teach and meaningfully practice hyperlinked writing in a classroom or professional learning environment, scan QR code 9.12 to begin exploring, which included activities to begin the process of building literacy and fluency with students and/or colleagues.

QR Code 9.12

Scan this QR code to read the blog post *Hyperlinked Writing in the Classroom— From Theory to Practice.*

http://langwitches.me/ hyperlinkedwriting

SUMMING UP

Incorporating audio and video documentation adds an engagement factor that hooks most learners. Platforms and tools for the documentation phases and learningflow routine steps will continue to expand due to innovative people and the demands and hopes of users.

It is important to be willing to be a risk-taker as a primary or secondary learner to try out new platforms tools. Do not be afraid to test, evaluate, re-evaluate, and switch platforms and tools in conjunction with experiencing a variety of documenting opportunities.

A blogging platform can be the glue that holds all of your documentation needs together. It allows for a wide range of documentation media and artifacts, as well as having built-in tools to insert and embed media and links, and connect to your past, present, and future documentation content. A blogging platform can also become a hub that inherently supports the share and amplify steps in the documenting learningflow routine.

As documenters share their digital work in online spaces, the skills involved in hyperlinked writing become a necessity to create meaningful, organized, and curated connections to the learning artifacts and the learning process itself.

GOING BEYOND

To amplify your reading beyond this book's pages, we have created *discussion questions and prompts* for this chapter, which are located at *www.documenting4learning.com*. To extend your thinking, reactions, and responses, you can connect with other readers by leaving comments on individual chapter's discussion posts on our documenting4learning blog.

We also invite you to contribute and share your artifacts in other social media spaces to connect with and learn from other readers around the world using the #documenting4learning hashtag on Twitter, Facebook, or Instagram; or by mentioning @documenting4learning on Facebook and Instagram, and @doc4learning on Twitter.

Documenting With Unpacking in Mind

The unexamined life is not worth living.

—Socrates

Unpacking, reflecting on, and analyzing captured artifacts are important facets of the post-documentation phase. As learners become fluent in the unpacking process, the cognition and metacognition involved positively influence choices about meaningful artifacts to be captured in the pre- and during-documentation phases.

UNPACKING DOCUMENTATION ARTIFACTS

The context for unpacking was first mentioned in Chapter 6 related to how the post-documentation phase's nine steps aid in transforming evidence of learning into meaningful artifacts. While there are myriad media that can be unpacked, this chapter focuses on six media platforms or tools commonly used in educational settings.

Unpacking Blog Posts

In Chapter 3, there was the example of a teacher extending her professional learning by contacting Mike Fisher and having him skype with a mixed fourth- and fifth-grade classroom. This documenting opportunity involved primary and secondary learners in the documentation process.

The teacher was Silvia, the 21st century literacy coach at the school at the time, who worked closely with Stephanie Teitelbaum, the students' Language Arts teacher. The two of them were working collaboratively on embedding documenting FOR and AS learning opportunities into Stephanie's classroom. Silvia and Stephanie connected with Mike and

QR Code 10.1

Scan this QR code to see the Blogging Rubric (first page).

http://langwitches.me/bloggingrubric

learned that he had written children's poems over the years. They saw this as a perfect opportunity for Stephanie's students to interact authentically with a poet.

The Skype call between Mike and Stephanie's students organically lead to him working on a project with her students wherein they illustrated a collection of poems Mike had written. The students embarked on an illustration-creation process that was iterative based on feedback from the poet and their classroom peers.

The students had been blogging throughout the year and continued to do so while they worked on their poetry illustration project. Based on the information gathered during their time skyping with Mike, they wrote a blog post expressing the key points of the project, as well as some facts about Mike. As in the past, when they drafted and eventually published their posts, they used a familiar blogging rubric for measuring their ongoing quality writing growth (scan QR Code 10.1 to access the rubric).

Silvia unpacked the blog post with the learning focuses and goals in mind, which Stephanie had discussed with her students prior to writing their posts. A portion of an unpacked artifact can be seen in Image 10.1. As primary learners, the students saw evidence of their writing being evaluated through the annotexted posts, which aided them in their ability to determine and defend their rubric scores. Stephanie, as a secondary learner, gained insights from Silvia in how documentation can aid in evaluating student work and the learning focuses and goals, including a digital writing genre (blog posts).

Image 10.1

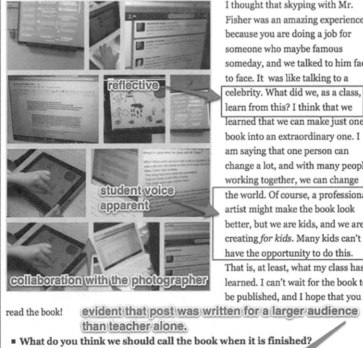

Silvia was both a primary and secondary learner. As a primary learner, she captured evidence of her own work concerning assessment practices in a modern classroom with *now* literacies applications, which she reflected on as an action researcher via her blog. As a secondary learner, she helped unpack evidence of Stephanie's teaching and her students' learning applications in their blog post writing samples.

As Silvia also shared her annotexted images and blog post reflection with Stephanie, they made additional observations: the annotexted artifacts helped Stephanie's students make connections among the project's focuses and their ongoing skill-building concerning grammar application, writing with an audience in mind, and digital writing skills (e.g., hyperlink writing, blogging as a conversation platform using first-person narrative).

In the unpacked Image 10.2, Silvia's annotations highlighted several learning applications for a particular student who provided evidence that he is being reflective and mentioned a posed question using proper dialogue punctuation, his enthusiastic voice, and attempting to engage the audience.

Image 10.2

Reflection written by: Ayden I

Recently, we did a skype call with the poet Mike Fisher. We're illustrating some of his poems and we managed to get him to agree to a skype call. The first person he talked to was Orli because she was the introducer. Everyone had different jobs. Evan was our transitioner, so he introduced everybody.(except Orli) Zach M. and Noah were our tweeters. Ayden Eliana, and Ariella were working on notetaking on a Google Doc. Jagger was the photographer. Jeremy and Griff were bloggers. He answered some of our questions like, "Why is the O poem in the shape of an O?" We learned that the reason the O poem is in the shape of an O is because it was a suggestion from one of his high school teachers. Next, we learned some interesting facts about Mr.Fisher, including he lives in Buffalo, New York which is five minutes away from Niagara Falls. He also is writing a mystery novel for young adults. Our whole class learned a few new words including: collaboration, cryptic, and emphatic. We learned a lot about our poems and Mike Fisher. Have you ever created a poem? This is just the beginning. We have to market! We have to publish! We have to find out how much we will make! All of this is going to be hard, but it's going to be worth it in the end. **author's voice**

(Annotation on image: previously taught grammar lesson on using quotation marks)

We still have many decisions to make.

- What should we name our book?
- How should we design the cover?
- What would be a reasonable price?
- Please respond and give us some feedback.

conversation starters

When unpacking blog posts, it is important to determine what details pertaining to the learning focuses or goals are going to be articulated as evidence in what has been captured. Possible considerations may include:

- What do I want to convey as evidence of understanding, relationships, and connections to current learning, past, or cross-discipline learning?
- What do I want to convey concerning the evidence of previous learning being applied in an authentic way?
- What do I want to convey that is evidence of growth over time?
- What do I want to convey concerning a specific image or other media form related to one or more of the *now* literacies that is present in the artifact?

The unpacked examples (see Images 10.1 and 10.2) involved students creating singular or collaborative blog posts. Silvia did not unpack every student's blog posts. Her goal was to make using blog posts as a formative assessment *and* reflection visible for Stephanie, as well as her *Langwitches* blog readers

As mentioned in Chapter 8, there is a variety of annotexting apps available to create superimposed text, highlights, frames, and directional arrows on an artifact. *Skitch* was used or the images above. Annotexting images can also be accomplished using PowerPoint or Keynote by importing the desired image into a slide frame and using the text box, shapes, and arrow features to create the annotext information. When the annotexting is complete, export the single slide as a .jpeg or .png.

Unpacking Twitter Feeds

Given a Twitter feed is an ongoing stream of tweeted messages, to follow a specific stream based on a conversation, an idea, value, or group, a hashtag is used to locate the crowd-sourced posts.

The first example of unpacking a Twitter feed will be from a professional learning perspective with Janet as a primary learner. She wanted to experience what is involved in hosting a Twitter chat, as she had been participating in educational chats for quite some time, but felt she did not truly grasp what it was like task-wise to host a chat.

QR Code 10.2

Scan this QR code to read three students' reflection posts based on their skype-with-Mike experience.

http://langwitches.me/digigogy

She learned as much as she could about the process and protocols prior to hosting. She created the #CDeduchat hashtag with the goal of connecting with educators around the theme of curriculum creation and decision making. She began hosting the #CDeduchat Twitter chat time at its pre-announced time, and created a conversation archive for asynchronous viewers and contributors after each chat time has ended.

After hosting her #CDeduchat for a few months, she wanted to capture evidence of her hosting capabilities at that time and get feedback from colleagues who were seasoned moderators. She took screen-capture images from the #CDeduchat stream and created a collage in a PowerPoint slide. Janet then used arrows and text boxes to annotext her images to convey her reflective observations. When she was done, she exported the slide as a .jpg file. Next, she shared her learning-thinking artifact via email with her colleagues who helped her gain insights into moderating chats. When she emailed her artifact (see Image 10.3), she included several questions she had based on applying what she learned and now realized having moderated and hosted a series of Twitter chats.

Image 10.3

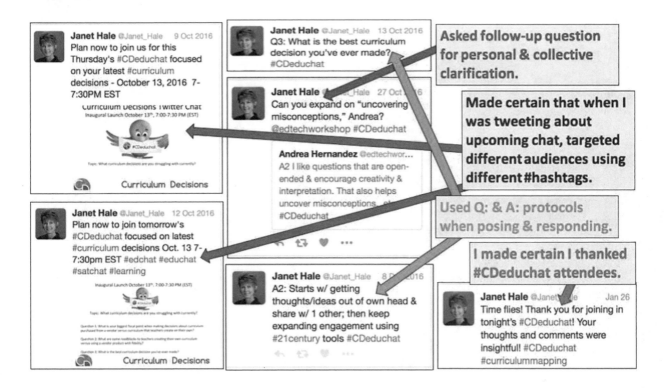

Assuming students have their own Twitter accounts or a classroom Twitter account, they can reflect on and analyze their own Twitter streams based on a learning focus or goal. Students or their teachers can unpack their posts to create reflective annotations or use a screencasting program or app to capture their reflective thoughts orally.

The second example for an unpacked Twitter feed features reflections made by Stephanie as a secondary learner with Silvia supporting her learning. They decided to unpack several tweets generated by her students while interviewing Mike during their *meet-a-poet* Skype session. Knowing the students had reached a comfort level with the various collaborative roles involved in conducting a Skype interview, they chose to capture evidence of the goals of authentic applications of quality expressive and receptive commenting and exemplary digital citizenship.

During the Skype call, Silvia and Mike were following the Twitter feed. Mike was using their tweets to aid in the conversation he was having with the Interviewers. Four students (two from Grade 4 and two from Grade 5) had been designated the Twitterers for the Skype call. Their job was to document and disseminate tweets that captured key points and interesting facts shared by Mike using their respective grade level's Twitter handle, which is the captured documentation that Stephanie unpacked (see Images 10.4 and 10.5).

Unpacking the classroom Twitter feeds proved insightful for both Silvia and Stephanie. Stephanie mentioned that she felt good about the instructional practices she had been providing based on the textual evidence in the two streams. She also mentioned that she noticed the fourth-graders' comments demonstrated little or no evidence of deep thought, since their tweets were mainly at a remember-and-recall level. Silvia and Stephanie agreed this concern could be addressed through practice lessons.

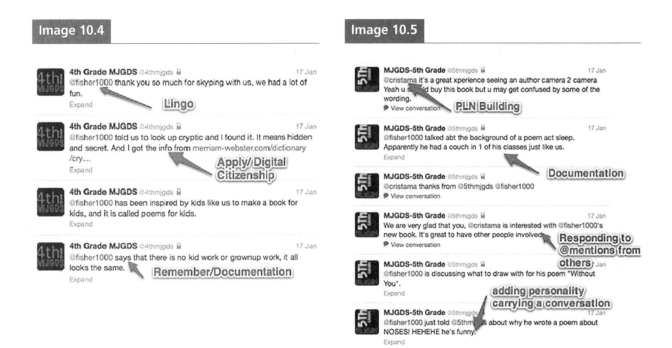

Stephanie shared that she would like to use these artifacts as a beginning benchmark and periodically capture and annotext their Twitter feeds to monitor their growth.

Twitter posts (tweets) involve applying unique skills and strategies that are beneficial to help convey one's intended message, which can take some time to apply effectively. For example:

- Concise articulation and summarizing of information or thoughts, given 280 characters or less limitation
- Accurate use of Twitter lingo and abbreviations (e.g., @username, #hashtag, Ss—students, Ts—teachers, TY—thank you, YW—you're welcome)
- Appropriate use of Twitter protocols (e.g., placement of third-party's @username mentioned in original post when responding to original Twitterer's comment)
- Ability to insert URLs or embed photos or videos
- Authentic application of digital citizenship and network literacies
- Awareness of potential influence on a larger audience by strategically amplifying
- Building one's professional learning network purposefully, as well as interacting with specific members of one's network

These unique capabilities can be focused on during the unpacking process, especially to measure improvement over time.

When unpacking Twitter feeds, it is important to remember that tweets rarely stand on their own. It is not easy to create a narrative context when reading only one tweet because it might be connected to a thread of tweets by the same person or group of people. Based on a specific hashtag being used, replies shared, links embedded, images attached, and/or tweets sent before or after specific tweets, a narrative emerges that expresses an idea or collective thoughts and resources concerning a topic or theme.

It is not easy to create a narrative context when reading only one tweet because it might be connected to a purposeful thread of tweets by the same person or group of people.

Unpacking Conference Hashtag Feeds

Brick-and-mortar conferences provide wonderful opportunities for crowdsourced learning by people with various:

- Background experiences and knowledge
- Perspectives and opinions
- Documenting learning methods and strategies
- Choices for attending workshop and session selections

Teachers tweeting throughout a conference using its designated hashtag creates collective crowdsourcing by attendees who are capturing, sharing, and amplifying their professional learning. Those attending often find that 280 characters are not enough to convey their desired information. When this happens, they add images or links to a blog post or article to generate further resources.

Conference Twitter posts can aid professional learning for a variety of reasons (Table 10.1). While some still perceive Twitter as a mundane way to share life's happenings, most educators realize the power of using this social platform to aid learning through

Table 10.1   Professional Learning Conference Twitter Posts

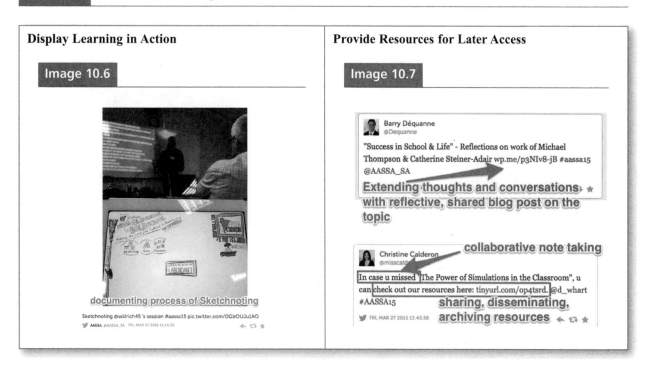

Display Learning in Action	Provide Resources for Later Access
Image 10.6	Image 10.7

(Continued)

Table 10.1   (Continued)

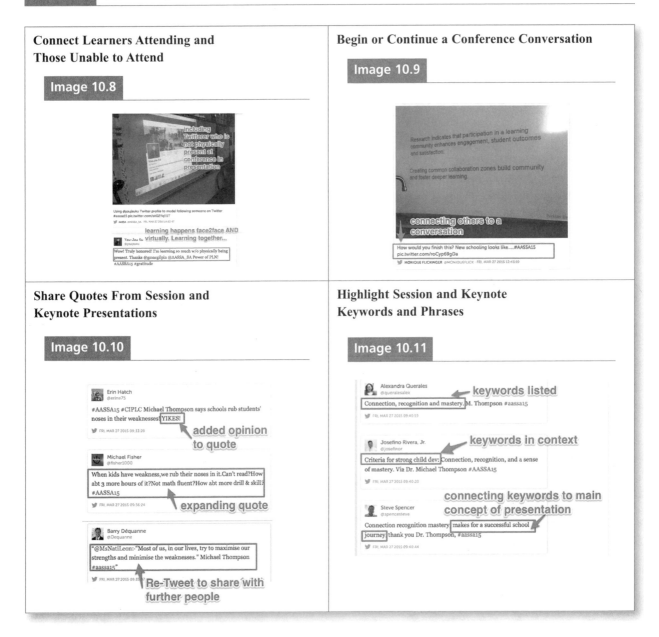

Connect Learners Attending and Those Unable to Attend

Image 10.8

Begin or Continue a Conference Conversation

Image 10.9

Share Quotes From Session and Keynote Presentations

Image 10.10

Highlight Session and Keynote Keywords and Phrases

Image 10.11

thoughtful posting, sharing, and strategic amplifying. Twitter brings educators from around the world together by threading their conversations that keep them connected and growing as ongoing learners.

When unpacking conference hashtag feeds, it is important to remember to strategically consider how to locate the desired crowdsourced posts. Twitterers who are cognizant of using a conference's hashtag will use it during or even after a conference to contribute information or thought-provoking ideas, which continuously adds personal perspective and voice to the hashtag's crowdsourced information and resources.

When reading and considering which conference hashtag Twitter posts or feeds are worthy of collecting, unpacking, and archiving, contemplating reflective questions to aid in the selection process can prove helpful:

- How does this tweet provide strong evidence of the content knowledge I am seeking to learn about or more about?
- Do I think I will want to revisit the resource embedded or attached to this tweet?
- What additional hashtag is included in this tweet that I may want to explore?
- Is there a specific person's @handle that I may want to follow or contact based on his or her tweet contributions?
- Is there a person's @handle included in another user's tweet that I may want to follow or contact?
- What is the added value to the conference topics or ideas based on this tweet?
- How are some of the tweets in the conference hashtag feed connected to each other?
- Does the tweet add to a specific curation story I am working on capturing, telling, and archiving?

It's Time to Take Action!

Chapter 10 Action Step

It is time for you to take action and select and unpack a Twitter hashtag conference feed. While much has been explained in the *Unpacking Conference Hashtag Feeds* section, when actually doing the unpacking, it begins to make more sense due to your personal cognitive and metacognitive processes.

Think of a conference that has taken place recently or within the last year. Oftentimes, conference hashtags will use one or more words in the organization's name or an initialism and simply change the year (e.g., ISTE18, ISTE19).

Important Note: You do not need to have attended the conference in person to complete this action step. You simply need to know the conference's hashtag. With this said, if you are attending a conference in person or virtually soon, plan to tweet out during the conference using its designated hashtag to add your perspective to the crowdsourced conference feed. After the conference is over, use some of the conference tweets to complete your selecting and unpacking process for this action step. If you prefer, you can unpack an already collected Twitter hashtag feed from the Association of American Schools in South America International Education (AASSA) 2016 conference by scanning QR code 10.3.

Begin the unpacking process by first accessing Twitter and searching for your desired conference's hashtag. Read through the hashtag tweets to determine

QR Code 10.3

Scan this QR Code to read through the captured #AASSA Twitter Chat.

http://langwitches.me/aassa-chat

(Continued)

(Continued)

the ones you consider worthy of selecting and collecting based on the reflective questions above this action step box.

After compiling your selected conference tweets, take a screenshot of several of the tweets and annotext the screenshot using an appropriate tool (e.g., PowerPoint slide with overlayed arrow and text-box images or Skitch annotation features; Screencast-o-matic with oral explanation while using pointer feature to highlight image areas as needed) based on the message you want to convey and share with a global audience.

Begin to annotext your collective tweets image to support your reflections and reasoning, (e.g., place an arrow over a tweet that is pointing to a URL link to a website that you found helpful for teaching your English language learner students).

When you have finished your annotexting reflective process, save your image and share it with others in person, or share and amplify your artifact using social media. Remember to use the #documenting4learning hashtag on Twitter, Facebook, or Instagram; or by mentioning @documenting4learning on Facebook and Instagram, and @doc4learning on Twitter. For this action step, remember to also include the conference's hashtag you are featuring.

Unpacking Backchannels Using TodaysMeet

An eighth-grade language arts teacher, Deb Kuhr, asked Silvia to aid her in a documenting opportunity wherein the focus would be on the proper use of copyright, public domain, fair use, and creative commons.

Deb and Silvia worked through the pre-documentation phase, which included developing instructional plans that would take place in the during-documentation phase. During the first lesson, they decided to begin by having the students watch the *Fair(y) Use Tale* video by Eric Faden.

The students were informed that, while watching the video, they needed to take collaborative notes in a TodaysMeet chat room their teacher had created. Silvia reminded them of key backchannel-posting etiquette. She also shared three notetaking focuses and guiding questions related to the learning goals that Deb wanted her students to consider prior to and when posting their thoughts during the video viewing:

QR Code 10.4

Scan this QR code to view the *Fair(y) Tale Use* video that the students watched.

http://langwitches.me/ fairytaleHabis, que con

- **Note Taking**—What am I seeing or hearing that is important to know concerning copyright, public domain, and fair use? What details will help us remember the key points of the content shared?
- **Note Organization**—What can we do to best articulate or frame when each new segment (chapter) begins and ends in the video? How will this be reflected in the backchannel notes?
- **Multitasking Capabilities**—How will I manage the task of needing to listen, summarize, write, and read simultaneously? What did I find you struggling to do concerning the need to multitask?

Silvia switched the TodaysMeet screen that was projected on the whiteboard to the video and reminded the students that she and Mrs. Kuhr would be the backchannel moderators and following along to view what they were collectively posting.

After each of the video's chapters, they paused the video and switched the screen back to the TodaysMeet room screen to have the class review the crowdsourced notes taken so far (see Image 10.12). They asked the students to predict what might be discussed next in the video, as well as asked a specific question they had wanted answered based on the next video-chapter segment.

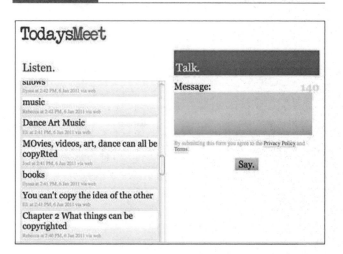

Image 10.12

By the end of the video, the main question every student had was, "How could the creator of this video have made it and published it on the Internet since it uses so much footage from Disney films?" Silvia shared that there had been a lawsuit by The Walt Disney Company against Professor Faden, who teaches English at Bucknell University. Eventually he won the case because the video was proven to be created and used for educational purposes, and therefore, allowed to be posted online and viewed under a Creative Commons Attribution-Noncommercial-ShareAlike 3.0 United States License.

Silvia and Deb directed the students back to the lesson focus and goal. The students' TodaysMeet transcript was copied and pasted into a Google Doc that was shared collaboratively with the class. They were tasked with unpacking the transcript to create an artifact. Silvia explained that their unpacking process would involve conducting a *Backchannel Clean-up* process based on the following tasks:

- Deleting the time stamp and author's name from each TodaysMeet entry (irrelevant for the purpose of unpacking, and could be distracting from main points)
- Deleting duplicate entries
- Double-checking fact accuracy (if a post's content or context "does not ring a bell," re-watch the video segment or search the Internet to prove or disprove the recorded statement)
- Bolding the video's chapter titles, as well as revise any of the chapter titles that are not worded accurately
- Adding bullets for visual clarity, when appropriate

These five tasks were accomplished in mini-teams that worked simultaneously in the document. After the clean-up tasks were completed, the students reflected on their unpacked artifact. They decided to add further notes they felt were missing and were needed based on the video and additional copyright/fair use information they found online while validating the video's content and completing the clean-up tasks.

Deb and Silvia annotexted the students' collaborative artifact (see Image 10.13 for a portion of the artifact) and debriefed on having the process of having the students unpacking their collective learning evidence as primary learners. Deb mentioned that she thought it was great to be able to see evidence of their organization of ideas based on how students grouped specific information.

Image 10.13

When unpacking back-channels using TodaysMeet, it is important to remember that it is a closed room versus a public backchannel like Twitter. A TodaysMeet room can be shared or amplified with a larger audience to add contributions while the room is active by providing its URL. Transcripts of backchannel feeds can also be shared or amplified while the room is active or after it is closed. TodaysMeet transcripts automatically place all of the post entries in chronological order, which is helpful when unpacking from a growth-over-time point of view.

Unpacking Backchannels Using Google Docs

Silvia and Janet attended a conference in 2010 wherein Alan November was one of the keynote presenters. They were familiar with his *digital learning farm* concepts, which include promoting students' responsibilities of contributing to the classroom's collective learning community.

Unbeknownst to them and the other conference attendees, Alan had asked three volunteers in the audience to share the responsibility of being the Official Scribes while he was speaking. Alan shared with the three that he had prepared a Google Doc containing a simple three-column table with these labeled columns:

- Keywords and Key Concepts
- Further Questions Emerging
- Resources and Links Shared

He asked the volunteers to decide among themselves who would be taking notes for each of the three focuses. While they were deciding, he added their email addresses to the document. They then went back and sat in the audience. Once Alan began speaking, they began filtering his keynote's oral and visual presentation through the lens of their respective column's focus and made appropriate contributions to the collaborative document to capture the key information shared.

Toward the conclusion of his presentation, which focused on the need for students to be actively involved and engaged in owning their learning, he revealed the Google Doc backchannel document on the large screen. He introduced the three audience contributors and discussed the power of using a Google Doc as a multifocus backchannel. The attendees were excited about the possibilities of using this form of backchanneling in their classrooms and professional development.

Both Silvia and Janet have since used this strategy when working in classrooms, schools, and districts. In one classroom, Mark Engstrom, an eighth-grade geography teacher, used November's backchanneling method for collaborative notetaking. While he did limit the roles to three students, he had multiple triads working in various Google Docs so that all his students were involved in a specific Scribe role. For this documenting opportunity, the three columns were General Notes, Data Collected, and Images Supporting Key Points. The lesson that included a PowerPoint titled, "Waiting for the Rains: The Effects of Monsoons in South Asia," which related to one of the course's overarching question: *Why Geography?*

After the collaborative notetaking process was completed, the students were asked as primary learners to unpack their collective notes per triad team. One student, Ben, added a reflection while reading the collaborative notes from his backchannel team:

> I found these very interesting because Florens and Tibet really try to link what is happening in India to our life in São Paulo, which for me is a smarter way to learn things; by comparing them with your everyday life.

Later the students were directed to access all the triad teams' backchannel artifacts. It was up to them to scan through the information in each Google Doc to determine what information was truly important to add to—curate—their content knowledge.

Curating information has become an important information literacy skill set. The ability to find, evaluate, analyze, categorize, present, remix, organize, and archive information is more important than ever given students now live in an information-overload era. Mr. Engstrom felt strongly that there was a natural connection between curation and the documentation phases, especially the post-documentation's nine steps (see Images 10.14 and 10.15).

Image 10.14

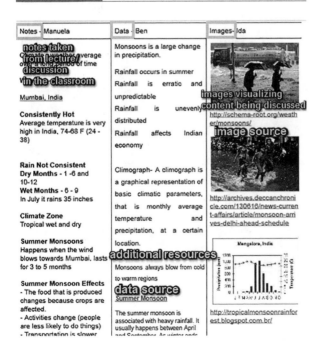

Image 10.15

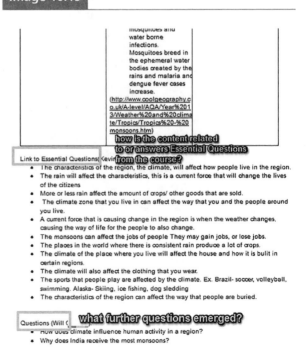

When a Google Doc is used as a synchronous experience where participants are contributing live to the backchannel, the logistics of adding information can sometimes be difficult because a Google Doc does not arrange the contributions in chronological order. There are times that contributors get frustrated due to their cursors being moved while they are typing due to someone else adding text above or below. To minimize this logistical problem, it is recommended to add columns and/or rows to the document and assign synchronous participants an individual cell, row, or column.

Google Doc backchannel collaborators can also take advantage of the comments function to add additional thoughts, ideas, resources, or questions that connect to the information expressed in the document.

Lastly, a unique feature within the Google Docs format enables students to view the document's history to see who contributed what and when it was contributed. This is a feature that often comes in handy when unpacking backchannels.

Unpacking Infographics and Sketchnotes

Rohde (2014) defines sketchnotes as, "Rich visual notes created from a mix of handwriting, drawings, hand-drawn typography, shapes, and visual elements like arrows, boxes, and lines" (p. 4). In comparison, infographics are not hand sketched (Images 10.16 and 10.17).

Sketchnotes are gaining popularity in educational environments as an introspective tool and reflective process on a personal level, whether being used by students or educators. A sketchnoter is constantly thinking about the visual image choices he or she is making when sketchnoting to best capture and internalize what is being read, seen, or heard.

While doing so requires purposefulness in the visual choice-making, the decision-making lens is based on creating content to be visualized for oneself, rather than shared with others. This is not to say that a sketchnoter cannot sketch purposefully for an audience beyond himself or herself, but an infographic is rarely created for personal use alone. Infographics are being used educationally to provide authentic applications of communicating with an audience foremost in one's mind.

Unpacking and interpreting sketchnotes and infographics provides excellent opportunities to document a pattern or trend regarding a creator's communication style and craft. For example, Images 10.16 and 10.17 convey Silvia's voice and style. Just as someone might say, "I know that is a Monet because . . ." Silvia's blog subscribers and Twitter followers instantly recognize her work. When students are provided frequent occasions to sketchnote and create infographics, not only can teachers and students use them as documentation artifacts, but the ongoing cognitive process involved in creating meaningful and purposeful content representation increases one's capability to convey clarity of thinking to oneself and a wider audience.

An additional benefit when creating sketchnotes or infographics is practicing digital citizenship by attributing the content source, unless the work is the creator's original work. Oftentimes, the source(s) are included along an edge in a sketchnote or at the bottom of an infographic. For example, in Silvia's sketchnote and infographic in Images 10.16 and 10.17, she states *By Alan November* around the curve of the number 5 as a content source attribution.

Sketchnotes and infographics take advantage of and strengthen the cognitive processes involved in

- Creating a text hierarchy by using different sizes and typography
- Grouping similar information by proximity or by color coding

Image 10.16 Sketchnote

Image 10.17 Infographic

- Connecting content elements using shapes and arrows to convey relationships or timelines
- Summarizing, categorizing, organizing, and breaking down into manageable "bites" that allow creator and readers to quickly comprehend information shared
- Applying metaphors and symbols to tell a learning story and aid in metacognition

It is important to remember that a sketchnote's primary purpose is for the information being synthesized to make sense to the sketchnoter, while infographics are most often created for conveying a message to a general or specific audience. Although many sketchnoters share their work and gain followers who enjoy their content and style of visual delivery, the primary purpose is about visualizing and making sense of one's thoughts with an emphasis on the cognitive thinking process *while* sketchnoting.

When unpacking a sketchnote or infographic, one's capability to convey an intended message in a concise and succinct manner can be evaluated by reflecting on questions such as these:

- What does the creator consider most important to support the information shared based on a font size hierarchy?
- How is the information grouped together? Does it appear random, or can you find evidence of a logical and purposeful placement of information using shapes, containers, numbers, or icons?
- How are arrows or other features used to convey connections between or among the content, sequence, or timeline?
- What metaphors, analogies, or symbologies are used to convey the overall message or specific components or details?

SUMMING UP

The reality is that most teachers will start unpacking their students' artifacts for their own learning and to improve their pedagogical practices. An important goal needs to also be creating a comfort level in modeling and coaching their students in being primary learners who are documenting their own learning through the process of unpacking captured-learning artifacts.

To do so, it is important to have students observe and reflect by taking an artifact apart, studying the individual components, and making connections between or among those pieces. By applying a maker culture to the unpacking process in the after-documentation phase, students become active participants in a co-creation learning environment.

Fostering students' skills over time to unpack their artifacts is a powerful tool that promotes students practicing ownership of their own learning and determining their next learning steps based on the evidence of learning visible in their artifacts.

GOING BEYOND

To amplify your reading beyond this book's pages, we have created *discussion questions and prompts* for this chapter, which are located at *www.documenting4learning.com*. To extend your thinking, reactions, and responses, you can connect with other readers by leaving comments on individual chapter's discussion posts on our documenting4learning blog.

We also invite you to contribute and share your artifacts in other social media spaces to connect with and learn from other readers around the world using the #documenting4learning hashtag on Twitter, Facebook, or Instagram; or by mentioning @documenting4learning on Facebook and Instagram, and @doc4learning on Twitter.

11

Documenting Challenge

21st Century Skills and the Now Literacies

I'm never sure what's coming next, but I'm an open-minded person and I welcome any challenge.

—Sarah Polley

FOCUSING THE CHALLENGE

This chapter has a twofold purpose: (1) to provide a detailed vignette that conveys the documentation phases and learningflow routine steps; (2) to challenge you to take your own learning, or your students' learning, and create a documenting opportunity.

Businesses are making it clear that employees, now more than ever, must display 21st century skills, known as soft skills, that aid in successful productivity. Buhl (2017) states that six essential soft skills needed are, "communication; teamwork and collaboration; problem solving; critical observations; and conflict resolution."

It is imperative that your students as engaged learners have authentic opportunities to learn and apply 21st century success skills in meaningful contexts throughout their academic years in preparation for their work life. Many learning organizations refer to these skills as the "*C*s," which most often include: *critical thinking, communication, collaboration,* and *creativity*, although they may also include other *C*s, such as *connections, citizenship*, and *character*.

There are times when you may want to be explicit about the *C*s being the learning focus or goal during a documenting opportunity (e.g., students capturing how they communicate and collaborate using various medias). Other times, the *C*s may serve as the mortar that

Image 11.1

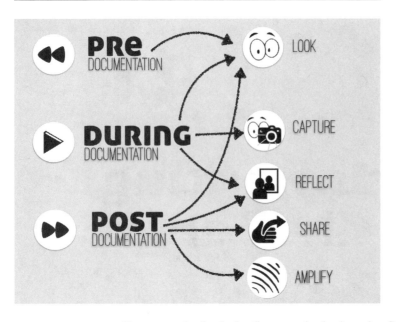

binds the documentation cohesively, such as in this challenge's vignette. You will recognize multiple moments wherein the students were critical thinkers, communicators, collaborators, and creators.

As you read through the challenge, you will experience how the *now* literacies, which were explained in Chapter 2, were infused with 21st century skills in a sixth-grade humanities class focused on metacognitively learning, while involved in literature circles. To create a context for this challenge, a brief summary of the three phases has been provided in Table 11.1.

Remember that the documentation phases and learningflow routine steps have points of intersection in a documenting opportunity (see Image 11.1).

For example, *look*, the first step in the learningflow routine is a facet in all three phases.

Therefore, you may notice that some of the bullets featured in Table 11.1 may be involved in the learningflow more than once when reading the "Framing the Challenge" section.

FRAMING THE CHALLENGE

A middle school teacher, Emily Vallillo, had been working with her students on documenting their learning as primary learners, as well as documenting her professional learning. She determined the focus she wanted her students to work on improving for this opportunity would be applying meaningful-engagement capabilities while participating in literature circle discussions. She also determined two clearly defined student learning goals:

- Participate meaningfully in high-quality, text-based literature circle discussions
- Support claims with relevant and specific evidence from the text

Emily met with her documenting action-research team (three other teachers in her school), and they agreed that students participating in literature circles was an excellent vehicle for both documenting her students' growth in becoming critical readers and their ability to be conscientious learners and critiquers. Emily shared her drafted criteria for high-quality discussion engagement and text-based evidence that needed to be visible in their discussion video. Next, they helped her generate a rubric that her students would use and refer to during their task. Before they concluded their meeting, Emily shared her professional-growth desire in relationship to this opportunity. She said, "My goal is to answer this question for myself: how do I help make my students aware of their personal strategies and behaviors when reading and discussing text?"

Silvia, who was coaching teachers at Emily's school in applying the documentation phases and routine, discussed the student-learning focuses and goals, as well as her personal-learning goal. They brainstormed documenting AS learning experiences that would aid students in their metacognitive processing that would make their behavior observations and

Table 11.1 Three Documentation Phases for 21st Century Skills and *Now* Literacies

Pre-Documentation Phase *Look*	During-Documentation Phase *Look, Capture, Reflect*	Post-Documentation Phase *Look, Reflect, Share, Amplify*
Teacher • Determine specific focus (literature circles) and clearly define learning goals (participate in text-based discussion; support claim with text-based evidence). • Articulate student text-based evidence expectations for determined learning focus and goals. • Establish engagement evidence expectations during discussion and in created video. • Create rubric based on learning focus and goals and evidence expectations. • Determine best platforms for documentation process. • Determine professional-learning focus and goal, as well as potential artifact evidence. **Students** • Clarify learning focus and goals (discussion task). • Generate potential visible and audible evidence of clarified goals; record suggestions on T-chart labeled: *We Will See* and *We Will Hear*. • Revisit discussion protocol and application to current literature circles discussion task. • Prepare for discussion by reading pre-determined passages and annotating text based on posed questions.	**Students** • Select video tool and set up camera in preparation for recording discussion and capture group displaying evidence of learning focus and goals. • Participate in discussion based on personal preparation and discussion protocol. • Refer to text-based evidence to support reasoning while probing and reflecting on points under discussion. • Self-correct personal participation, or re-direct participants, if off topic. • Orally debrief and reflect on observations (evidence of, or lack of evidence) related to learning focus and goals while participating in literature circle discussion. **Teacher** • Record quotes voiced by students while listening in on literature circle discussion groups. • Capture visual discussion moments with camera to use as next-step conversation starters at the onset of the post-documentation phase.	**Students** • Unpack captured documentation. • Look for visible and audible evidence in group's recorded discussion video. • Decide what is usable and what is irrelevant to create annotexted video evidence based on learning goals. • Create video by trimming and splicing raw video. • Annotext video by adding subtitles, phrases, and sentences to provide evidence of learning goals: high-quality discussion engagement and text-based evidence to support their claims. • Create and post a reflective personal blog related to the latest literature circle discussion and evidence of learning focus and goals. **Teacher** • View student-created videos using rubric to determine appropriate feedback. • View student blog reflections and leaving personalized feedback comments. • Share and amplify students' artifacts via professional blog and social media. • Evaluate and reflect on personal professional focus and goals based on student artifacts and personally captured documentation. **Students and Teacher** • Debrief documenting opportunity's phases and routine steps and brainstorm application to new learning opportunities.

textual reflections visible to themselves and others. This was important, given Emily's desire for her students to become more aware of their personal engagement strategies and behaviors. Silvia mentioned that she would be a secondary learner and aid in capturing evidence of the students' learning since she would be in the classroom for the task components as well. They then discussed what would be considered worthwhile captured evidence of learning based on the two student goals and Emily's professional goal.

A few days later, Emily began the documenting process by posting a task summary and asked her students to think-pair-share regarding their initial reactions to the scope of the task:

> Your task is to digitally analyze your group's literature circle discussion. With images, words, and quotations from the text, you will show evidence of how your participation in your literature circle discussion met or exceeded high-quality expectations, including providing constructive comments. For the culmination of your task, you will create a reflective blog post on your own participation in your discussion group. You will embed your annotated video in your post as a documentation artifact.

Emily had backward planned the necessary outcomes to reach the culminating blog post expectation and provided her students with a task calendar highlighting the various components' deadlines (e.g., reading and annotating pre-selected text, literature circle discussion time, analyzing recorded video of meeting, creating annotexted video, drafting blog post). Given the designated due dates, students in their literature-circle groups discussed the details of the task and generated clarifying questions to ask Emily. Once they conferenced with her, they determined what needed to be accomplished individually and as a group and filled in checkpoints on their calendars appropriately.

On the following pages, you will read and see highlights from each learningflow routine step during the literature circle discussion task. Be thinking about how the 21st century skills and *now* literacies are interwoven into these students' learning experience.

Image 11.2

Look for Learning

Students individually focused on a literature-discussion question Emily had provided and made sticky note annotations in their text in preparation for using text-based evidence to support their claims in their discussion groups (see Image 11.2). Part of the preparation also included each student creating two or three questions that required text-based evidence that would be asked during the literature circle discussion.

Prior to beginning the discussion time, Emily reminded her students of the discussion focus and two goals, and asked them to begin to brainstorm what each goal may visually look like and audibly sound like when they record their discussion. She noted their suggestions on a T-chart labeled: *What We Will See* and *What We Will Hear.*

Next, she displayed and had her class review their previously agreed-on discussion protocols, which would be applied in their literature circle discussion:

Discussion Protocols

1. Read discussion norms:
   - Come prepared.
   - Share in the flow of conversation.
   - You can read/think ahead, but don't talk ahead.
   - Stay on topic.
   - Be respectful.
   - Be responsible for everyone's knowledge.
   - Follow protocol.

2. Be certain everyone is ready to transition.

3. Ask clarifying questions.

4. Participate in deep discussion.

5. Take time to debrief and reflect on points shared.

6. Listen closely as each person shares their reflective thoughts.

Lastly, Emily asked each student to write a personal goal to actively work on during the discussion that could be captured via the video recording of their discussion. For example, Felix noted in his reflective journal: *Be better at keeping my group on topic.*

As Silvia prepared to capture the learning displayed by all the discussion groups, Emily provided each group with a reminder statement summarizing the purpose of the discussion in relationship to the two class goals, their personal goal, and the documenting task: *The purpose of your camera recording is to create evidence of your discussion skills and your literary analysis of the read text.*

Capture Learning

Everyone joined in their respective literature circle group and collaboratively determined (a) where they wanted to meet and (b) how to best capture their discussion on camera (see Image 11.3). One group decided their camera angle was "just right" when it was leaned up against a brick wall, while another group found a group member's pencil case worked fine (see Image 11.4).

Each group began by reviewing the protocol norms and reflecting on the summary statement Emily had just given them. They used the remainder of their discussion time to address the provided and student-generated questions by answering them using text-based evidence and collaborative conversations.

Image 11.3

Image 11.4

camera

While the discussions were taking place, Emily and Silvia individually recorded quotes being voiced by students while they listened in on the discussion groups, as well as reflective anecdotes for two reasons: one, as evidence of the students' skill abilities concerning the documenting opportunity's focuses and goals; and two, to generate learning evidence for Emily's professional learning goal. Here are a few examples of the recorded quotes and *corresponding anecdotes*:

- "I have a deep discussion question. What made me think of it was on page . . ." (*fueling discussion, supporting claims with relevant evidence from text*)
- "I think it is on page 1 . . . " (*supporting claims with specific evidence from text*)
- "What if he could . . ." (*fueling discussion, looking at different points of view*)
- "But how can he see the future without bamboo?" (*fueling discussion*)
- "Guys, we have to focus." (*being responsible for everyone's knowledge, being respectful*)
- "What else? Do you have anything?" (*being responsible for everyone's knowledge, being certain everyone is ready to transition*)
- "In the book, it said. . . . Right? . . . Yes, there is also evidence earlier in the book. Turn to page . . ." (*supporting claims with relevant and specific evidence from text*)
- "I have a counter-argument I'd like to share." (*being respectful, fueling discussion*)
- "This is off topic." (*staying on topic—Felix said this. He is owning his learning!*)
- "I still don't understand why they left him. It is still confusing. Can someone . . ." (*asking clarifying questions*)

Emily signaled when it was time for the discussion groups to begin debriefing and reflecting within their respective groups in preparation to share out as a class. She reminded her students that it is very important to

Listen closely to your own words when describing yourself and your actions, as well as when others share their critiques, both in your own discussion group and as a class. This information will help guide you when you begin to reflect deeper on your personal learning strategies and behaviors.

Reflect on Learning

The following day, each student began the next learningflow routine by metacognitively reflecting on what he or she personally said and conveyed during the peer critiques, as well as each group's share-out time.

Emily followed this personal reflection time by letting the class know that they would now begin one of the most challenging components of the task—looking for visible and audible evidence of what was conveyed in their recorded discussion videos based on seeing and/or hearing:

- High-quality discussion capabilities, or lack thereof, based on the protocols and rubric expectations
- Text-based evidence to support the claims made based on the posed discussion questions

She then conducted a mini-lesson on what low-to-high quality literary text-based analysis and discussion behaviors look and sound like using their rubric to spark conversation. When Emily addressed the rubric-level requirements for the two video sections, she asked her students to brainstorm examples of what they might observe for a rating of Level 4 to Level 1. She had them use their previously brainstormed T-chart *What We Will See* and *What We Will* suggestions as a springboard, as well as reflecting on what had happened during their literature circle discussion time.

After they shared their ideas and examples, Emily facilitated her students calibrating what each level's measurable attributes would be.

She then segued into the next component of their documentation task: annotexting their group-discussion videos to generate learning-thinking artifacts. She reminded them that, "Annotexting is annotating digitally by overlaying text, directional arrows, and frames at specific moments in the video," and added, "Remember why you are annotexting—to provide evidence of your two learning goals: high-quality discussion engagement, and text-based evidence to support your claims." She demonstrated how to annotext a video clip that she and Silvia had created for the purpose of the mini-lesson using iMovie. Her students instantly got the idea of what they needed to do and were excited. They could not wait to get started annotexting their own videos (see Image 11.5)!

To conduct the annotexting process, each group was given the choice of using iMovie, Movie Maker, or any other video-creation tool they preferred. They referred to the last row of the rubric: *Overall Professionalism*, as well as annotexting guidelines for their literature circle video during this post-documentation phase (Table 11.2).

During the video annotexting and editing footage process, Emily and Silvia circulated to the different student groups to observe and document collaboration in action among each group's members. They noticed that some students requested help from a peer (for shortcuts or tech support). For example, a few needed some assistance with how to cut individual movie clips and add subtitles, while others needed reminders or asked for feedback regarding audio quality and volume.

Silvia and Emily noted that some students chose to share the screen and took turns in annotexting their group's video clips, while others split the headset's headphones and listened to the videos simultaneously, alternating turns to work on their respective clips, adding transitions, and typing the subtitles (see Image 11.6).

Image 11.5

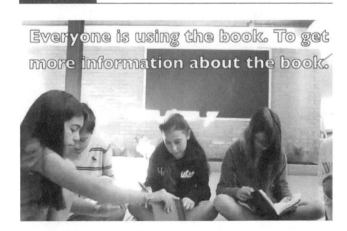

Everyone is using the book. To get more information about the book.

Table 11.2 Guidelines for Annotexting Literature Circle Videos

General

- Cut out *dead air* when no one is speaking and nothing productive is happening in your literature circle discussion.
- Do not use last names when embedding text for security reasons. Only use first names throughout video.
- Constructive criticism is helpful to others. Make certain your words are positive and kind. For example, do not annotate: *Here is Emily goofing off again.* Instead, write: *Emily is having difficulty staying on topic.*

Literary Analysis Discussion

- Clearly identify points in the discussion that represent clarifying questions being addressed by deeper discussion.
- Highlight and annotate moments in your video where you see yourself or a group member displaying high-quality, text-based discussion points:
  - Evidence from the text is being used to support the claim.
  - Quotes from the text are being used to spark discussion or ask a deeper question.
  - Questions are asked that fuel discussion.
  - Questions are asked to clarify something that is confusing.
  - Claims, inferences, opinions, connections, and/or predictions are being made.
- Highlight and annotate moments in your video where you see yourself or a group member displaying engaged discussion behaviors:
  - Tracking a speaker with your eyes.
  - Actively listening based on body language.
  - Verbally inviting others to join in the discussion.
- Highlight and annotate moments in your video where you see yourself or a group member who is displaying strategies or behaviors that need improvement based on your two goals and specific personal goal:
  - Explain specifically how you will personally improve, or suggest improvement to another group member, in a constructive manner.

Image 11.6

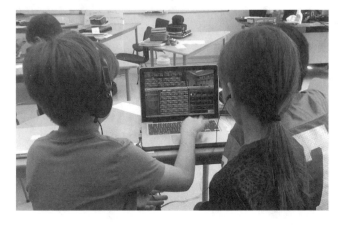

The students were provided two 45-minute blocks of time to edit and annotext their videos. They then published their videos online using YouTube or Google Video in preparation to embed the team video into their personal reflective blog post.

Share the Learning

For the *share* learningflow routine step, each student drafted a blog post that highlighted his or her key points related to the two learning goals (high-quality discussion skills, text-based evidence), personal goal, and the task rubric's criteria: *Blog Post Reflection*.

Emily also shared guidelines for the reflective post expectations:

- Explain the purpose of your Literature Circle Video Analysis and why or how it has helped you improve, and reflect upon your ability to participate in a discussion group and your ability to use text-based evidence to support your claims.
- Reflect on your own participation in your literature circle group. Share with your audience what you did well, and what you realized you can improve on, based on the video's evidence.
- Embed your group's video into your blog post as an artifact.
- Choose an engaging and relevant title for your blog.
- Check your punctuation and spelling.
- Check your professionalism: *Does your blog post look and sound professional when someone views and reads it?* For example, in your blog text:
  - This is not professional: My group's video is AWEsome!! XOXOXOX!!!
  - This is professional: I learned a lot by creating our group video. I realized that I need to get better at having evidence ready for my reasoning.

QR Code 11.1

Scan this QR code to view *Literature Circle Video Analysis— Annotexting.*

http://langwitches.me/literaturecircles

The students worked on their reflection drafts and participated in content revision and editing feedback meetings with their respective discussion group members, as well as with Emily. Based on the task calendar's due date, each student added the post to his or her blogfolio. Figure 11.1 is an excerpt from one of the posted reflections by a student whose second language is English.

To access GianLuca's group's annotated video, scan QR Code 11.2.

As a follow-up to posting their personal reflective blogs, Emily had her students visit one another's posts and leave comments that conveyed positive feedback, and if appropriate, caring critique based on the rubric expectations.

QR Code 11.2

Scan this QR code to view *Annotexted Literature Circle Discussion—Student Reflection.*

http://langwitches.me/litcircle

Figure 11.1   GianLuca's Reflective Blog Post Excerpt

I participated in a way that I didn't just express my thoughts, (talked) but I also participated in a way that I also writed "stuff" in a way that I also participated on the discussion, but in an "un-verbal" way, coming up with a simple word called: writing. Actually it is five words: Expressing my thoughts by writing. Or even maybe seven words: Expressing and communicating my thoughts by writing.

I used this "ability" to participate in a literature circle before in all of the discussion, but every discussion we had, I "evoluted" this ability, making me better every time. I also will use this skills again not only in literature discussion, but yes, in life! (So I can communicate with people all over the world! That's also my core value: communicator).

I think that something that I still could had improved on my participation on the literature discussion was to use the book just a bit more, because I simply felt that the amount of times that I used the book on the discussion wasn't enough for my group. That is because there wasn't enough information about the book that I told the group, but yes, instead of information, I expressed thoughts and questions for the group, which made the discussion more interesting and "fueled" until it ended. So I came up with a solution. For next time, I'll improve my "ability" of participating by, well, using the book a little more often!

Amplify the Learning

While the sharing and commenting of their reflective allowed for some degrees of amplification, Silvia reached out to her Twitter professional learning network, as well as wrote and posted a reflective professional blog post. This level of learningflow amplification created an unexpected and exciting extension to this documenting opportunity.

The co-creator of *Habits of Mind*, Dr. Bena Kallick, follows Silvia on Twitter. She sent her a direct message to share that she was intrigued by the metacognitive mindfulness displayed in both the textual aspects of Emily's students' blog posts, as well as their embedded annotexted videos. Silvia asked Bena if she would be willing to skype with Emily's class so they could be connected with an expert in metacognition and the *Habits of Mind* behaviors. Bena shared that she would love to do so, and the amplification and continuation of the 21st century skills and *now* literacies began!

To prepare for the virtual call, Emily's students learned about Dr. Kallick by researching her professional work on the Internet, as well as investigated the *Habits of Mind* characteristics. Given this was the first time Emily's students would be involved in a Skype interview call, Emily and Silvia provided descriptions and examples of the video conferencing call roles they would be fulfilling.

After being certain that the students understood each role's function, the students shared with one another the roles they were most interested in performing during the video call:

- **Videographer** (records Skype call)
- **Photographer** (takes visual notes with images)
- **Speaker** (begin introduction, keeps the flow of conversation going)
- **Live Blogger** (creates a post for the classroom blog)
- **Official Scribe** (notes the key points shared during the Skype conversation)
- **Notetaker** (takes individual notes for personal learning and making connections)

While it can vary depending on the purpose of a virtual conference call, the responsibilities of the first five roles are often assumed by one to three students. Emily had her students volunteer to take on these roles. The students who did not want any of these roles became notetakers.

The students discussed in small groups how they could personally display evidence of learning related to eight *I Can . . .* statements Emily posted related to participating in the upcoming Skype call:

I can explain why sharing with a global audience amplifies my learning.
I can explain why it is important to network using social media with a global audience.
I can explain how my learning and information does not only come from books.
I can explain my thinking about my personal learning habits.
I can make connections to my own learning and work.
I can express my communication skills in an authentic way.
I can use my collaboration skills to help my classmates learn new information.
I can take notes that are meaningful to me, as well as to others.

Emily visited with each group's members and listened to their *I Can* evidence ideas. When appropriate, she coached them on additional suggestions for how they might capture evidence of their learning.

Lastly, she facilitated her class's efforts to collaboratively create their upcoming Skype call's agenda:

1. Introduce our class to Dr. Kallick.

2. Explain our two literacy circle discussion goals, including the process we used to create our annotexted videos and reflective blog posts.

3. Listen to Dr. Kallick share how she found out about our Literature Circle discussion work.

4. Ask our interview questions (if we have not already asked them):

    a. What are the Habits of Mind?

    b. How did you make connections between our work and the Habits of Mind?

    c. How are the Habits of Mind connected to our learning goals for the task we did?

5. Participate in an open question and answer time with Dr. Kallick.

6. Conclude our meeting with Dr. Kallick by summarizing what she shared with us.

7. Thank her for spending time with us.

Finally, the interview day arrived! Dr. Kallick was inspirational. She was impressed by the students' professionalism and depth of questions. Throughout the virtual meeting, the students were engaged as the primary learners. Emily and Silvia were engaged as secondary learners, observing the learning taking place around them in order to create evidence for Emily's professional growth learning, as well as for her students as primary leaners (see Images 11.7 and 11.8).

Image 11.7

Image 11.8

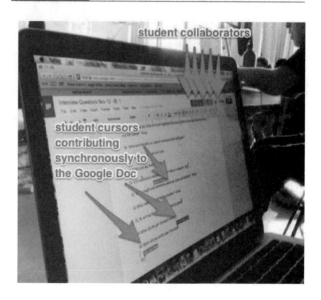

All of her students were enthusiastically and authentically involved throughout their 30-minute call (see Images 11.9 and 11.10).

While observing the students in action, Silvia commented to Emily,

It is impressive to witness an entire conversation flow between your collective students and Dr. Kallick. Bena is talking to the students via a screen, looking at the two speakers directly. Yet the rest of the class is equally experiencing and being involved in the conversation with Bena (see Image 11.11).

Silvia continued to explain to Emily that while the rest of the class was listening in on the conversation transpiring between Bena and the two speakers, a sharing degree of amplification was taking place through the Google Doc because it was serving as a backchannel extension of the conversation. Students were responding live to Bena's comments by adding their thoughts and questions in the backchannel, which was being moderated by a student sitting next to the speakers. He was able to read the backchannel created by his classmates and choose worthwhile questions or comments, while he simultaneously eliminated non-essential or duplicate ones, and passing the relevant ones on to the speakers to ask Dr. Kallick directly. The conversation flow continues as Dr. Kallick responds live to the posed questions (Image 11.11).

Image 11.11

Silvia adds, "This ebb and flow of conversation, and intertwining of synchronous conversation with technology tools to aid in amplifying the interaction and crowdsourced perspectives is 21st century skills and the *now* literacies in action!"

Here are two of the anecdotes Emily and Silvia wrote during the Skype call that were shared with the students (along with the appropriate photographs) during their debriefing time after the call was concluded.

- Speakers took charge of introducing our school and class. They were prepared to ask the planned questions, as well as ones that surfaced during the conversation based on the collaborative Google Doc that had been shared with all the students to add questions that they had for the expert.
- The Live Blogger, who was in charge of preparing a post on the classroom blog, was taking notes and jotting down ideas for which images to incorporate from the photographer and videographer segments once the video was edited.

To view the Skype interview Emily's students conducted with Dr. Kallick, scan QR Code 11.3.

During the interview call's debriefing time, Emily and her students realized that they had collected a lot of information that was stored in various media formats, including the following:

- Mental models (what is personally in their own minds)
- Flip camera recordings
- Smartphone and iPad photographs
- Google Doc with posed questions and responses
- Google Doc with the Official Scribe's text
- Live Blogger textual notes
- Notetakers' journal textual and sketched notes

QR Code 11.3

Scan this QR code to view the Skype call with Dr. Bena Kallick: *Habits of Mind.*

http://langwitches.me/ habitsofmind

Emily posed the question to her class, "What do you think would be the best media selections to aid you in providing evidence of your learning when interviewing Dr. Kallick when considering your learning goals?" The students brainstormed and decided that (a) having an interview transcript would be beneficial to closely read later, (b) important moments captured and annotexted would highlight key learning points, and (c) creating a collaborative reflective document—*What We Remember the Most*—would help them to think about their thinking.

The students broke into teams to create evidence in the three selected forms. For example, the Official Scribe and a few other students worked collaboratively to generate a text-based interview transcript by reviewing the scribe's notes and listening (and re-listening) to the Flip camera recording. Here are three excerpts from their transcribed text:

Dr. Kallick: What kind of questions do you ask at the circles?

Brenna: Clarifying questions and deep discussion questions.

Dr. Kallick: How does that extra person help? The person taking notes in the discussion.

Maya: At the end of the discussion, they tell us what we do well on, what we should improve, what they liked about the discussion.

Dr. Kallick: Are you using Habits of Mind? I think it would help, sort of help, you guys to discover new things.

Maya: No, but I think we might start to.

Brenna: Where did you get the idea for Habits of Mind? And, when did you make it?

Dr. Kallick: I had the idea since I worked with my partner, and we started looking at all those different ways to think like in those literature circles. All of those skills, like comparing and contrasting. Disposition for thinking, not only do you know how to compare and contrast, but you dare to do so. Disposition attitudes are called Habits of Mind. Listening is a habit of mind, and empathy is too, because you are not just going to say something, you ask questions and try to understand the points of view. When you hear another person's perspective, you try to understand, which helps your mind be as flexible as possible.

Maya: Can we have this for other subjects?

Dr. Kallick: You can use Habits of Mind for any area, and even outside school. I worked with students working with Habits of Mind. Some people started getting bored at a party and they thought flexibly and used Habits of Mind skills. I hope you can bring them everywhere. Bring it to some of your classes and show them about it.

Brenna: Have all your books been about Habits of Mind?

Dr. Kallick: They have been about educational things. Not all Habits of Mind, but all about how to think and ways of thinking. Higher-level thinking is how the world is right now. You are asking good questions, which is a habit of mind. Communication, which you guys are doing. From Mrs. Tolisano, I noticed you guys work hard, and maybe you can start mapping things out. I have co-authored all my 16 books! Thinking collaboratively, is also a habit which is why I worked with a partner."

Maya: Why did you choose us?

Dr. Kallick: You are special. I was interested in what you guys were doing. Since I was following Mrs. Tolisano, I saw it. I wanted to bring Habits of Mind to your work, so you don't just use ordinary skills, but you understand them. I skyped with other classes. What makes you special is that you guys brought in technology.

In their collaborative *What We Remember the Most* Google document, Emily's students contributed their personal thoughts. Here is an excerpt of their comments:

- I remember that she said, "Habits of Mind are everywhere" that affected me because it made me think that we think all the time and we don't even notice it. —*Jess*
- What I remember the most from the conference was how she talked about how you should be flexible, so that creativity will come to you. Also, you will learn more. —*Maya*
- I remember that she said that habits of mind can be used outside of school. —*Jack*
- I remember how she said that it [HoM] wasn't only for humanities or English but it is for everything. —*Martin*
- One thing I remember is how she said that people need to learn how to use more exquisite language in our everyday talking instead of saying "that was awesome," but saying why it was "awesome" and making our conversations meaningful. —*Claudia*
- I remember when she mentioned that she made a museum for a good reason that really was an inspiring thing to help kids understand about how important Habits of Mind are. —*Juan Pablo*
- One thing that I remember she said was that "two people are better than one" so she likes to write books with other people. —*Samuel*
- One thing that I remember is that she said that not all [her] books are about habits of mind, but all of them have a connection to education. —*Juan*
- I remember is that she said she worked with partners because of the habit of thinking interdependently. Also, how she worked with a partner for all of the books because it is better to work with two minds that have two perspectives, than one mind that thinks on its own. —*Yael*

After they all contributed and read each other's comments, Emily asked her class, "What trend or pattern do you see in your collective comments? Why is it important for us, as learners, to recognize a trend or pattern?" This began an interesting dialogue that allowed Emily to segue back to reflecting on the focus and goals of the task. She provided one more time for reflective thoughts to be shared centered on their experiences during each of the learningflow routine steps, followed by celebrating their many accomplishments throughout the documenting opportunity. After the shared their thoughts and ideas collaboratively, the students recorded their personal thoughts in their reflection journals.

SUMMING UP

Silvia met to debrief with Emily regarding her personal professional learning. They began by revisiting Emily's documenting question: *How do I make my students aware of their personal reading strategies and behaviors when reading and discussing text?* Emily reflected on some of the photographs, annotexted videos, and blogfolio examples that best conveyed evidence of her desired outcome.

Silvia then asked her, "Where did you see or hear evidence of your goal?" Emily was introspective for a few moments and then shared, "Reading the annotated commentaries embedded in their videos was the most powerful for me as a learner. They were very specific about their exhibited behaviors, both positive and those areas that needed improvement." She added,

> I think that my interactions with them, coaching them really, helped them to determine their personal strengths and weaknesses. Reading through their reflective blog posts also provided evidence of each student's personal awareness of the reading strategies or characteristics that they were feeling good about, as well as those that were missing or needed to be worked on.

At the conclusion of their debriefing time, Emily mentioned,

> It is such a valuable way to grow as a professional learner to visibly see and hear my students thinking and reflecting, as it informs me in ways that I would only have been able to infer without them creating their own learning-thinking artifacts. It is also given me another set of strategies for better personalizing instruction and mini-lessons for my students.

APPLYING THE CHALLENGE

Your Turn!

This challenge focused on providing students with an authentic opportunity to document their learning focus and goals through the infusion of 21st century skills and the *now* literacies.

Now that you have read through the vignette, consider these questions as you brainstorm your own challenge:

- What can I do to create a 21st century skills and *now* literacies documenting opportunity for my students (or teachers) that will cause them to meaningfully and purposefully capture evidence of learning related to specific learning focuses and goals?
- What will the discipline's or cross-disciplines' content and specific focuses and goals be for my challenge that will cultivate an engaging and authentic opportunity to apply the 21st century skills and *now* literacies?
    - What will be the evidence of learning for my challenge's focus and goals that enable the learningflow routine to be visible, meaningful, shared, and amplified (see Image 11.12)?
    - How will I articulate how my challenge involves the documenting OF or AS learning characteristics?

    Explain why you believe it reflects the characteristics. (Be certain to share your thoughts beyond yourself to ensure you are increasing your sharing amplification degree.)

    - What do I think I will need to do to plan for the three documentation phases: pre-documentation, during-documentation, and post-documentation?

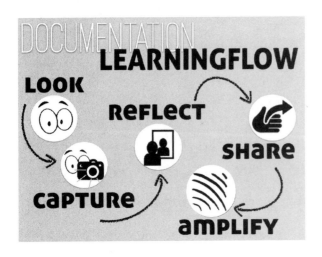

Image 11.12

Now What?

Remember that the key purpose for this challenge is to allow your learners (and yourself) to authentically apply specific characteristics, behaviors, and actions involved in the 21st century skills and *now* literacies combined with content learning in a purposeful documenting opportunity, whether an activity, task, or project.

Here are several questions to spark your personal and collaborative thinking during your Pre-Documentation Phase's planning time:

21st Century Skills and the *Now* Literacies

- Who do I think I may need to contact in my Orbits of Ability for my challenge that has expertise in one or more of the 21st century skills and the *now* literacies?

QR Code 11.4

Scan this QR code to view a #21stcenturyskills Twitter feed.

http://langwitches .me/21stcenturyskills

Note: Think out of the box. If you do not have anyone in your learning environment that meets the question criteria, try connecting with experts on Twitter using an appropriate hashtag, such as #21centuryskills, #nowliteracies, #contemporarylearning, and #documenting4learning. Scan QR Code 11.4 to view the current #21stcenturyskills feed.

- Who can help me make each of the learningflow routine steps happen successfully in relationship to the 21st century skills and *now* literacies coupled with my learners' content learning focuses and goals?
- How will I extend my personal professional learning as a primary learner and/or secondary learner related to the 21st century skills and *now* literacies as I plan for and carry out my challenge?

Content-Specific Learning Focuses and Goals

Ask colleagues in person or virtually to listen to your learners' focuses and goals (e.g., standards-based learning, applying school mission/vision behaviors, improving a specific skill or habit). Explain how they will be authentically applied in the upcoming documenting opportunity. Ask them to provide you with feedback based on the question: *Is this challenge truly an authentic way to improve my learners' capabilities based on their need to _____?*

Next, brainstorm your colleagues to answer this question:

- How can I and my learners find and engage experts, eyewitnesses, or people of interest related to the challenge's learning focuses and goals locally, as well as using social media to reach a global audience?

QR Code 11.5

Scan this QR code to access the Documenting Planner PDF.

http://langwitches.me/ documenting-planner

Now it is time to plan your challenge's three documentation phases and five learningflow routine steps. *How about creating a sketchnote?* You can reproduce the template on page 242 in the Appendix to help you get started.

If you prefer to use a text-based planner, you can either reproduce the template on page 243 or scan QR Code 11.5 to access a *Documenting Planner* PDF. After you download the PDF to your selected device, choose your preferred tool to annotate the saved file.

QR Code 11.6

Scan this QR code to access the Google Sheets Documenting Planner.

http://langwitches.me/
documenting-planner-
sheets

If you prefer to use a spreadsheet planner, scan QR Code 11.6 to access a Google Sheets document. Once you make a copy of the file, you will be able to edit the template to customize your plans by filling in the various cells.

12

Documenting Learning and Branding

Administrative Actions

We should want our community to see all the amazing things happening in school, and we should want our children to have a strong connection with the community around them.

—Tony Sinanis and Dr. Joseph Sanfelippo

I n Chapter 4, it was mentioned that schools and districts can use documenting learning as institutional memory:

Institutional memory for a school or district is a collective set of facts, events, best practices, learning experiences, values, and knowledge that represents who they are and what they believe in as an educational institution at a specific moment in, as well as over time. From an administrator's school or district perspective, documenting learning can begin to replace traditional ways of communicating the teaching and learning taking place. When a school or district is willing to be transparent about its institutional processes and results of teaching and learning over time, all stakeholders benefit and grow.

When viewed through the documenting learning layers, teachers and administrators are the primary learners, while the local community and global network are the secondary learners.

SCHOOL AND DISTRICT BRAND IDENTITY

Sinanis and Sanfelippo (2014) note that branding provides a visibility, or identity, that a brick-and-mortar or online school cannot convey in traditional forms:

> We want to ensure that OUR voices are the ones telling OUR story—we cannot let anyone else tell our story for us! The idea of branding schools isn't about selling kids or making false promises: it's about promoting the amazing things happening in our schools for those who don't have the opportunity to experience them on a daily basis. (p. 9)

When the voice of a school is shared and amplified, it reveals who they are and what they believe in, similar to what a product brand evokes in consumers' minds. For example, when someone hears *Apple,* he or she associates the name with *innovation and outstanding design* (Benson, 2014). This association did not happen overnight. It took years to brand this product, which included, and still includes, innovative ad campaigns that collectively convey and share what Apple stands for in the marketplace.

While brand-identity building needs to be intentional, there are times when a school's or district's branding will be organic. For example, Silvia was working together with Andrea Hernandez in a Jewish day school in Jacksonville, Florida, as the school's 21st Century Learning Specialists. They implemented schoolwide classroom blogs as a communication platform for teachers to document day-to-day and special-event happenings taking place in the K–8 classrooms to replace the weekly newsletters and reach out and inform the school community.

Dr. Jon Mitzmacher joined the school the following year as the new head of school. Under his leadership, the school's ability to document learning grew from classroom blogs to include individual blogfolios for every student, as well as a private faculty blog for teachers to reflect on their own learning and teaching practices.

The public classroom blogs and student blogfolios aided in the school's commitment and promise to stakeholders to embrace and practice a 21st century approach to teaching and learning. The local and global Jewish day school field (community) throughout North America responded to the school's transparency of sharing and amplifying their learning. More and more schools came to visit and observe the teachers to see their 21st century learning in action.

The sharing of the school's innovation birthed the idea for a new professional learning conference: edJEWcon, a 21st century teaching and learning institute. Twenty-five schools from around the United States and Canada made their way to Florida to participate in two edJEWcon conferences. They were hosted and held at their school with teachers and students showcasing their work and forging new collaborative connections to advance the collective work of the Jewish day schools across North America. The conference themes were *building awareness*, *fostering and sharing understanding*, and *documenting best practices in Jewish education* around 21st century skills and the *now* literacies. To document the learning taking place, students and teachers captured the learning during the conference through multiple school blogs that were created.

Following the conferences, the 21st century leadership team continued to coach teachers in documenting on the school's private blog where they transparently reflected on their classroom successes and failures and professional learning. It was also a place where the faculty could share resources, book recommendations, and reflect on feedback left as comments by their colleagues. When appropriate, documentation artifacts were cross-posted from the private faculty blog to the public edJEWcon blog.

After an initial period of getting comfortable with the logistics of the private blogging platform from a reading, writing, and commenting-contributing perspective, Dr. Mitzmacher took a bold move to the edge and announced to the teachers that they no longer had to turn in weekly lesson plans. His upgrade required them to publish a weekly quality blog post that highlighted reflections on that week's classroom content and skills learning, best practices, and new ideas related to 21st century and the *now* literacies.

The collective artifacts and evidence of learning visible in the classroom, student, faculty, and edJEWcon blogs contributed to an archived institutional-memory history of the school.

When teachers share their students' and their own professional growth over time openly and transparently, it provides authentic opportunities for administrators to strategically embed artifacts in the branding of a school and/or district. McLane and Lowe (2015) remind educators that, "One dilemma education faces today is invisibility. So many great things are happening in schools around the world that, for the most part, no one knows about" (p. 2). Branding removes the invisibility and illuminates its identity by sharing and amplifying evidence of learning via online platforms that include websites, blogs, wikis, and social media.

Rubin (2017) describes one reason for branding a school in a fast-paced changing world:

Schools must be resolved in building a brand and sharing the range of messages and stories of the good work they produce daily. Amplifying messages has never been more important. We live in a new decade, an era of acceleration, where communication around real stories and fake news touches a school community. Schools can be known for their authenticity through building a brand and being a digital leader in education.

Documenting on a school or district level requires going beyond traditional forms of sharing documenting OF learning artifacts, including

- Posting photographs of important events
- Tweeting out scores of sporting events
- Live streaming award ceremonies

Artifacts that represent documenting FOR or AS learning opportunities enable a school or district to communicate who it is and what it stands for in visible ways that include annotations that convey the implicit messages that the explicit text, visual images, videos, and audio recordings cannot do on their own. It also invites local and global communities to be engaged participants and contributors by posting comments on the school's or district's blog posts, liking its videos or tweets, or contributing artifacts that support the school's or district's story and brand.

Given a school or a district is an organization, branding in an educational context is not exactly the same as branding a product or cause, but the principles apply. Sheninger and Rubin (2017) explain:

Educators are not selling a product or services. But [a] brand is a fit for us in a modern, digital view of professional learning and progressive school thinking. This brand is made up of three foundational school elements: An image, a promise, a result. The concepts of image, promise, and result can powerfully frame a school's brand-building communication effort, but with a distinct difference from the way these terms are used in the business world. . . . In schools, brand is a personification of a community. . . . Offering a strong institutional persona across various channels through a clear brand presence is not an option in our age of visibility. "Define before being defined" is part of the leadership agenda of visibility in a digital and social age. (p. 13)

Sheninger and Rubin clarify that an institution's *image* is developed through sharing authentic stories, which is beautifully supported by the learningflow routine. An institution's *promise* can be promoted through sharing artifacts that provide evidence of the institution's mission, vision, and core values. An institution's *result*, which implies *after*, is reflected through sharing artifacts as *ongoing* assessments that convey evidence of learning, which can be shared in its infancy, as it is moving forward, and upon completion.

A school's or district's brand provides its members (students, teachers, and administrators) a platform to share and amplify their learning with its stakeholders, community, and ultimately, the world. For some institutions, branding can be viewed as a form of marketing.

Documenting Learning and Branding Identity

While branding a school or district to convey and promote its identity, there are five strategic considerations in using documentation for branding purposes (see Image 12.1).

Documenting the Big Picture of Learning on Campus

As students and teachers document their learning, they can capture only a sliver of all the learning that takes place on any given day on a school campus or throughout a district. Teachers and students are busy within their specific grade or courses and do not often see or experience connections with the teacher next door, among grade levels, or across course disciplines. This is true for content knowledge, soft skills, and the *now* literacies.

Administrators have an excellent opportunity to look for, capture, reflect, share, and amplify evidence of the learning to brand the big picture of what is taking place from a macro lens to a wide-angle lens regarding content learning and/or the institution's mission, vision, and values. They can strategically connect the student and teacher documentation artifacts and provide their own learning-thinking perspectives and experiences by adding personal narratives and comments to the in-process artifacts on a campus or throughout a district. Administrators become the curators of the evidence of learning that collectively paints a portrait of a school's or district's learning community.

It is important to paint a teaching and learning portrait as a shared experience. Portraits have for centuries conveyed more than just a face. They express one's status in society and conveying memory-laden moments in time. In modern times, the paintbrush has been traded in for a camera and the portraits are often selfies or USies. According to *Merriam-Webster's* (2017), *selfie* is defined as an image of oneself taken by oneself using a digital

Image 12.1

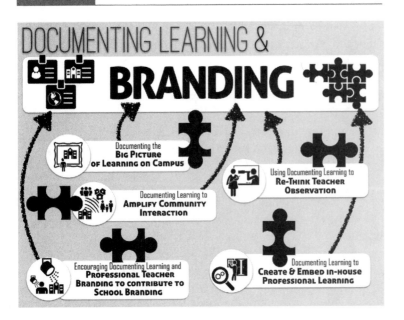

camera especially for posting on social networks. Selfies might have started out by being a shot of oneself, and they more often now include oneself in a group shot, referred to as *USies*. They capture special moments in time to be shared with a network or the world.

Who is holding the camera to convey the heartbeat of those living and learning in an educational institution? Too often non-educators, politicians, and the media paint a grim picture of the educational system. It is time for teachers, schools, and districts to take selfies and USies to become their own storytellers. By sharing and amplifying artifacts that represent slow-and-steady progress toward successes, it overshadows false or negative press.

Educators who strive to continuously learn and hone their craft expressed through documenting opportunities via a classroom, school, or district website or other social media platform speak volumes. When sharing and amplifying documenting FOR or AS learning artifacts, a school or district provides its local and global communities the chance to connect *while the learning and growth is taking place.* In-person and online communities interacting with the learners (e.g., commenting to posts, participating in online polls, using #SchoolName while attending an event) creates shared experiences, and relationship-building extends to the highest degrees of amplification. Scan QR Code 12.1 to see a school's collaborative effort in creating a brand-identity video that highlights and documents the learning that takes place on their campus, as well as invites comments by viewers.

QR Code 12.1

Scan this QR code to view the *#thisismyschool 2017* **video.**

http://langwitches.me/ this-is-my-school

Documenting Learning to Amplify Community Interaction

When students, teachers, and administrators authentically share their ongoing documentation, they automatically communicate to parents, stakeholders, and the local and global communities who they are and who they are striving to be. Branding a school or district is a journey. A journey is not a once-in-a-while event. It is an evolving accumulation of experiences. By keeping to oneself and interacting with no one else or just a few people, the growth and potential for expanding one's learning and understanding along the journey's way diminishes. When constantly and purposefully interacting with others, the journey is more fulfilling. This storytelling sharing and amplifying provide ongoing opportunities for school or district community communication interactions to take place.

It is also important to remember that branding is not just about conveying a story, but also about interacting with the reactions, comments, and re-sharing by others. In order to encourage a school's or district's local community to amplify their branding story, the institution needs to take into consideration what Burgess (2017) points out, "There is a huge difference between 'communicating' with your students' families and ENGAGING them."

Traditionally schools have used analog materials and direct mail (e.g., newsletters, flyers, handbooks, occasional write-ups in the local newspaper) to share information about their institution to the community. The content most often is to inform the community about what has happened on campus, upcoming events, policies, or new initiatives. Community interaction, if any, is minimal, such an inquiry phone call to a school or district office to clarify content or ask a personalized question.

Interaction increases when special events take place (e.g., theater productions, concerts, sporting events, STEAM fairs), but traditionally, these are passive interactions where the community members in attendance are only receptive. When there are exceptions, it most often involves conversations between a community guest or two, and one student or small group of students explaining what *has already happened* (e.g., STEAM fair—prototype with specific criteria that has been created to solve a particular problem). This traditional method does not provide insights into what is currently taking place as schools move toward the attainment of desired outcomes or learning goals.

For example, think of an instrumental performance where students are beginners to playing an instrument, let alone playing in an orchestra or band. Oftentimes administrators require the teachers to have the students performing pieces that are more difficult than should be allowed to showcase the school or district. Unfortunately, the reality is that this type of demand is detrimental to the students' learning. When beginners are encouraged to play ability-appropriate pieces, learning becomes less stressful for all. During the community performance, the conductor/director should explain to the audience why the students are playing the pieces from a learner-in-progress point of view. Better yet, the performance should be filmed from various vantage points in the theater or room, including a post-playing question-and-answer time when audience members can ask the student-players questions related to their struggles and successes in learning to play the performance pieces. Back in the classroom, the students can unpack the concert performance footage and Q & A interactions from various perspectives, such as band/orchestra performance skills or communication skills.

Strategically using targeted email lists with interactive components and engaging in active social media network to increase and amplify a school's or district's reach in defining, developing, and strengthening its brand is important to do. A co-created journey is developed by reaching out and asking the community to go beyond merely consuming the shared information to contributing their perspectives to the organization's story. Visible community social media interactions based on incremental degrees of amplification include

- Providing an emotional reaction (e.g., like, heart, favorite, sad face)
- Re-disseminating content (e.g., re-tweet, re-pin, re-share)
- Leaving a comment
- Creating artifacts and sharing one's perspective on the learning (e.g., a parent creates Facebook post that features student interviews about a school's maker-faire event)

To encourage ongoing community interaction, a school or district can take advantage of popular social media content ideas and relate them to the student learning and professional learning taking place on one or multiple campuses. Six strategies that can aid in establishing or expanding an educational brand-identity are highlighted: *memes, challenges, selfies/USies, throwbacks, crowdsourcing,* and *visual quotes.*

Memes. According to Google (2017), *meme* is a humorous image, video, or piece of text that is copied, often with slight variations, and spread rapidly by Internet users.

One popular meme: *What I Really Do* can easily be personalized to *What They Think I Do* for a student, teacher, administrator, or stakeholder to share and amplify using his or her photos and perspectives (see Image 12.2).

Image 12.2

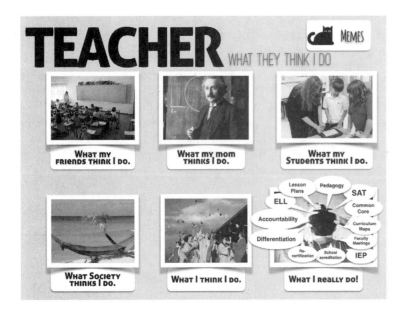

Challenges. Consider promoting participation in a monthly or semester educational-oriented challenge that embraces a school's or district's mission, vision, goals, or recently implemented learning or teaching initiative.

Participants, both in-house and in the community, are encouraged to post their contributions to the learning organization's designated social media platform or platforms. A challenge can be one that

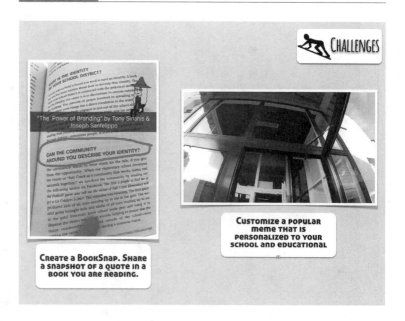

Image 12.3

- is already established and has an educational feel or theme (e.g., book bucket challenge);
- can be modified with an educational twist (e.g., mannequin challenge where the scene is in various locations on a campus that collectively convey a specific type of learning moment); or
- is a new challenge that is strategically shared and amplified using multiple social-media platforms and networks (see Image 12.3).

Using hashtags (e.g., #bookbucketchallenge) purposefully will only heighten amplification degrees and encourage additional local and global community interactions.

Selfies/USies. As mentioned previously, selfies and USies are intended to be taken and shared via a networking platform. Therefore, they are perfect for branding!

If selfies or USies are uploaded *as is* to social-media platforms for branding purposes, they only represent a documenting OF learning moment, given the photograph captured what has happened as display; and, there may not be any annotations included to convey the identity/purpose for the selfies or USies. To make certain these types of images serve the dual purpose of representing FOR and AS learning, a selfie or USie cannot stand on its own. The image needs to be part of a collection, such as a contribution in a crowdsourced action, or documentation over time.

For example, a teacher or principal can brand himself or herself as a lifelong learner by posting a selfie of each book he or she has read, holding up the book so the cover is visible and giving it a thumbs-up. The brand-identity does not happen when one or two selfies are posted; it happens after 10 or 20 selfies are shared because the cumulative selfies convey the message that reading and the act of learning new information is important to the selfie taker. To amplify this teacher's or principal's sharing of his or her love for reading and calling for community members to also share their own selfies reading their favorite books will contribute to painting a story of the importance of a reading community (see Image 12.4).

Throwbacks. According to Wikipedia, *throwback days* are a trend among social media sites where users post or repost older photographs, often from childhood. Engage a community by strategically sharing nostalgic photographs of school- or district-related past events or

Image 12.4

memorable moments (e.g., first-day-of-school pictures, graduating seniors as freshmen, field trips, alumni's favorite school/district memory). Encourage them to contribute their own throwbacks from past learning experiences at a school or while in a district.

By conducting throwback days, a brand-identity is being built or expanded because the interaction provides visual and emotional connections among in-house and local community members. When the community is invited to provide an emotional reaction, re-disseminate, leave a comment, or add their own throwback images, it continues to deepen the human connectivity. For example, a teacher, principal, or superintendent shares a throwback in-a-school-sport-uniform photograph on Facebook and asks the following in the description field: *Please like if you played sports in school and add your own "I played in school sports" photo. Go Saber Cats!*

Throwback images encourage community members to find connections to their own learning and lives, as well as help them gain an insight into the lives of the educators caring for and teaching their children. For example, Image 12.5 includes a photo collage representing three of Janet's *firsts*. The key message she is sharing in her curated descriptions is that who she is as a teacher has been affected by her youth, as well as the love and loss of her mother. When colleagues, stakeholders, and community members are afforded transparent glimpses into the people they work alongside or interact with, the institution adds emotional and empathic perspectives that convey *who* the collective school or district is, rather than only identifying *what* the institution believes in, strives for, or represents.

Image 12.5

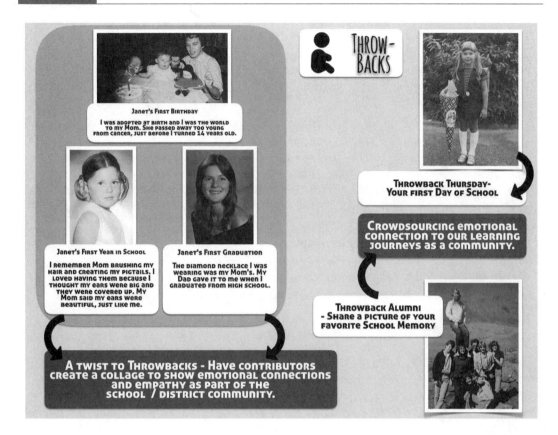

It's Time to Take Action!

Chapter 12 Action Step

It is selfie, USie, or throwback time! Based on what you have read in these sections, use one of the ideas or examples shared to experience a brand-identity opportunity for your classroom, grade level, department, school, or district office. Or if you prefer, brainstorm with colleagues and come up with your own idea.

Remember to invite your community to contribute a selfie, USie, or throwback photograph. When sharing and amplifying your call for a crowdsourced image (e.g., how you take care of the environment, the love for your pet, your first or favorite family road trip memory), be sure to use the #documenting4learning hashtag on Twitter, Facebook, or Instagram; or by mentioning @documenting4learning on Facebook and Instagram, and @doc4learning on Twitter.

Crowdsourcing. While crowdsourcing has been addressed in previous chapters, thinking about its purpose adds a branding layer to its usefulness. Oxford English Dictionary defines *crowdsourcing* as the practice of obtaining information or input into a task or project by enlisting the services of a large number of people, usually online.

Schools and districts can aid their online branding efforts by engaging their community in creating crowdsourced content that conveys learning topics and themes happening on its campus or campuses.

Asking the community to elicit a one-word or one-sentence perspective pertaining to a posed question can be powerful (see Image 12.6).

For example, responses to "What do you think is one skill future leaders need to learn now?" can become a posted video containing the one-sentence submitted answers with background music.

Another crowdsourcing idea is to create a collage of selfies with written responses to a posed question, such as, "What does documenting learning mean to you?"

Visual Quotes

Visual quote cards were explained in Chapter 8, including examples of creating them while attending a conference or reading a book (see Image 12.7). Sharing quotes from books, magazines, films, music, artwork, and other forms of media related to a learning focus or supporting vision, mission, and core values can also contribute to a school's or district's branding.

Community members can be invited to share comments about the posted visual quotes or share their favorite media-based quotes to be added to a visual quote showcase.

Image 12.6

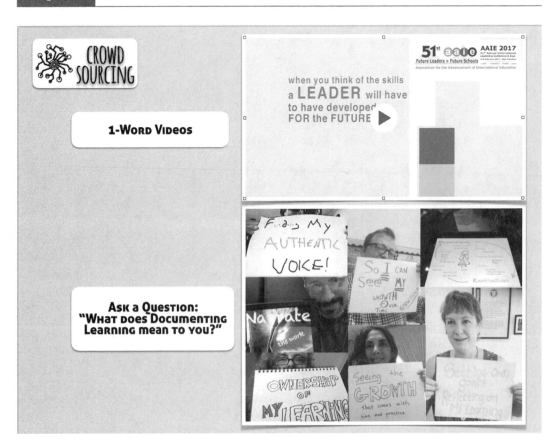

Using Documenting Learning to Re-think Teacher Observation

The documenting learning framework is not meant to be a must-do addition to an already full plate for educators. It is meant to be a learning-and-teaching replacement model that supports students and teachers who authentically own their own learning while the learning is taking place.

When a teacher is required to be formally observed, his or her learner engagement and classroom culture should be captured, reflected on, and shared over time. Artifacts that convey curricular focuses and goals need to be made visible multiple times to express a teacher's pedagogical patterns and trends (see Image 12.7).

While officially observing a teacher in person has its purpose, do traditional classroom observations two or three times a year or via random walk-throughs truly

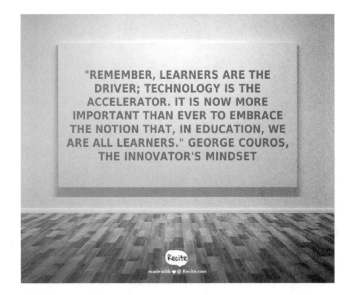

Image 12.7

"REMEMBER, LEARNERS ARE THE DRIVER; TECHNOLOGY IS THE ACCELERATOR. IT IS NOW MORE IMPORTANT THAN EVER TO EMBRACE THE NOTION THAT, IN EDUCATION, WE ARE ALL LEARNERS." GEORGE COUROS, THE INNOVATOR'S MINDSET

- Paint an accurate picture of a teacher's learning and teaching capabilities?
- Provide adequate evidence of a schoolwide or districtwide initiative's implementation or its sustainability?
- Provide adequate evidence of a teacher being a risk-taker and innovative?

A learning organization that meaningfully incorporates the framework throughout the year can upgrade teacher observations and evaluations by using a teacher's students' artifacts, as well as his or her professional learning. When re-thinking teacher observations and the inclusion of documentation artifacts, here are a few more questions to ponder:

- What will we accept as evidence of learning for professional growth related to a pedagogy or practice?
- Could a teacher blogfolio that includes annotexted images or videos better reflect his or her growth over time?
- How could a teacher's engagement in a year-long, self-selected area of growth within a local or global network provide authentic documentation evidence of his or her learning journey?

Since teacher observation and evaluation procedures are often controlled by policymakers (e.g., school boards, unions), current practices for now might not easily be changed or modified. Armed with pedagogical reasoning, it calls for educators to become disruptors of the status quo and present relevant alternative measures to policymakers. Since sustainable change takes time, an immediate action can be incorporating professional and student artifacts in post-classroom observation meetings. These authentic documents can aid in spearheading meaningful conversations and thoughtful decision making that can offer stronger evidence of what has been taking place in a classroom beyond an in-person observation time.

Another re-think that leverages the use of documenting FOR and AS learning artifacts from a teacher-evaluation perspective is to use the documentation as an evidence component for an accreditation or reaccreditation process. While accreditors have policies and procedures they must follow (which most of them need to be upgraded as well), it is refreshing when they have opportunities to analyze these types of artifacts of student, teacher, and administrator learning and teaching over time. The availability of authentic documented evidence over time eliminates the need for the in-house accreditation task force to develop evidence to satisfy accreditation requirements.

Documenting Learning to Create and Embed In-House Professional Learning

Everyone in a school struggles to find time to learn and work collaboratively in meaningful ways. There are plenty of meetings scheduled, but many times, teachers comment that they leave the meetings feeling as if the time or content did not contribute at all or significantly to their students' learning or their teaching in a personalized manner.

Jacobs and Alcock (2017) name *participation in a learning network* as one of the most powerful tools of a professional learner:

> Making connections and participating in a community with purpose empowers the participant as an educator. Finally, there is a power in publishing. Participating in a network above the level of observer indicates a commitment to the community. That commitment is rewarded by increased connections, feedback, and a sense of emotional ties to the community. It is also an investment in the strength of the community, achieved by sharing learning and active research with other participants, and sharing reflections about process and product development in the fastest way possible. The combination of rewards and investments makes participation in a learning network among the most powerful tools of a professional learner in the field of education. (p. 43)

Throughout our book, the call for participating in digital learning networks or in-person learning communities to aid in making documenting opportunities meaningful and purposeful has been emphasized. These professional learning hubs do precisely what Jacobs and Alcock advocate: increase connections, invite feedback, and evoke emotional ties to a community of learners. And, it causes the educators as learners to walk the talk, not just talk the talk. If educators want students to

- Be avid digital readers and writers, they need to model what digital readers and writers do when they are learning
- Learn to collaborate and work on a local or global learning team, they need networking opportunities to apply the skills necessary to learn and work collaboratively in a virtual environment
- Share their learning with peers and experts for feedback, they need to be transparent and openly share their learning with colleagues and experts to engage in feedback experiences
- Become network literate, they need to have personal experiences with strategically using network platforms and tools, including creating a professional identity and gaining understanding of network capabilities through authentic experiences
- Leverage the power of a learning network to solve problems and find answers beyond Googleable questions, they need to be connected and actively engaged in social media inquiry networks

- Own their own learning by actively participating and contributing, the teachers need to own their own learning too and the evidence thereof by producing artifacts that represent their growth in understanding and application over time

To brand a school or district as a strong learning community and/or network, teachers and administrators need to be empowered as professionals by self-selecting personalize learning topics of interests, similar to the Edcamp model. This allows them to be heutagogically engaged while growing as educators and leaders who foster and support the learning of those in their care.

Using the learningflow routine steps will not only benefit an individual educator as a learner, but it contributes knowledge and understanding to an entire community, which serves as evidence of a school's or district's collective ongoing professional development. The teachers and administrators' learning-thinking artifacts can be captured, unpacked, shared, and amplified using the social media platforms and tools mentioned in Chapters 8, 9, and 10 to aid in the branding process.

Encouraging Documenting Learning and Professional Teacher Branding to Contribute to School Branding

The personal professional branding of an educator can easily be confused with bragging and the efforts of one person to put himself or herself in the limelight. This is not the case when sharing and amplifying are the norm in an educational institution. As Muhammad Ali put it so well, "It's not bragging, if you can back it up" (see Image 12.8).

Many in the educational profession consider sharing to be a moral imperative (Sharski, 2013). Teachers' and administrators' professional documentation purposefully contribute to the collective school's or district's brand. Sheninger and Rubin (2017) make it clear when they ask schools to, "Look at your teachers as brand ambassadors" (p. 27). They add that the branding of a school or district cannot, "Rest on the shoulders of one person. It is a distributed, collaborative, service-oriented school improvement effort" (p. 34)

Teachers' branding via the use of artifacts tells the stories of who they are as learners and what they are exploring and applying in their learning environments. The visible telling of their stories promotes the development of skills that aid in defining, valuing, monitoring, and managing their digital identities (brand), which in turn enables them to better foster these

Image 12.8

Martin J Gottlieb Day School
Yesterday at 12:03pm ·

We hate to brag - okay not really - but hopefully by now you know that our graduating 8th graders can take up to four high school credits with them when they leave us. We are proud to report that ALL of our students who took the Geometry EOC (State of Florida's end of course exam) to acquire that credit not only passed, but ALL received the highest possible score. Yasher koach to them and our awesome Middle School math teachers, Amy McClure and Lauren Resnick!

skills in their students. Students, teachers, and administrators collectively contribute to a school's brand. And, if applicable, when joined with one or more other schools in a district, the collective brands lead to conveying a district's brand.

SUMMING UP

Schools and districts are experiencing cultural shifts that ask educators, administrators, and learning communities to re-evaluate and re-think traditional notions of brands and branding. Branding for educational institutions is relatively new. Stakeholders may be hesitant to take risks in transparently sharing a school's or district's learning journeys. Starting to think about an institution's identity in the face of a "business as *un*usual" culture is important, given the accelerated leading and managing changes occurring in the world (Pritchett & Pound, 2014).

Educators with a strong personal brand become aggregators of their school's or district's brand. These teachers and administrators constantly evaluate who they are as professionals and make their cognitive and metacognitive thinking visible by sharing and using social media platforms. For example:

- When a teacher documents by capturing strategic moments while presenting at a local, national, or international conference, he or she is branding the school and/or district.
- When teachers are actively engaged in professional learning by blogging, they are contributing to the brand of their school and/or district.
- When two or more teachers from a school attend conferences and consistently share and amplify their learning while using social media platforms, the school automatically and over time is being branded as an environment that supports ongoing learning for both its students and its teachers.

Therefore, administrators need to re-think the following:

- Granting permission for teachers (and themselves) to attend and present at conferences
- Providing adequate time for their teachers to learn digital networking skills and *now* literacies and applying them authentically in classrooms and professional learning environments
- Encouraging, supporting, and celebrating the efforts of teachers who are willing to be risk-takers and transparent learners in local and global communities

Teachers and administrators need to understand that they play a significant role as members in a collective community of learners. They also need to realize that they have a responsibility to go beyond just being consumers to being producers who create quality contributions that continually add to the learning and teaching stories that define their professional brands, as well as the collective school's or district's brand.

For educators and institutions creating and maintaining a branding identity can express, facilitate, and encourage the openness of their learning process. It is a strategic choice to move beyond documenting OF learning to sharing and amplifying documenting FOR and AS learning artifacts that represent learning journeys over time. By advocating and providing a visible and audible voice of a school's or district's learning stories as institutional memory, it conveys a commitment to lifelong learning.

Possibly for your school or district, it is a *you don't know what you don't know until you try it* situation. Sharing learning as an individual teacher, school, or district will bring amplified documenting learning opportunities for oneself, students, and administrators. The action of branding involves and embeds building meaningful relationships and connections within and outside the walls of a classroom, school campus, and district offices.

GOING BEYOND

To amplify your reading beyond this book's pages, we have created *discussion questions and prompts* for this chapter, which are located at *www.documenting4learning.com*. To extend your thinking, reactions, and responses, you can connect with other readers by leaving comments on individual chapter's discussion posts on our documenting4learning blog.

We also invite you to contribute and share your artifacts in other social media spaces to connect with and learn from other readers around the world using the #documenting4learning hashtag on Twitter, Facebook, or Instagram; or by mentioning @documenting4learning on Facebook and Instagram, and @doc4learning on Twitter.

Documenting Learning

Moving Forward

Actions have consequences.

—Tom Cotton

otton's phrase often evokes negative connotations, when in reality, there are often positive consequences to one's actions. When someone decides to eat healthier and starts exercising, the consequences are a stronger body, a clearer mind, and a better ability to focus on complex tasks.

Choice making in conjunction with considering consequences is not foreign to educational environments. Decision making followed by deliberate actions happen often concerning curriculum, instruction, assessments, learning environments, and community relations.

WHAT TO CUT? WHAT TO KEEP? WHAT TO UPGRADE?

When making decisions about documenting OF, FOR, and AS learning opportunities in a classroom, school, or district, consider why the documenting learning framework is a necessary and worthwhile action for moving forward.

Jacobs (2010) shares in *Curriculum21*

We need to overhaul, update, and inject life into our curriculum and dramatically alter the format of what schools look like to match the times we live in. Our responsibility is to prepare the learners in our care for their world and their future.

She reminds educators of two positive consequences that result from modernizing learning and teaching:

When students are engaged in the types of products and performances that are ongoing in the larger contemporary world, they are more motivated to respond to those forms and to create them as well. The deliberate and formal work of identifying new options and working to target replacements is a sensible place for a faculty to begin.

To move toward or expand a contemporary learning environment that targets replacements and mirrors the real world that students and educators experience outside of school time, Jacobs poses three straightforward questions that need to be asked, explored, and actionably answered:

What do we cut? What do we keep? What do we create?

In reality, these separate questions intermingle. For example, when something is cut, it makes room to create. Likewise, when something is kept, it may be tweaked, which means creating is taking place. Jacobs often refers to the action of *creating* as *upgrading*. For example, while sharing a modernizing-learning experience she had with a school, she mentions

Given how overwhelming it might seem to change an entrenched curriculum, we needed a reasonable place to commence *upgrading*. . . . As a lifelong student of curriculum, I am aware that curriculum has three basic elements: content, skills, and assessment. Each element needs to be revised for timeliness and aligned for coherence. . . . I suggested that we start small, we start focused, and we start with assessments.

While there are myriad learning and teaching replacement practices that can be considered through Jacobs's three questions, from a documenting perspective and this concluding chapter's purpose

- *What to cut* focuses on *mindsets.*
- *What to keep* focuses on *learning requirements.*
- *What to create* focuses on viewing assessments through an *upgrading* lens.

What to Cut?

To foster and nurture the documentation phases and learningflow routine steps, four mindsets need to be cut (see Image 13.1):

- Documenting learning is too time consuming.
- I do not have any learning worth sharing or amplifying.
- We cannot document learning using the entire learningflow routine because of policy.
- Documenting is about taking pictures or using technology.

Documenting learning is too time consuming. No one ever has enough time. That is the reality of living in a fast-paced world, both inside and outside of the school day. Because learning something new takes time, effort, and causes moments of disequilibrium and disruption, learning and teaching practices are often based on tradition—*we have always done it this way.* This mindset—"Why change, if it is working?"—leads to complacency and a sense of irrelevance for students. The reality is that it may only appear to be working on the surface.

Image 13.1

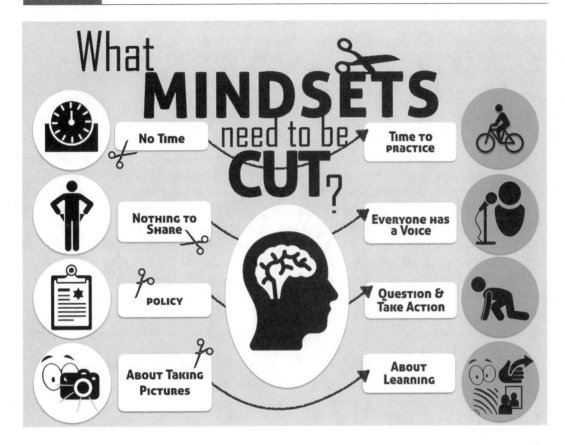

If you ask or survey students, they will often reveal that they are disengaged and not finding purpose or connections in their learning.

Finding the time to engage in meaningful learning opportunities must be a priority. Providing authentic experiences where students and teachers mingle with and learn from people in the local and global community of learners and experts needs to slowly and steadily become *just the way we do things*. Participating in documenting OF, FOR, and AS learning opportunities strategically aids in cutting dated content and pedagogy.

The reality is that the documenting learning process will be time consuming at the onset. When thinking about the documentation phases' components and the learningflow routine steps, they involve acquiring a new set of skills, which when first put into practice takes time, just like learning to ride a bike or play a complex game. Klosowki (2013) notes that when people learn new skill sets

> The more adept you become at a skill, the less work your brain has to do. Over time, a skill becomes automatic and you don't need to think about what you're doing. This is because your brain is actually strengthening itself over time as you learn that skill. . . . As those connections get stronger, the less we have to think about what we're doing, which means we can get better at other facets of a set of skills.

The good news is that it does not take too long for the documenting process skills to become effortless when practiced regularly.

Engaging in documenting opportunities does not mean all or nothing. The most important four words to remember are, *not all at once.* It is about taking one step at a time and allowing time to reflect on the struggles and successes of implementing and experimenting with a cohort (in person or virtually) who is involved the same or similar documenting opportunity in their learning environments. Hale and Fisher (2013) note, "Slow-and-steady transformations, in which teachers (and students) work collaboratively to make strategic and specific modifications to current curricular elements, lead to modern, meaningful, and engaging experiences" (p. 3).

I do not have any learning worth sharing or amplifying. A producer-consumer culture, which is foundational for a documenting environment to thrive, is built on sharing and amplifying. This culture is the norm for many students (and adults) when not in school. Connecting with others is ubiquitous in their everyday lives. Updating one's status on Facebook, adding a book review on Amazon or reviewing a product purchased online, sharing photographs on Instagram, posting videos on Snapchat and YouTube, sending out #hashtag tweets, and tagging photos are just a few ways active online participants choose to connect with peers to express their moments, milestones, and memories.

Educational systems need to acknowledge this reality and create or enhance the sharing and amplifying taking place from within a classroom, school, or district. Doing so takes advantage of behaviors and mindsets that students naturally embrace. Likewise, they relate better to their academic environments when they observe their teachers and administrators sharing and amplifying as well.

Learning is social now more than ever. Educationally speaking, teachers and administrators are establishing and growing their professional learning networks (PLN) to leverage their students' and their own authentic learning experiences. Networking is built on a concept of sharing. As previously mentioned, the Internet was developed so people could connect in purposeful and meaningful ways.

Networking is defined as the exchange of information or services among individuals, groups, or institutions. The key word is *among,* which indicates *three or more*, not one or two. In order for multiple digital exchanges to take place concerning a topic, idea, or event someone has to step up to the plate (device) and begin the sharing. Others then take, give, add, and re-share to amplify to their own networks. Godin (2017a) reminds global citizens:

> *You go first.* That's the key insight of the peer-to-peer connection economy. Anyone can reach out, anyone can lead, anyone can pick someone else. But if you wait for anyone, it's unlikely to happen. It begins with you.

The importance of building a network and reaching out to one's PLN members to interact with his or her learners cannot be overlooked. If creating and building a social media network is out of an educator's comfort zone, he or she should ask someone who is comfortable with the desired social media platform to serve as a mentor or coach, or search among the many self-guiding tutorials available online.

For educators who have never explored social media platforms and interactions in a personal or professional context often believe they have nothing worthwhile to say or share. Dave Burgess (2016) addresses why a nothing-worth-sharing belief needs to be cut from a teacher's or administrator's mindset:

> The first is the belief that their ideas are either not worthy of sharing or not unique enough to warrant adding into the conversation. This is a false belief! You have

amazing ideas and experiences that are unique to you and your path as an educator. And what you have to add to the conversation may be exactly what someone needs to hear. Share everything! The things that were successful as well as all the stuff that didn't work! You may help others . . . or save them from making the mistakes you've made. I constantly hear teachers say, "I'm sure everyone does this." No! They don't! Even if your idea is not new, you have probably put a personalized spin on it. Others can build on your idea to create something powerful for themselves. Furthermore, if you share something in a chat that others already know or do, that doesn't annoy people; it validates their practices and experiences. By talking about an idea they're trying to implement, you reinforce their belief in the soundness of the practice. You'll also encourage those who may be under fire for trying something innovative. Hearing your experiences raises their confidence and enables them to continue to fight the good fight.

We cannot document using the entire learningflow routine. Many educators participating in our documenting learning workshops are enthusiastic about the new possibilities that the documenting learning process provides, but then thoughts of school or district policy creeps into their minds, and they become paralyzed concerning implementation when they return to their schools. Unfortunately, this causes many participants to instantly snap back to a fixed mindset during the workshops. Here are a few comments that are often overheard:

- What a fantastic way to foster authentic feedback and global connections, but this won't work in my school. We have password-protected student portfolios that only the teacher, student, and parents have access to reading.
- I am so excited about having my students document their learning with annotexted images and videos, but we just don't have enough devices available for a full class-room of students. And there is a strict no-cell-phone policy in our district, even though almost every student has one, even kids in upper elementary.
- I would love to use blogs and Twitter posts as documentation artifacts for my professional learning portfolio, but it would not count toward credits or points I need for re-certification in my district because it is not on the pre-approved list.

When policies are put into place, they are often appropriate. Other times, they are not. They are knee-jerk reactions to situations, incidents, or believing urban legends that cause the policies to be created and initiated. Just as education adapts, grows, and changes over time; school and district policies need to grow, adapt, and change as well. Educators willing to pioneer new pedagogies through documenting opportunities must be willing to advocate for their students and themselves by questioning outdated policies that do not support the *now* literacies.

An example of a change over time involves a 180-degree turn in Silvia's mindset and one of her instructional practices. She remembers over a decade ago when she used to advise students to not share any personal glimpses of themselves online. *Why?* Potential college counselors and employers could search for them online by name, and they could not be accepted or hired if compromising information was found. Fast forward to the present. Silvia encourages all student and adult learners to share and amplify their learning as much as possible online. Her concern is no longer that college counselors and employers will find evidence of a learner online. On the contrary, her fear is they might not find anything at all.

Teachers and their students are typically motivated and enthusiastic to start documenting at their school, but the Internet Technology (IT) department has or creates guidelines, which can make strategic sharing and amplifying impossible to implement. When educators are eager to implement new forms and ways to use technology for learning, IT departments need to be flexible to adapt to these new requests. When pedagogically sound reasons are behind a request, IT departments should not be allowed to say *no*, but work collaboratively to find ways to make it happen. While there may be valid relational concerns regarding adequate bandwidth throughout the school day for all learners—network security and vulnerability concerns or equity for device accessibility—the IT department and general policy makers need to serve contemporary learning and teaching environments, not the other way around.

Educators cannot hide behind policies that prevent them from contemporary teaching and learning. They need to take positive actions to upgrade outdated policies to modernize learning and support what is in the best interests of their students.

Documenting is about taking photographs or using technology. Documenting opportunities involve much more than simply taking photographs or using a technology device, platform, or tool, which have been expressed throughout this book.

Based on our experiences working alongside teachers and administrators, this mindset can be a difficult one to change. The traditional understanding of visual documentation is ingrained in many educators' minds as taking photographs of what is happening and posting them as what happened. No annotexting. No reflecting. No analyzing.

It is possible to document learning without the use of modern technology (think paper and pencil) when it involves asking learners to be cognitive and metacognitive about what the evidence (e.g., a drawn sketchnote, a long-hand written fairy tale) they created conveys through unpacking and reflecting on explicit and implicit learning in the artifact. Sharing analog artifacts can be increasingly powerful when the amplification moves beyond oneself, especially when others include local experts (e.g., sketchnotes—local artists; fairy tale—local authors). Whether analog or digital artifacts, the captured evidence must go through the documenting learningflow routine steps to create process-based outcome.

The art of reflection does not happen instantly. Therefore, it is understandable why educators who have participated in documenting FOR and AS learning opportunities often slip back into a product mindset when coaching or support is removed. Similar to a bungee cord reverting back to its original position (even though it had a great time being stretched), teachers are in danger of reverting back to taking photographs or using the technology tools and platforms to simply display snapshots and refer to what they have done as documenting learning.

Documenting involves a mindset that values the learning process. In preschool to professional environments, capturing evidence of the learning while it is taking place via unpacking, analyzing, sharing, and amplifying artifacts is essential. The learningflow routine steps embrace and showcase multimedia evidence of learning that involve textual and photographic images, video actions, and auditory recordings that collectively provide insights into learners' thinking, as well as how they learn and apply their learning to new contexts over time.

What to Keep?

The *what* to keep that needs to be captured, reflected on, shared, and amplified is threefold:

- *Curricular focuses and goals* based on the standards used to aid in determining the learning
- *The vision, mission, and values* of the school or district
- *Action research* to improve learning engagement and teaching practices through meaningful projects and application opportunities

Calibrating Curricular Focuses and Goals. Calibrating is defined as adjusting to take external factors into account. In a documenting setting, this refers to adjusting the way in which teaching has been traditionally delivered to allow students' learning-thinking to be made visible.

Curricular focuses are the concepts, content, and skills birthed from standards that students need to know and be able to do, and provide evidence of their understanding and application in multiple contexts. This requisite is the same in traditional classrooms as well, although it is not as easy to capture and unpack evidence of learning and assessing students' visible thinking over time to strategically analyze their learning patterns and trends.

As one teacher put it in a cohort coaching session,

I am beginning to see the difference in my room between my students owning their own learning by having them unpack and reflect on captured learning evidence, and the way I've been teaching for years, which was more of a do-it-for-them method rather than a see-it-for-yourself method. What they are learning is the same, but I am finding they see their learning as a progression, rather than a "I have to pass a test at the end, and that is all that matters" mentality.

Curricular goals embrace the soft skills, mindsets, behaviors, and habits that meaningful and authentic learning environments provide. These dispositions need to be nurtured and practiced in conjunction with curricular focuses. Kallick and Zmuda (2017) convey this when considering the infusion of the Habits of Mind in personalized learning environments:

The teaching of disciplinary knowledge and dispositional thinking are complementary, not competing, aims. When schools include Habits of Mind as an intentional component of practice, they are ignoring that teaching for thinking is as important as teaching content knowledge. Their curriculum, instruction, and assessment intentionally address how to think critically and creatively and how to problem-solve. . . . The student's role is to use—and further develop through use—the Habits of Mind needed to fully experience a self-directed performance. Not only should the level of cognition remain high in terms of the learning and the performance, but also the level of metacognition should bring about a consciousness and an intention concerning decisions about where and when to use the habits for effective thinking. (pp. 13–14)

Documenting OF, FOR, and AS learning opportunities are founded on curricular focuses and goals. Documentation provides authentic experiences for learners to express their knowledge and understanding through pre-planned focuses and goals, as well as unforeseen learning opportunities. The documenting learning framework is a pedagogical and heutagogical methodology, not a learning goal in itself.

Conveying the Vision, Mission, and Values. When a school deeply believes in their vision, mission, and core values, they look for every opportunity to make them come alive in their classrooms and building(s). These statements need to live and breathe in the school beyond simply being displayed on the school's brick-and-mortar walls, website, in a handbook, or in marketing materials.

- Can every student, faculty member, administrator, and local community member give examples of what the vision looks like in reality?
- Can students and parents or caregivers articulate the mission statement in their own words?

- Can evidence of the core values be visibly seen or audibly heard in schoolwide assemblies and referred to often during learning experiences?

Documenting learning supports and encourages making a school's or district's mission, vision, and core values visible. They are not only idle words as part of a marketing package, but truly represent and convey the tapestry of the learning environment. Conveying an institution's mission, vision, and values in action takes thoughtful and strategic planning and implementation based on the documentation phases and learningflow routine.

A middle school faculty wanted its core values to be evident in their students' artifacts (see Image 13.2). While everyone could recite the core values by heart, there was currently no clear evidence of the values present in their students' thinking processes or academic behaviors.

Image 13.2

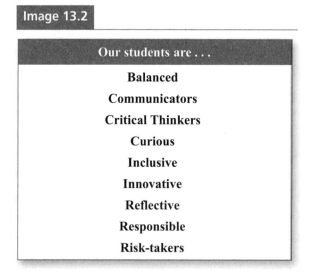

Our students are . . .

Balanced

Communicators

Critical Thinkers

Curious

Inclusive

Innovative

Reflective

Responsible

Risk-takers

During the pre-documentation phase, which took place just prior to the beginning of the school year, the teachers and administrators met as a full faculty to brainstorm possible ways in which their students could provide visible core-value evidence. After some discussion and negotiating, they reached consensus. They decided that since their students were already comfortable with the use of blogfolios, they would ask them to add a layer of core-value documentation when writing their posts throughout the school year.

In the during-documentation phase, students were asked to use the appropriate core value terms as a category or label for each post they wrote and published (see Image 13.3). Over time, regardless of the class period, the students were creating visible core-value connections between and among the disciplines.

Image 13.3

Posted by Unknown at 1:29 PM

Recommend this on Google

Labels: 7th Grade, Advisory, Critical Thinker, Reflective, SLC

In the first round of the post-documentation phase, which was just prior to the school's first grading period student-led conferences (SLC), students had to dig deep into their understanding of each core value's characteristics to justify their reasoning for how they chose to label their blog post artifacts with a particular core value or values.

What surfaced was that the students were inconsistent in their understanding of what constituted evidence of each core value's characteristics, which the teachers discussed during their next faculty meeting. They noted that this occurrence was not specific to a particular grade, cultural group, or boys versus girls. This realization led the faculty and staff to determine specific and strategic actions and activities to provide consistent in-school exemplars, as well as real-world applications for each core value to aid in their students understanding.

Based on the continued expectation for their students to document their content learning as well as the core-value visual connections in their blog posts, the teachers began to see an improvement pattern emerge during the next three quarters. They commented that the majority of students improved their abilities to articulate the connections between their artifacts' indicated core values that they chose to share with their parents/guardians during the SLC meetings.

Toward the end of the fourth quarter, the teachers were challenged to sit in grade level teams, rather than by disciplines, during a faculty meeting. The principal asked each grade-level team to use the network labels in their customized blogging platform and choose one of the core values that the team would like to reflect on and analyze from a year-long learning-application lens. One team of teachers chose *communicators* because they agreed it was a challenging year for this group of students to communicate well, especially when working on group projects or tasks. The principal provided two reflective questions to aid in each team's conversation once they scanned through and read the search-result blog posts:

- How was the specific core value evident among students' blog posts in your grade level?
- What trend or pattern, or lack thereof, did your team notice? (Be ready to provide evidence when we meet again as a large group.)

After the large-group sharing was completed, the principal posed another question:

- Which core value was embedded strongly in the school's culture and evident in the students' blogfolios?

Small-group discussions led to a large-group discussion. In conclusion, everyone agreed that the year-long core-value documentation process posed challenges, such as getting some students to not just be compliant when creating their blog post entries. They were also pleased that their students were building ongoing evidence. These data revealed to the students, themselves, board, and local community that the school's core values are alive, well, and visible.

The students' blogfolios initially served as documenting OF learning. The students, as primary learners, had to select blog posts they felt best conveyed evidence of their growth as a learner over time. Students then shared the data in their SLC meetings.

When the faculty used the students' blog posts in a collective analysis through a core-values lens at the end of the school year, documenting FOR and AS learning was taking place. A larger degree of sharing and amplification also happened because more people were viewing and reflecting on the blog posts beyond a student blogger, his or her parents/guardians, and his or her classroom teacher.

Conducting Action Research. Chapter 1 mentioned that mindful documenting educators purposefully have the inquisitive minds of scientists and the curiosity of researchers.

In classroom or professional learning environments involved in documenting opportunities, the learners—whether students or teachers—actively participate in the learning by asking questions, analyzing data, and communicating their findings while conducting the research.

Hagel, Brown, and Davison (2012) note that when people want to expand their knowledge boundaries, they do so based on *knowledge flows*, where new information flows from multiple people, experiences, and resources to gain or evolve the current knowledge of a topic, or the ability to better apply the understanding:

> Knowledge-flows naturally flourish on the edge. Why? Because, by definition, participants on these edges are wrestling with how to match unmet needs with unexploited capabilities and all the uncertainty that implies. Edge participants therefore focus on ways to innovate and create value by connecting unmet needs with unexploited capabilities and then scaling these opportunities as rapidly as possible. In the process, they create significant new knowledge. (p. 53)

Culberhouse (2017) observes in reference to Hagel, Brown, and Davison's note:

> It is at the *"edges"* not only where new ideas, new thinking and new knowledge are discovered and formed, but where we learn to overcome the "genetic" drift that often entrenches our organizations in stasis, status quo, and eventual irrelevance for the future. Most organizations tend to push creativity and innovation to the outer edges. . . . Creative and innovative leaders not only tap into those edges, they find ways to fold them back into the core.

Modernizing classrooms and professional learning needs to include students and educators who perceive themselves as action researchers willing to go beyond the edges. When learners share their questions and findings through documentation artifacts and strategic amplification they are promoting and fostering research as collaborative inquiry. Price (2013) acknowledges that:

> [In] a culture of collaborative enquiry – educators see themselves as researchers and developers. They are encouraged to look outside education for inspiration and innovation. They are required to share those enquiries, involving students, parents, and other staff. Their learning spaces welcome the disruption of visitors, because, as Stephen Harris [Founder/Director of Sydney Centre for Innovation in Learning] says 'the more students have to articulate their learning, the more they live it.' (p. 186)

Remember, conducting action research requires innovation to improve learning engagement and teaching practices through meaningful projects and application opportunities, which means thinking outside the edges of the box to get beyond *the way in which I or we have always done it.*

Documenting embraces educators as action researchers who have read a professional learning book and participated in a workshop or coaching cycle, and who are open to now applying new practices in their learning environments, but want to make that application (action) visible and shareable with local and global learning communities as they search and re-search their professional growth. The same is true for students who desire authentic applications of their learning and research and learn about themselves from analyzing their evidence of learning over time and in various contexts.

What to Upgrade?

Documenting FOR and AS learning can be viewed as a modern assessment methodology. It provides opportunities for deeper meaning and authentic purposes to apply what is being learned to inform learners, teachers, parents/guardians, administrators, and the local/global community. Kashin (2017), who works specifically with young learners, points out

> When documentation has meaningful content that depicts learning and development, early learning teachers share it with children, families, the community, and with each other as a way to demonstrate children's competency and capacity. This is a form of assessment of children's learning as it is visible, transparent and meaningful. During this process, educators seek to make meaning in their continued reflection of the documentation in order to seek ways for it to authentically influence the direction future teaching and learning will take.

As we work with educators from around the world on implementing and sustaining the documenting learning framework in their environments, there is often a clash between traditional assessment measurements and documenting's new forms of evidence of learning. This clash is often due to traditional grading practices and the perception that the captured and analyzed artifacts do not fit the norm of what is permissible as evidence to determine their students' grades.

Sadly, the opposite is true. Sackstein (2015) comments on this false dichotomy:

> Every time a grading period ended, I struggled with how to assess my students meaningfully and became increasingly less satisfied with how the system expected me to do it. Something had to change—I was doing my students a disservice even if they didn't realize it. Assessment must be a conversation, a narrative that enhances students' understanding of what they know, what they can do, and what needs further work. Perhaps even more important, they need to understand how to make improvements and how to recognize when legitimate growth has occurred. (pp. 13–14)

Due to her frustration, Sackstein asked her administration for permission to experiment with a non-graded measurement system. Reflecting on her initial implementation, she shares

> As with any new endeavor, running a no-grades classroom came with some challenges. Although I'd taught all of the classes before I hadn't done so without grades, and time management became an issue. At times, the shift away from traditional grades was exceptionally challenging: it was much easier, I realized to "just" put a grade on student work. However, the immediate impact of the new system on my students and encouraged me to persevere through these difficulties. My lower-level students were enticed by the idea of a no-grades classroom, often asking why other teachers weren't taking the same approach. They like the idea of not being judged; they hadn't had success in a traditional space, often being negatively labeled because learning was more challenging for them. . . . My highest level students weren't as

excited by the idea; after all, most of the 12th grade advanced placement class define themselves as "A" students and if I took this away from them, how would they know they were excelling? [As a former honor student myself] looking back, the grade had little to do with the learning and more to do with my need to feel smart . . . I can't imagine how much more I would have learned if I didn't feel the need to compete for better grades and instead had just focused on learning. Hard conversations had to happen. Tough questions had to be answered. What is achievement? (pp. 14–16)

The concept of using a scaled grading system began at Yale College in 1785, with traditional letter grades first appearing at Harvard in 1883 (Durm, 1993). Upon hearing this, most educators agree that upgrading a century-plus practice is an absolute necessity.

And herein lies the 21st century assessment-evaluation dilemma: With encouragement and support from their administrators, teachers are upgrading many areas of their pedagogical practices to facilitate authentic tasks and the *now* literacies, but struggle when they are required to simultaneously use standard assessment measurements by the same administrators. Rather than allowing upgraded assessments that showcase students' visible cognitive and metacognitive thinking that is clearly evident in documentation artifacts, teachers and students are supposed to still find value in a letter, number, or percentile grading system that no longer makes sense to them as engaged learners.

Dr. Evelyn Mahler, an educator who teaches high-school health and environmental science courses, has been struggling with the rich work her students have been producing via their thought-provoking artifacts and the over-simplification of having to create grading-period letter grades:

Documenting for learning is a trendy concept that did not mean too much to me until I decided to give it a try. The motivation for transforming my Health Ed lessons into something more meaningful to the students, and less oriented to the overwhelming curriculum, challenged me to a whole new approach. And I thought that documenting these processes could, hopefully, help me to reflect. I had never documented in a systematic manner (but now I do it using a professional blog). Moreover, I decided not only to document my own teaching and learning processes, but also asked my students to document their own.

As we were working on projects, their documenting turned out to be an amazing way to follow up with their progress. Working collaboratively in the cloud allowed me to closely follow up their tumbles, falls, and achievements; along with continuous feedback by commenting and encouraging them to analyze their learning in a more reflective manner. It was incredible how in less than 4 weeks, the quality of their own documentation improved, with metacognitive thinking becoming deeper. It was exciting to see how they got motivated, how they felt that someone listened to them seriously, accepting their doubts, their cognitive conflicts, fairly praising their successes. The feedback on their learning was not only online, but I also tried to take my time to sit with the groups and conference with them, trying to follow their thinking, making it visible, inquiring. It was difficult to get them to the point of true understanding: that they were working not for me and their term grade, but for themselves (and in the case of this community-oriented prevention action, for the whole school community).

Our system demands grading. How could I possibly demote and simplify all this rich work together to a term grade, a plain number? Does it make any sense?

Unfortunately, we are still far away from getting rid of grades. I will keep on trying and find the way to assess their learning in a more significant and transparent manner, getting closer, getting nearer, from *learner* to *learners*, letting the motivation be much more than a grade. The path is made by walking, and documenting this trip is an incredible companion.

The documenting learning framework can be used in parallel with gathering evidence that meets traditional assessment and grades practices. The purpose of the learningflow routine steps is meant to be an occasional or full-time replacement model for traditional grading.

The phases and learningflow routine celebrate new forms of learning, teaching, and assessing that confront traditional evaluation systems head on. When we talk with teachers who are attempting innovation by combining documenting pedagogy and heutagogy with their traditional assessments and grading requirements, they share their frustrations:

- We are sending the signal to stakeholders (e.g., parents, other educators, local community) that we are not sure what our institution truly values as learning, which is why we do both. If we and our students had our way, we would not choose to do traditional forms at all, or keep the traditional ones to a bare minimum.
- We find that while administrators and other teachers say they want to do what is best for students, they are really not ready to let go of what might not, at first, appear to make sense anymore when thinking about new forms of teaching and learning.
- We are conveying a duality message to our students that on one hand their evidence of learning, captured through their artifacts are valued, but on the other hand not a priority when it comes to getting their quarter grades.
- Some teachers look at us like we are crazy because our workload is actually greater, given we have to run parallel tracks through our classrooms. One track captures the traditional assessment requirements, while the other is capturing student learning engagement while they are capturing evidence of their thinking through their documentation artifacts.

For a classroom example of this dilemma, meet Josh (whose name has been changed for privacy reasons). He is a high school history and social studies teacher who has been attempting to live in both assessment worlds. He upgraded a year-long course focused on social issues affecting their country and required his students to use a blog to convey their learning-thinking evidence as the year progressed. He explained to them that their blogs would be viewed as a form of documenting their understanding, reflections, and findings, as well their peers and his feedback to push the boundaries of their thinking.

QR Code 13.1

Scan this QR code to read one of Evelyn's reflective professional blog post.

http://langwitches.me/ grading-tension

Josh's students reacted positively to working with this social media platform throughout the year. He was thrilled with the ongoing and cumulative evidence of learning that each student's collective blog posts conveyed. His desire was to celebrate this evidence and have them conduct a reflection forum. Unfortunately, he could not do this because an end-of-course requirement steeped in school tradition meant his students had to create a PowerPoint coupled with a research paper that would be printed out and evaluated by a panel of teachers as each student conducted an oral presentation with the PowerPoint as a presentation aid. (Note: The teachers on the panel had not read any of his students' blogs throughout the year.)

As his students were going through the required motions to prepare their presentations, they voiced their frustrations to him and questioned their year-long blogging experience as it now appeared to be "useless" and an "unnecessary" workload. They no longer saw the act of blogging and the evidence of patterns and trends over time as authentic assessment of their learning.

Josh began to also question the significant amount of time he had invested in his students' blogging, not to mention the time it personally took him to evaluate and provide meaningful feedback to all of his students. The biggest blow was when he realized that what he had done throughout the year was not being valued by his colleagues or administrators in terms of worthwhile assessment and evaluation. They told him that the blogs can only serve as a form of anecdotal assessment. In Josh's personal reflection concerning his students' blogging year and its perceived value versus actual value, he shared

> Blogs offer enormous possibilities for not only autonomous student work, but also collaborative work that would have been unthinkable just a few years back. Blogs give students a great broadmindedness, since they can connect with other online resources, people, and organizations from different parts of the world. Blogs also give students concrete evidence how they have constructed their own knowledge, because they were able to make their thinking visible along the way. For us teachers, their blogs are valuable tools to help us guide them, they show their prior knowledge and demonstrate evidence of which knowledge they actually incorporated in their process.

> But, I have no doubt, that many times external conditions go exactly against these possibilities. Some schools will only accept as evidence "formal and traditional" forms of assessment. Sometimes the time invested using these new forms of teaching and learning is much more complex work that the majority who are not familiar with the tools and platforms cannot imagine. They do not recognize the time it demands to do it well and do it right.

> Last, but not least, there is also a tension that has to do with the open mindset from teachers in accepting non-traditional forms of evaluation. I would even say, more than an open mindset, is the need to be prepared and possess the skills to work with the tools and platforms.

A second example of how new forms of documenting cause disruptive tensions with traditional notions of accepted evidence of learning happened during a *Middle School Admissions and Transitions* night at a private K–8 school attended by eighth graders and their parents or guardians.

A variety of high school admission directors and guidance counselors were present to share their school's admission-and-placement procedures and answer any questions about their schools for the students and parents in attendance. Some parents asked if their child's comprehensive student portfolios would be taken into consideration for admission. Given this was not the norm for the feeder-pattern schools present, they were hesitant to reply. In the end, their responses were not what the parents and students wanted to hear,

> We might take a look at the portfolios, but only if standardized test scores, report cards, and teacher recommendations don't give us clear picture of where that student is. . . . We also might use the portfolio for academic placement when considering a student for being in honors classes, or not.

The purpose in sharing these two vignettes is to point out the urgency to upgrade what a school's or district's community (e.g., students, teachers, administrators, parents, the feeder pattern schools) perceives as valued evidence of learning. Sackstein states in the conclusion to *Hacking Assessment*

> In the 21st century, we nurture critical thinkers and collaborators, innovators and problem solvers; we must if we want our world to thrive. The way we assess our students affects their perception of learning, so if we take the negative or superficially positive away from the experience, more students will be able to see the brilliance that lies beneath the number and letter grades. What can you change about your assessment practices tomorrow? What will you change in the future? . . . If you're ready to see your students thrive and to bring joy and curiosity back to your classroom, take a risk: Make the change to a non-grades classroom and watch it happen. The work will be worth it. (pp. 129–131)

Upgrading means replacing traditional evaluation methods with contemporary forms. As long as schools and districts cling solely to traditional assessment systems, they will continue to not reflect valuing their students as deep thinkers involved in authentic experiences, nor contributor-producers who reach out to local and global communities.

SUMMING UP

After reading this chapter and reflecting on what has been shared from a documenting learning perspective, it is obvious that changes need to be made. What to change and how to begin making the change—whether a mindset, overcoming barriers, or rethinking what is valued—involves being a risk-taker, as Sackstein mentioned.

Most importantly, it involves a willingness to dive in, head first, and be a transparent example to others. In a Twitter #i2chat focused on innovation, Sherratt (2017) summarized how to best do so when he responded to the question:

> Q3 Schools don't always love change. What advice do you have for others when facing resistance?

> By tweeting:

> A3. My biggest advice is "Show, Don't Tell". Telling works for a few people, but showing the way things can be done is more powerful #i2chat

Godin (2017b) inquires, *"But what if it works?* Fear of success is at least as big a challenge as fear of failure. Because if it works, things are going to change. Are you ready for that?"

Change in the context of the documenting framework includes meaningful and purposeful learning opportunities for students, teachers, and communities. These changes support answering action-oriented questions such as the following: *Who owns the learning? Who do we learn from? How does cognition and metacognition become centerpieces for learning how to learn?*

Change will also set cogs in motion that will affect related cogs to move in new ways and in new directions throughout an institutional organization (see Image 13.4).

Image 13.4

Are you ready for the documenting learning framework and documenting FOR and AS learning opportunities to disrupt your status quo and clash with traditional ways you and your colleagues have always done things?

It's Time to Take Action!

Chapter 13 Action Step

This is the last, and most important, action step! It is time for you and your colleagues to discuss, brainstorm, and plan how you will begin or expand the application of the documentation phases and documenting learningflow routine steps in your learning environment.

What will you cut? What will you keep? What will you upgrade? How will you and your colleagues turn the

- *ideas,*
- *processes,*
- *procedures,*
- *suggestions, and*
- *provocations*

that you have read, reflected on, and visualized in the thirteen chapters into actionable steps?

To get you started, you and your colleagues can use the KWHLAQ chart in the Appendix (page 244) to aid in addressing your first learning and teaching action step (e.g., using technology strategically to transform learning, globally connected project, going gradeless, having students use documentation artifacts during student-led conferences to justify their acquisition and application of knowledge and understanding).

When you have filled in your documenting learning KWHLAQ chart, share your artifact and reasoning with additional colleagues or experts and ask them for their feedback and suggestions.

If sharing and amplifying your KWHLAQ artifact and reflections, remember to use the #documenting4learning hashtag on Twitter, Facebook, or Instagram, or by mentioning @documenting4learning on Facebook and Instagram, and @doc4learning on Twitter.

GOING BEYOND

To amplify your reading beyond the book's pages, we have created *discussion questions and prompts* for this chapter, which are located at *www.documenting4learning.com*. In order to extend your thinking, reactions, and responses, you can connect with other readers of the book by leaving comments on individual chapter's discussion posts our documenting4learning blog.

We also invite you to contribute and share your artifacts in other social media spaces in order to connect and learn with and from other readers from around the world via the #documenting4learning hashtag on Twitter, Facebook, or Instagram, or by mentioning @documenting4learning on Facebook and Instagram, or @doc4learning on Twitter.

Appendix

Image A.1

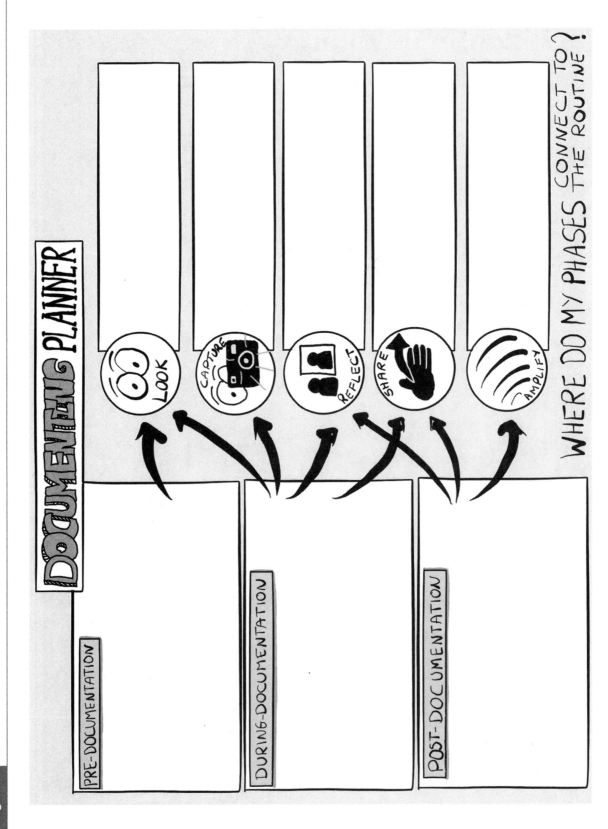

Image A.2

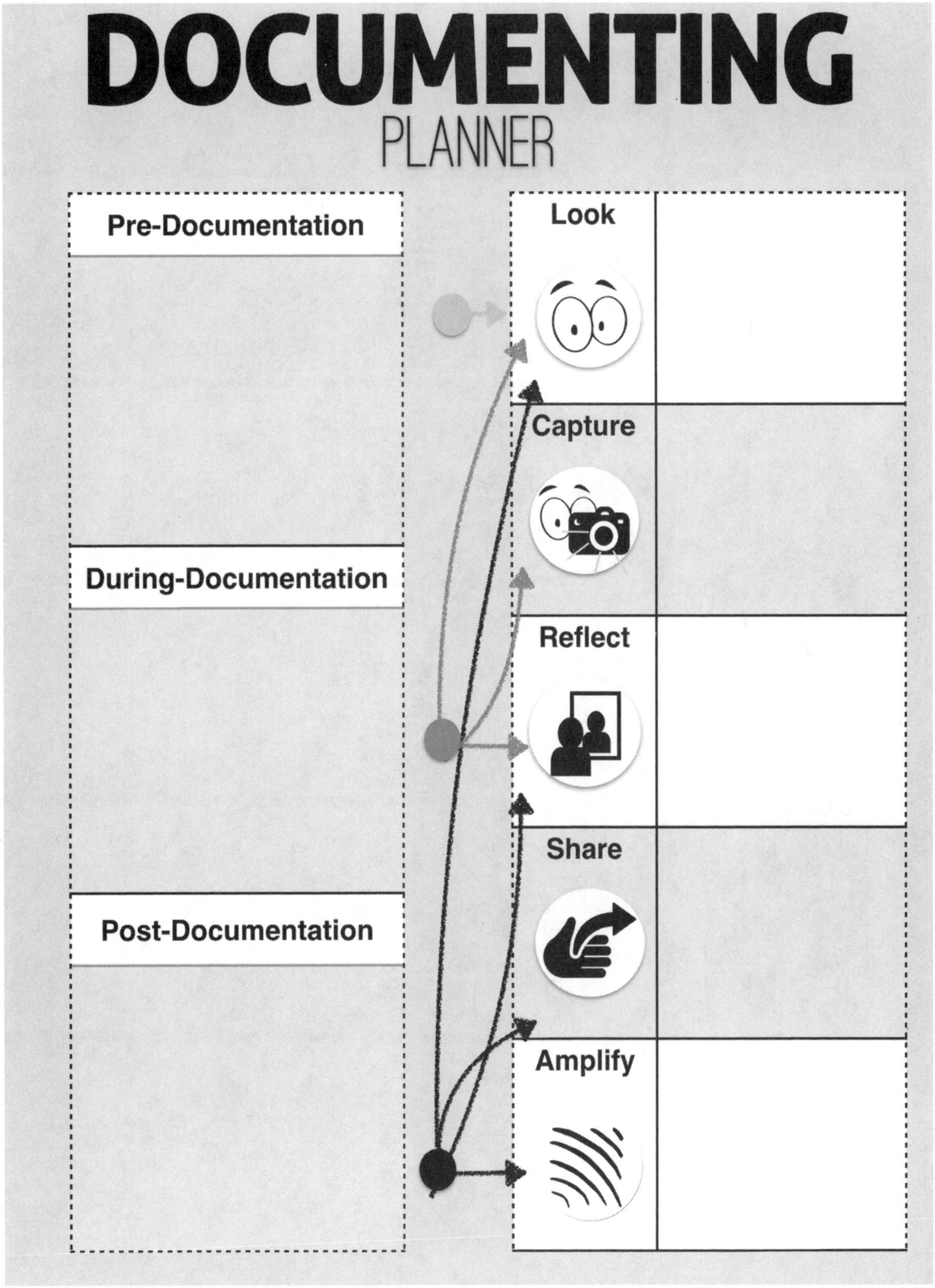

DOCUMENTING
PLANNER

Pre-Documentation

During-Documentation

Post-Documentation

Look

Capture

Reflect

Share

Amplify

KWHLAQ

Documenting Learning Action Step

based on John Barell's inquiry strategy in: <u>Why Are School Buses Always Yellow?</u>

Following the KWHLAQ sequence, document your thinking process related to your chosen action step.

K	W	H	L	A	Q
 What do we **KNOW** ?	What do we **WANT** to know ?	**HOW** will we find out?	What have we **LEARNED** ?	What **ACTION** will we now take?	What further **QUESTIONS** do we have?

Glossary

Amplification: Extending teaching and learning opportunities and one's influence; make thinking and learning visible beyond own mind and zip code; make learning available to others by inviting them to contribute; action of impacting the learning of others

Amplify: To make larger or greater; increasing audience reach using social media

Analog: Paper based; opposite of digital (e.g., analog chart versus digital chart)

Annotate: Act of adding notes or comments alongside text, image, video to aid in processing or explaining the media content

Annotext: Annotate digitally by overlaying text, directional arrows, and/or frames at specific moments on a still image or in a video

Artifact: Analog or digital media (e.g., text, visual, audio, video) used for documentation purposes

Bite-size Information: Bite-sized nuggets of content that are easy to consume, sometimes they're images or image-based, whose meaning can be grasped quickly, and often create deeper meaning by referencing shared experiences or stories (Gutierrez, 2014)

Blogfolio: Combination of a blog and portfolio characterized by providing learners opportunities to (a) develop writing skills, increase reflective practices, and connecting with authentic audiences; and (b) use as a platform that embraces creativity, communication, connections, and applications of digital citizenship (term coined by Andrea Hernandez)

Cognition: mental action or process of acquiring knowledge and understanding through one's thoughts, experiences, and senses

Community: Group of people living in same area; group of people with common interests

Crowdsourcing: Obtaining information or input into a task or project by enlisting the services of a large number of people (*Oxford Dictionary*)

Curate: Act of determining a resource's or artifact's value for current or future learning need or task

Curation: The Critical Thinker's collection, and involves several nuances that make it an independent and classroom-worthy task (Fisher & Tolisano, 2014)

Digital: Electronic based; opposite of analog

Digital Citizenship: Quality of habits, actions, and consumption patterns that impact the ecology of digital content and communities (Heick, 2013a)

Digital Curation: Selection, preservation, maintenance, collection, and archiving of digital assets which establish, maintain, and add value to repositories of digital data for present and future use. (Wikipedia, 2017)

Digital Portfolio: Compilation evidence of learner's growth, development, and accomplishments over time that is usually collected, curated, and shared online

Documentation: Captured, collected, and/or curated evidence of learning

Documenting AS Learning: Curation decision making for capturing and explaining purposeful moments as evidence of learning. Documentation is strategic, embedded, and ongoing, component of the learning process.

Documenting FOR Learning: Explanations of selected artifacts to convey purposeful moments during and as a result of learning. Documentation is strategic and purposefully captures learning so that it can be reflected upon to support learning of oneself and/or others.

Documenting OF Learning: Product or performance documentation display during or after learning has taken place, but no reflection is involved

Edit: Prepare for publication by correcting, condensing, or otherwise modifying

Explanation: Describing facts in a way that makes them understandable (LeFever, 2012)

Global Literacy: Ability to understand how the world is organized and interconnected, including four global competencies: ability to investigate the world; recognize perspective; communicate ideas; and take action on issues of global significance

Hashtag: Hash or pound sign directly followed by a word or phrase that conveys topic or concept used strategically on social media platforms

Heutagogical Documentation: Documentation focused on self-motivated and self-directed learning that aids self-awareness, fueling motivation, and supporting decision making concerning desired learning

Heutogogy: Self-motivated and self-directed learning

Hyperlink: Clickable online image- or text-based link that transfers user from one location or another

Hyperlinked Writing: Multilayered writing that takes advantage of the power of hyperlinks to connect personal writing to further content, concepts, ideas, or other sites on the web; writing that transforms static, linear, one layered writing into multilayered, connected, non-linear writing

Information Literacy: Ability to filter and find information, analyze, evaluate, tag, categorize, organize, archive, store, find again, connect, curate, present, re-mix, and create new types of information

Institutional Memory: School's or district's analog/digital collection and curation of events, experiences, best practices, values, and beliefs accessed by local and global audiences

Learningflow Routine: Series of steps that creates a fluidity, and ultimately a habit, within the three documentation phases designed to create a flow from documenting initiation to completion based on content-specific focuses and articulated goals

Linktribution: An attribution via a web link or offering (Levine, 2006)

Media Literacy: Ability to express informed and critical understanding of mass-media purposes and influences, both explicit and subliminal

Metacognition: Thinking about one's thinking; refers to processes used to plan, monitor, and assess one's understanding and performance

Network Literacy: Ability to obtain a basic understanding of network technology, being able to craft one's own network identity, understand network intelligence, and understand network capabilities (Hellweg, 2012)

Orbit of Ability: A given person's knowledge, talents, or expertise (Hale & Fisher, 2013)

Pedagogy: Methods, techniques, and strategies used by teachers to facilitate learning

Personal Learning Network (PLN): Group of people who interact (most often) digitally based on common interests and passions

Platform: Social media environment enabling a community to meet, share, communicate, and learn together

SAMR: Four-level taxonomy (Substitution, Augmentation, Modification, Redefinition) developed by Ruben Puentedura that classifies technology, pedagogy, and content knowledge infusion based on teaching and learning impact

Schoolware: Education-specific platforms and tools, purchased through a vendor or online educational company

Screencasting: Act of recording and producing a video of what is transpiring on a screen, which can be recorded via screencasting tools and voice-overs through the device's microphone

Screenshooting: Act of taking a screenshot

Sketchnoting: A form of taking notes wherein the sketchnoter visually represents his or her thoughts and ideas, which can be created using a digital screen or analog paper format (Rohde, 2014)

Synthesizing: Act of combining what is known to create a new or more complex understanding

Tool: Device or implement used to carry out a particular function (*Oxford Dictionary,* 2017b)

Transmedia Documentation: Narrative that extends beyond multiple media forms that also plays to the strength of those forms (Heick, 2014b)

Unpacking: Decision-making regarding the usefulness of captured documentation; analyzing media to determine and inform learners of their current capabilities

Worldware: Denote materials that are created and marketed mainly for purposes other than teaching and learning, but which are also used for teaching and learning (Ehrmann, 1995)

References

Addison, J. (n.d.). Addison quote [Quote website]. Retrieved from https://www.brainyquote.com/quotes/quotes/j/josephaddi104348.html

Ali, M. (n.d.). Ali quote [Quote website]. Retrieved from https://www.brainyquote.com/quotes/quotes/m/muhammadal167367.html

Anderson, P. (2011). Developing & using models [Informational video]. Retrieved from http://www.bozemanscience.com/ngs-developing-using-models

Anderson, W., Krathwohl, D. R., Airasian, P. W., Cruikshank, K.A., Mayer, R. E., Pintrich, P. R., Raths, J., & Wittrock, M. C. (2000). *A taxonomy for learning, teaching, and assessing: A revision of Bloom's taxonomy of educational objectives.* Upper Saddle River, NJ: Pearson.

Asia Society. (2015). Global competence outcomes and rubrics [Informational website]. Retrieved from http://asiasociety.org/education/global-competence-outcomes-and-rubrics

Benson, P. (2014, January 23). Quoted in "20 iconic brands—and why they work" [Blog post]. Retrieved from http://www.creativebloq.com/branding/most-iconic-brands-11121149

Buhl, L. (2017). 6 soft skills everyone needs and employers look for [Blog post]. Retrieved from https://www.monster.com/career-advice/article/six-soft-skills-everyone-needs-hot-jobs

Burgess, D. (2016, June 10). The critical importance of 127 [Blog post]. Retrieved from http://daveburgess.com/the-critical-importance-of-127/

Burgess, D. (2017, January 8). #YourSchoolRocks tweet [Twitter post]. Retrieved from https://twitter.com/burgessdave/status/818153865765752832

Cable News Network. (2017, March 14). #MyFreedomDay [Event web page]. Retrieved from http://www.cnn.com/specials/world/myfreedomday

Casa-Todd, J. (2017). Social LEADia: Moving students from digital citizenship to digital leadership. Dave Burgess Consulting: San Diego, CA.

Clark, B. (2007). Zen and the art of remarkable blogging [Blog post]. Retrieved from http://www.copyblogger.com/zen-and-the-art-of-remarkable-blogging/

Clark, T. (2017). Metacognition. [Infographic]. Retrieved from https://www.smore.com/ncec?utm_content=buffer04353&utm_medium=social&utm_source=twitter.com&utm_campaign=buffer

Costa, A., & Kallick, B. (2010). Describing the habits of mind [Online chapter]. Retrieved from http://www.ascd.org/publications/books/108008/chapters/Describing-the-Habits-of-Mind.aspx

Cotton, T. (2017). Cotton quote [Quote website]. Retrieved from https://www.brainyquote.com/quotes/quotes/t/tomcotton771331.html

Couros, G. (2015b, March 7). New project: #EDUin30 [Blog post]. Retrieved from http://georgecouros.ca/blog/archives/5121

Couros, G. (2016, March 17). The (nearly) invisible portfolio [Blog post]. Retrieved from http://georgecouros.ca/blog/archives/6131

Culberhouse, D. (2017, June 7). Folding back the "edges" [Blog post]. Retrieved form https://dculberh.wordpress.com/2017/06/07/11615/

Downes, S. (2013, October 23). A few words on ePortfolios [Blog post]. Retrieved from http://halfanhour.blogspot.com/2013/10/a-few-words-on-eportfolios.html

Durm, M. W. (1993). An A is not an A is not an A: A history of grading. *Educational Forum,* *57*(Spring), p. 2.

Earl, L. (2003). *Assessment as learning: Using classroom assessment to maximize student learning.* Thousand Oaks, CA: Corwin.

Ehrmann, S. C. (1995). "Asking the right questions: What does research tell us about technology and higher learning?" *Change, 27*(2), 20–27.

Fisher, M. (2010, October 10). No one who ever bought a drill wanted a drill. They wanted a hole. —Perry Marchall quote [Flicker image]. Retrieved from http://bit.ly/2qOS32t

Fisher, M., & Rosenthal Tolisano, S. (2014). Digital masters: Becoming a blogmaster, annotexter, or web curator. In H. H. Jacobs (ed.) *Mastering digital literacy* (pp. 5–28). Solution Tree: Bloomington, IN.

Fry, D. (2016, January 22). Where's the beef? [Blog post]. Retrieved from http://blog.donnamillerfry.com/collaboration-2/wheres-the-beef-610/

Fryer, W. (2008, June 30). Nuggets from NECC 2008 (1) [Blog post]. Retrieved from http://www.speedofcreativity.org/2008/06/30/nuggets-from-necc-1-2/

Gauss, C. F. (n.d.). Gauss quote [Quote website]. Retrieved from http://www.brainyquote.com/quotes/quotes/c/carlfriedr319895.html?src=t_learning

Gerstein, J. (2015, March 29). Sharing: A responsibility of the modern educator [Blog post]. Retrieved from https://usergeneratededucation.wordpress.com/2015/03/29/sharing-a-responsibility-of-the-modern-educator/

Godin, S. (2017a, April 27). You go first [Blog post]. Retrieved from http://sethgodin.typepad.com/seths_blog/2017/04/you-go-first.html

Godin, S. (2017b, June 11). "But what if it works?" [Blog post]. Retrieved from http://sethgodin.typepad.com/seths_blog/2017/06/but-what-if-it-works.html

Google. (2017, June 19). Meme definition [Information search result]. Retrieved form https://www.google.com/search?q=memes+definition+humorous+image%2C+video%2C+piece+of+text%2C+etc.+that+is+copied%2C+often+with+slight+variations%2C+and+spread+rapidly+by+Internet+users&ie=utf-8&oe=utf-8#q=memes+definition

Gutierrez, K. (2014, April 15). The age of bite-sized learning: What is it and why it works [Blog post]. Retrieved from http://info.shiftelearning.com/blog/bid/342367/The-Age-of-Bite-sized-Learning-What-is-It-and-Why-It-Works

Hagel III, J., Brown, J. S., & Davison, L. (2012). *The power of pull: How small moves, smartly made, can set big things in motion.* New York, NY: Basic Books.

Hale, J. A., & Fisher, M. (2013). *Upgrade your curriculum: Practical ways to transform units and engage students.* Thousand Oaks, CA: Corwin.

Halliwell, G. (n.d.). Halliwell quote [Quote website]. Retrieved from https://www.brainyquote.com/quotes/quotes/g/gerihalliw544997.html

Hattie, J. (2011, October 28). Presentation by John Hattie: Maximising the dividend of professional learning [Edited transcript]. Retrieved from https://visible-learning.org/2013/02/john-hattie-presentation-maximising-the-impact-video-transcript/

Heick, T. (2013a, May 3). The definition of digital citizenship [Blog post]. Retrieved from http://www.teachthought.com/the-future-of-learning/digital-citizenship-the-future-of-learning/the-definition-of-digital-citzenship/

Heick, T. (2013b, August 31). The definition of transmedia [Blog post]. Retrieved from http://www.teachthought.com/uncategorized/the-definition-of-transmedia/

Hellweg, E. (2012, March 1). Are you network literate? [Blog post]. Retrieved from https://hbr.org/2012/03/are-you-network-literate/

Hunt, B. (2008, March 10). Thinking 'bout linking [Blog post]. Retrieved from http://budtheteacher.com/blog/2008/03/10/thinking-bout-linking/

Hunt, B. (2011, September 25). Ruminations on implications: Notes from the thesis [Blog post]. Retrieved from http://budtheteacher.com/blog/2011/09/25/ruminations-on-implications-notes-from-the-thesis/

Hyatt, M. (n.d.). Hyatt quote [Quote website]. Retrieved from http://www.azquotes.com/quote/1427664?ref=amplify

Jacobs, H. H. (Editor). (2010). *Curriculum 21: Essential education for a changing world.* Alexandria, VA: ASCD.

Jacobs, H. H., & Alcock, M. H. (2017). *Bold moves for schools: How we create remarkable learning environments*. Alexandria, VA: ASCD.

Kallick, B., & Zmuda, A. (2017). *Students at the center: Personalized learning with habits of mind*. Alexandria, VA: ASCD.

Kashin, D. (2017, January 7). What about the what? Finding the deeper meaning in pedagogical documentation [Blog post]. Retrieved from https://tecribresearch.wordpress.com/2017/01/07/what-about-the-what-finding-the-deeper-meaning-in-pedagogical-documentation/

Klosowski, T. (2013, July 25) The science behind how we learn new skills [Blog post]. Retrieved from http://lifehacker.com/the-science-behind-how-we-learn-new-skills-908488422

Krechevsky, M., Mardell, B., Rivard, M., & Wilson, D. (2013). *Visible learners: Promoting Reggio-inspired approaches in all schools*. San Francisco, CA: Jossey-Bass.

Krochmal, M. (2010, December 1). Hyperlinks: The secret sauce of the world wide web [Slideshare presentation]. Retrieved from https://www.slideshare.net/krochmal/hyperlinks-6001289

Lapowsky, I. (2013, October 4). Ev Williams on Twitter's early years [Blog post]. Retrieved from https://www.inc.com/issie-lapowsky/ev-williams-twitter-early-years.html?cid=em01011week40day04b

Lee, R. (2017). Private communication [Virtually shared document].

LeFever, L. (2012). *The art of explanation: Making your ideas, products, and services easier to understand*. San Francisco, CA: Wiley.

Levine, A. (2006, October 25). Linktribution [Blog post]. Retrieved from http://cogdogblog.com/2006/10/linktribution/

MacMeeking, M. (2013, April 22). Digital citizenship [Blog post]. Retrieved from https://anethicalisland.wordpress.com/2013/04/22/digital-citizenship/

Merriam-Webster (2017, June 19). Selfie definition [Dictionary website]. Retrieved from https://www.merriam-webster.com/dictionary/selfie

Martin, A. J. (n.d.) Martin quote [Quote website]. Retrieved from https://www.brainyquote.com/quotes/quotes/a/amyjomarti529774.html

Martin, K. (2016, March 14). Martin quote [Twitter post]. Retrieved from https://twitter.com/cuelosangeles/status/709929132935655424

Martinez, S. L., & Stager, G. S. (2013). *Invent to learn: Making, tinkering, and engineering in the classroom*. Torrance, CA: Constructing Modern Knowledge Press.

Mayer, M. (n.d.) Mayer quote [Quote website]. Retrieved from https://www.brainyquote.com/quotes/m/marissamay746990.html?src=t_collaboration

McLane, R., & Lowe, E. (2015). Your school rocks . . . So tell people!: Passionately pitch and promote the positives happening on your campus. San Diego, CA: Dave Burgess Consulting, Inc.

Moberg, L. (2012, August 28). Teaching is the loneliest profession? [Blog post]. Retrieved from http://www.storiesfromschoolaz.org/teaching-is-the-loneliest-profession/

November, A. (2010). *Empowering students with technology* (2nd ed.). Thousand Oaks, CA: Corwin.

November, A. (2012). *Who owns the learning?: Preparing students for success in the digital age*. Bloomington, IN: Solution Tree Press.

November, A. (2017, February 20). How making thinking visible helps teachers and students [Blog post]. Retrieved from http://novemberlearning.com/educational-resources-for-educators/teaching-and-learning-articles/making-thinking-visible-helps-teachers-students/

Oxford Dictionary. (2017a, June 19). Definition of crowdsourcing [Informational website]. Retrieved from https://en.oxforddictionaries.com/definition/crowdsourcing

Oxford Dictionary. (2017b, June 19). Definition of tool [Informational website]. Retrieved from https://en.oxforddictionaries.com/definition/tool

Pink, D. (2009, August). The puzzle of motivation [TED Talk video and manuscript]. Retrieved from https://www.ted.com/talks/dan_pink_on_motivation/transcript?language=en

Polley, S. (n.d.). Polley quote [Quote website]. Retrieved from https://www.brainyquote.com/quotes/s/sarahpolle329325.html?src=t_challenge

Price, D. (2013). *OPEN: How we'll work, live and learn in the future*. United Kingdom: Crux Publishing.

Pritchett, P., & Pound, R. (2014). Business as unusual: The handbook for leading and managing organizational change. Pritchett, LP: Dallas, TX.

Project Zero. (2017, June 19). Why Make Thinking Visible [Informational website]. Retrieved from http://www.visiblethinkingpz.org/VisibleThinking_html_files/01_VisibleThinkingInAction/01b_WhyMake.html

Proust, M. (n.d.). Proust quote [Quote website]. Retrieved from http://www.brainyquote.com/quotes/quotes/m/marcelprou107111.html

Puentedura, R. (2008, October 27). The horizon report at five: Strategies for innovation. "A toolkit for decision making and design: TPCK + SAMR" [Blog post]. Retrieved from http://hippasus.com/blog/archives/24

Puentedura, R. (2011). SAMR and change [Blog post]. Retrieved from http://www.hippasus.com/rrpweblog/archives/2011/10/27/SAMR_And_Change.pdf

Raindance.com (2014, March 30). The 13 steps of post-production [Blog post]. Retrieved from http://www.raindance.org/the-13-steps-of-post-production/

Ritchhart, R., Church, M., & Morrison, K. (2011). *Making thinking visible.* San Francisco, CA: Jossey-Bass.

Rohde, M. (2014). *The sketchnote workbook: Advanced techniques for taking visual notes you can use anywhere.* Berkeley, CA: Peachpit Press.

Rosen, J. (2008, April 8). Ethics of linking: Jay Rosen [YouTube video]. Retrieved from https://www.youtube.com/watch?v=RIMB9Kx18hw

Rosenthal Tolisano, S. (2011, August 8). The next step: Amplification . . . amplify . . . [Blog post]. Retrieved from http://langwitches.org/blog/2011/08/08/the-next-step-amplification-amplify/

Rubin, T. (2017, June 8). 5 reasons why every school needs to brand NOW [Blog post]. Retrieved from https://www.eschoolnews.com/2017/06/08/every-school-needs-brand-now/?all

Sackstein, S. (2015). Hacking assessment: 10 ways to go gradeless in a traditional grades school. Hack Learning: Cleveland, OH.

Sharski, D. (2013, June 9). Sharing: The moral imperative by Dean Shareski (2010) [YouTube video]. Retrieved from https://www.youtube.com/watch?v=ELelPZWx7ZsSha

Sheninger, E. & Rubin, T. (2017). *BrandED: Tell your story, build relationships, and empower learning.* San Francisco, CA: Jossey-Bass.

Sherratt, S. (2017, May 30). #l2chat [Twitter hashtag chat]. Retrieved from https://twitter.com/sherrattsam/status/869512395336564737

Sheskey, B. (2010). Creating learning connections with today's tech-savvy student. In H. H. Jacobs (ed.), *Curriculum 21: Essential education for a changing world* (pp. 195–209). Alexandria, VA: ASCD.

Shirky, C. (2011). *Cognitive surplus: How technology makes consumers into collaborators.* New York, NY: Penguin.

Sinanis, T., & Sanfelippo, J. M. (2014). *The power of branding: Telling your school's story.* Thousand Oaks, CA: Corwin.

Sivers, D. (2011, June 28). Obvious to you. Amazing to others. [YouTube video]. Retrieved from https://www.youtube.com/watch?v=xcmI5SSQLmE

Socrates. (n.d.). Socrates quote [Quote website]. Retrieved from https://www.brainyquote.com/quotes/quotes/s/socrates101168.html

Sokanu.com (2017). What does a filmmaker do? [Informational website]. Retrieved https://www.sokanu.com/careers/filmmaker/

Spencer, J. (2017, January 12). How action research sparks innovation and boosts creativity in the classroom [Blog post]. Retrieved from http://www.spencerauthor.com/2017/01/how-action-research-sparks-innovation-and-boosts-creativity-in-the-classroom.html/

Stiggins, R. J., Arter, J. A., Chappuis, J., & Chappuis, S. (2006). *Classroom assessment for student learning: Doing it right—using it well.* Princeton, NJ: Educational Testing Service.

Stockman, A. (2015). *Make writing: 5 teaching strategies that turn writer's workshop into a maker space.* Cleveland, OH: Times 10 Publications.

Technopedia. (2017, June 19). Social platform definition [Information website]. Retrieved from https://www.techopedia.com/definition/23759/social-platform

Watson, L. (2015, May 15). Humans have shorter attention span than goldfish, thanks to smartphones [Blog post]. Retrieved from http://www.telegraph.co.uk/science/2016/03/12/humans-have-shorter-attention-span-than-goldfish-thanks-to-smart/

Wayans, K. I. (n.d.). Wayans quote [Quote website]. Retrieved from https://www.brainyquote.com/quotes/quotes/k/keenenivor282291.html

Wien, C. A. (2013). Making learning visible through pedagogical documentation [Online article]. Retrieved from http://www.edu.gov.on.ca/childcare/Wien.pdf

Wien, C. A., Guyevskey, V., & Berdoussis, N. (2011). Learning to document in Reggio-inspired education [Informational website]. Retrieved from http://ecrp.uiuc.edu/v13n2/wien.html

Wikipedia. (2017, April 29). Digital curation definition [Information website]. Retrieved from https://en.m.wikipedia.org/wiki/Digital_curation

Wise, R. (2004, June). Dopamine, Learning and Motivation. *Nature Reviews Neuroscience, 5,* 483–494.

Yousafza, M. (n.d.) Yousafza quote [Quote website]. Retrieved from https://www.brainyquote.com/quotes/quotes/m/malalayous569369.html

Index

Images/figures, boxes, and tables are indicated by f, b, or t following the page number.

Helping educators make the greatest impact

Laura Fleming

Tinker, doodle, and create in this workbook for building a GREAT makerspace.

Grade: K–12 • ISBN: 978-1-5063-9252-3

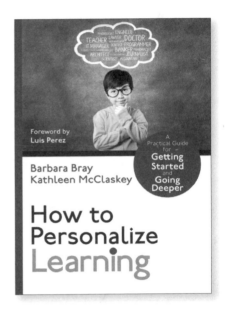

Barbara Bray, Kathleen McClaskey

Find tools, skills, and strategies needed to develop independent learners.

Grade: K–12 • ISBN: 978-1-5063-3853-8

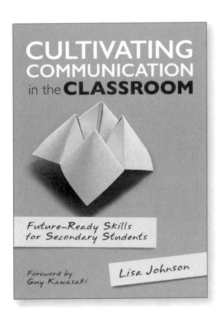

Lisa Johnson

Teach your students how to communicate their ideas persuasively with modern technology.

Grade: K–12 • ISBN: 978-1-5063-5637-2

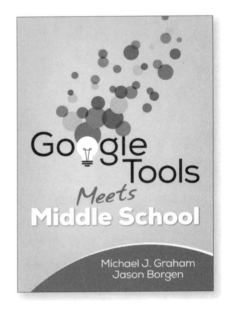

Michael J. Graham, Jason Borgen

Mastering 21st century technology and its integration in modern classrooms for day-to-day lessons.

Grade: 6–8 • ISBN: 978-1-5063-6016-4

Corwin books represent the latest thinking from some of the most respected experts in K–12 education. We are proud of the breadth and depth of the books we have published and the authors we have partnered with in our mission to better serve educators and students.

Catlin Rice Tucker, Tiffany Wycoff, Jason T. Green

Transform your classroom using the blended learning model built for the 21st century.

Grade: K–12 • ISBN: 978-1-5063-4116-3

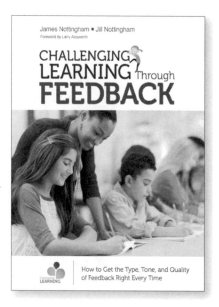

James Nottingham, Jill Nottingham

Get tools your classroom needs to channel success with high quality feedback.

Grade: K–12 • ISBN: 978-1-5063-7647-9

James Nottingham, Jill Nottingham, Martin Renton

Teach your students the power of effective dialogue with clear and precise communication skills.

Grade: K–12 • ISBN: 978-1-5063-7652-3

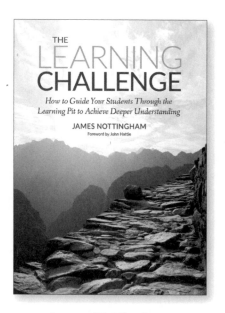

James Nottingham

Dive into the learning pit and show students how to promote challenge, dialogue, and a growth mindset.

Grade: K–12 • ISBN: 978-1-5063-7642-4

A SAGE Publishing Company

CORWIN HAS ONE MISSION: to enhance education through intentional professional learning.

We build long-term relationships with our authors, educators, clients, and associations who partner with us to develop and continuously improve the best evidence-based practices that establish and support lifelong learning.

Solutions you want. Experts you trust.
Results you need.